JAMES MARTIN'S

COMPLETE

Home

Comforts

JAMES MARTIN'S

COMPLETE
Home
Comforts

Over 150 delicious comfort-food classics

Hardie Grant

QUADRILLE

Publishing director: Sarah Lavelle
Creative director: Helen Lewis
Art direction and design: Gabriella Le Grazie
Photographers: Peter Cassidy and Yuki Sugiura
Food stylists: Janet Brinkworth, David Birt,
  Chris Start... and James Martin
Props stylist: Rebecca Newport
Home economist: Janet Brinkworth
Production: Nikolaus Ginelli, Stephen Lang

First published in 2017 by Quadrille,
an imprint of Hardie Grant Publishing

Quadrille
52–54 Southwark Street
London SE1 1UN
quadrille.com

Text © James Martin 2017
Photography © Peter Cassidy and
  Yuki Sugiura 2017
Design and layout © Quadrille Publishing
  Limited 2017

Cataloguing in Publication Data: a catalogue
record for this book is available from the
British Library.

ISBN: 978 1 78713 651 9

Printed in Germany

Reprinted in 2020
10 9 8 7 6 5 4 3 2

Notes:
* All eggs are medium-sized unless otherwise
  stated. Use free-range eggs.
* When keeping cooked rice for another use,
  cool it quickly, cover and put it straight in
  the fridge. Use within 1 day.

Photography credits
Yuki Sugiura pages 6, 8, 9 (below), 11, 13, 16, 19, 23, 24, 28–29, 42, 43,
41, 65, 50–51, 53, 57, 58, 62, 63, 64, 75 (below), 77, 80, 83, 105 (above),
109, 111, 112, 117, 119, 140, 143, 145, 146, 151, 152, 157, 159, 160,
180, 181 (below), 183, 185, 186, 189, 191, 192, 195, 197, 207, 218, 235,
239, 241, 244–245, 248, 253, 255, 258, 261, 262, 274, 276, 277 (below),
279, 281, 282, 285, 289, 290, 295.

Peter Cassidy: 2, 4, 9 (above), 31, 34–35, 37, 39, 40, 67, 71, 72, 74, 75
(above), 87, 89, 90, 100, 101, 103, 104, 105 (below), 122–123, 127,
131, 134–134, 136, 139, 141, 149, 165, 167, 168, 171, 173, 174, 176,
177, 179, 181 (above), 198, 201, 205, 208, 211, 214, 215, 217, 219, 227,
236, 240, 267, 269, 272, 273, 277 (above), 297, 300, 305, 307, 308, 311,
313, 320.

Contents

Introduction

Like most of us, I work harder now than I've ever done, with longer hours and more stress. And after all those long days, there is nothing that I like more than chilling out at home with some delicious, comforting food. I don't mean what we traditionally call 'comfort food', such as pie and mash or rib-sticking steamed puddings with custard (though those are brilliant, too); to me, comforting food can just as easily be a beautifully made and cleverly dressed salad, a magnificent fish with a piquant salsa verde, or a fresh raspberry and vodka jelly.

Over the years, I've been lucky enough to have worked with some amazing people and in some of the best kitchens around, so I've packed this book full of the hints, tips and shortcuts I've learnt along the way. Food should be enjoyed in the eating and the cooking. Let's face it, none of us wants to spend hours behind the stove sweating to make lunch and supper – it's all about making life easier.

From great simple starters, to main courses that will impress at the dinner table, to desserts I can't resist, this book is full of all the food I really love to cook at home. It's food that is accessible to all and that you crave the moment you arrive home and get into the kitchen. We could all do with more home comforts; I hope you love these recipes as much as I do.

Comforting
Little Lunches

Quick tomato and basil soup with roasted garlic bread

San Marzano are the best canned tomatoes I know; they are sweet and have fewer seeds. I use them for pizza sauce, too. You will find them in the supermarket if you read the label. And making your own butter is nothing new… well, not to me anyway. Roasting the garlic softens it and turns this into the best garlic bread out there.

Serves 2–3

1 garlic bulb

500ml double cream

leaves from a large bunch of basil, roughly chopped, 2 sprigs reserved

75ml extra virgin olive oil

½ banana shallot, finely chopped

2 x 400g cans of San Marzano tomatoes

1 small baguette, halved lengthways, then halved widthways

sea salt and freshly ground black pepper

Preheat the oven to 180°C/350°F/gas mark 4. Wrap the whole garlic bulb in foil then place on a baking tray and roast for 40–45 minutes until soft. Set aside until cool enough to handle, then cut the top off of the bulb, squeeze out all the soft garlic and finely chop it.

Pour the double cream into the bowl of a food mixer and beat for 3–5 minutes until the mixture turns into solid lumps with a liquid base. You have made butter!

Tip out into a muslin or cloth-lined colander over a large bowl, wrap the muslin tightly around it and squeeze out all the liquid so that you have a solid mass of butter in the muslin, then discard the liquid.

Return the butter to the bowl, add the roast garlic and a generous pinch of salt, then stir in one-third of the chopped basil and mix once more.

Heat a large sauté pan until hot, add all but 2 tbsp of the extra virgin olive oil and the shallot and cook without colour for 1 minute. Add the canned tomatoes and the remaining basil (except the 2 reserved sprigs), then simmer for 2–3 minutes.

Meanwhile, heat a griddle pan until very hot and char the bread on both sides. Slather with the garlic butter and keep warm in a low oven.

Blitz the soup with a stick blender – or place in a blender and blitz – to a fine purée. If using a blender, make sure to fill it only one-third full. (You will probably have to blend the soup in batches.) Season with salt and pepper. You'll know your blender better than I do, but you need to make sure the centre part of the lid is slightly ajar, or it can create a vacuum which can pop the lid off and spray hot soup around the kitchen. Be careful.

Serve the soup in bowls with some of the reserved olive oil drizzled over the top and a scattering of shredded basil leaves from the reserved sprigs, with the garlic bread alongside.

Tip

Making butter really is very easy and it is a great way to use up leftover double cream. It freezes well, too.

Butternut squash soup with flowerpot bread

I first made this while working on menus for the NHS. Butternut squash is packed full of flavour and the soup takes little time to make. The bread comes from a ready mix my mum uses and the idea of baking it in flowerpots is not new, but it just makes a fun way of presenting rolls.

Serves 4

450g packet ready-made pain de campagne bread mix

25g unsalted butter, plus more for the flowerpots

1 tbsp olive oil

½ onion, thinly sliced

450g butternut squash, peeled and cut into 1cm pieces

500ml vegetable stock

375ml milk

finely grated zest and juice of 2 limes

sea salt and freshly ground black pepper

Make the bread dough according to the packet instructions, then leave to prove in a large bowl in a warm place for 1 hour, or until doubled in size. Meanwhile, clean four small clay flowerpots, butter them and line with twists or strips of double-sided silicone kitchen paper.

Take the dough out and knock it back, then divide into four and place into the flowerpots. Leave to prove again for 30 minutes.

Preheat the oven to 220°C/425°F/gas mark 7. Place the flowerpots on a baking tray in the oven and bake for 10–15 minutes until golden brown and cooked through.

Meanwhile, heat the remaining butter and olive oil in a large saucepan or sauté pan, add the onion, cover and cook without colour for 3–4 minutes. Add the butternut squash and sauté for 2–3 minutes, then add all the remaining ingredients except the lime zest and juice.

Bring to the boil, then reduce the heat to a simmer and cook for 6 minutes, or until the butternut squash is cooked.

Pour into a blender, making sure to fill it only one-third full, cover with the lid and blitz to a purée. (You will probably have to blend the soup in batches.) You'll know your blender better than I do, but you need to make sure the centre part of the lid is slightly ajar, or it can create a vacuum which can pop the lid off and spray hot soup around the kitchen. Be careful.

Return the soup to the saucepan to heat through, then adjust the seasoning and finish with the lime zest and juice. Serve the soup with the flowerpot bread alongside.

Tip

I love these as they look great on the table. If there is space in your oven you can use a larger pot, too, to make a loaf.

Ham hock and pea soup

The main thing about this soup is not to overcook it once you add the peas, or it will end up muddying the clean flavour you are after and tasting like mushy peas from a chippy.

Place the ham hock into a deep saucepan, add the vegetables, herbs and peppercorns and cover with water. Bring slowly to the boil, then reduce the heat and simmer for 1½–2 hours. Turn off the heat and leave to cool slightly.

Remove the ham hock from the stock and shred the meat from the bone. Strain and reserve the stock.

To make the soup, place a saucepan over a medium heat, then add the butter, peas and parsley, 750ml of the hot ham stock and the cream and bring to a simmer. Pour into a blender, making sure to fill it only one-third full, cover with the lid and blitz to a purée. (You will probably have to blend the soup in batches.) You'll know your blender better than I do, but you need to make sure the centre part of the lid is slightly ajar, or it can create a vacuum which can pop the lid off and spray hot soup around the kitchen. Be careful.

Return the soup to the saucepan to heat through, then season with salt and pepper.

Heat a griddle pan until hot, drizzle half the rapeseed oil over the cut side of the bread, then place on the griddle cut-side down and cook until charred, then scrape with the cut side of the garlic cloves.

Ladle the soup into a bowl, top with some of the shredded ham, a drizzle of cream and the last of the rapeseed oil.

Serves 4

For the ham hock

1 small ham hock, about 1kg
1 large onion, thickly sliced
1 shallot, thickly sliced
1 garlic bulb, halved horizontally
2 carrots, cut into chunks
1 celery stick, cut into chunks
3 sprigs of parsley
1 sprig of thyme
1 bay leaf
small handful of peppercorns

For the soup

25g unsalted butter
400g frozen peas
1 large bunch of flat-leaf parsley, roughly chopped
150ml double cream, plus more to serve
sea salt and freshly ground black pepper
2 tbsp rapeseed oil
1 long baguette, halved lengthways, then halved widthways
2 garlic cloves, halved

Parma ham-wrapped mozzarella with plum chutney

I'm lucky to have mozzarella made just down the road from me. You can now buy it online and in supermarkets and it needs to be as fresh as possible. Buying it in the UK from a UK supplier is a bonus. Plus the farmer is an old F1 world champion… what more encouragement do you need to buy some?

Serves 4

For the plum chutney

75g caster sugar
500g plums, pitted and roughly chopped
1 shallot, finely chopped
50ml malt vinegar
1 star anise
½ tsp ground cinnamon
sea salt and freshly ground black pepper

For the wrapped mozzarella

8 slices of Parma ham, halved lengthways
4 balls of buffalo mozzarella, drained and quartered
3 tbsp olive oil
2 tsp sesame seeds
8 slices of ciabatta

For the chutney, heat a frying pan until hot, add the caster sugar and cook without stirring until melted and a light golden brown colour, swirling the pan from time to time. Add the plums, shallot, vinegar, star anise and cinnamon and cook for 5–8 minutes until tender and slightly pulpy. Season with a little salt and pepper. Set aside.

Wrap a slice of Parma ham around each quarter mozzarella ball to encase the cheese. Ideally, it should cover as much of the cheese as possible.

Heat a large frying pan until hot, add 1 tbsp of the olive oil and fry the parcels on each side until just crispy and the mozzarella is starting to ooze. Sprinkle over the sesame seeds.

Heat a griddle pan until searing hot, then drizzle the rest of the olive oil over the ciabatta and place on to the griddle. Char on each side for 1–2 minutes until golden brown.

Spoon some chutney on to plates, lay wedges of the mozzarella alongside, then add a couple of slices of bread.

Adding the basil leaves to the pasta gives it some colour. Try making your own pasta as it's simple, plus you will probably have a pasta machine gathering dust in the cupboard anyway. You can fill the pasta with whatever cheese you wish, but nothing too strong as the basil flavour needs to come through.

Basil tortellini with ricotta and pine nuts

Serves 4 as a starter or light lunch

For the pasta

200g '00' pasta flour, plus more to dust

2 eggs, lightly beaten

12 large basil leaves, plus about 20 small basil leaves, plus more to serve

225g buffalo ricotta, or cow's milk ricotta

60g toasted pine nuts, to serve

grated Parmesan, to serve

For the pesto

50g basil leaves

10g toasted pine nuts

25g Parmesan, grated

1 garlic clove, bashed

25ml extra virgin olive oil

50ml olive oil

sea salt and freshly ground black pepper

Place the flour and eggs into a food processor and pulse until the mixture forms crumbs. Tip it out on to a work surface and squish into a ball, then knead for a few minutes until smooth. Wrap in cling film and chill for 20 minutes in the fridge.

Meanwhile, make the pesto. Place the basil, pine nuts, Parmesan and garlic into a mortar and pestle and bash until deep green and broken down, then gradually add both the oils, pounding all the time. Season with salt and freshly ground black pepper.

Lightly flour the business end of a pasta machine. Cut the pasta into three and flatten out about 1cm thick. Starting at the lowest (thickest) setting, feed a piece of dough through the machine, turning the handle with one hand and holding the dough as it comes through with the other.

Change the setting on the pasta machine to the next-thickest setting, flour it again and feed the pasta sheet through the machine again, as before.

Repeat this process three or four more times, flouring the machine and changing the setting down each time, until the last-but-one setting. It helps to cut the pasta into smaller pieces during this process, as this will mean it is less likely to dry out; you should end up with about six sheets. (Any pasta you are not working on should be covered with cling film.) Take one long sheet and place two of the large basil leaves on to the bottom half of it, then fold

the other half over to cover and pass back through the pasta machine on its finest setting; you should get two elongated basil leaves running through it. Repeat with the remaining pasta and large basil leaves.

Cut the pasta into 9cm discs with a pasta cutter or cookie cutter.

Place a small spoonful of ricotta on to a small basil leaf, then place this in the centre of each disc. Brush around the edges with a little water. Fold the top over to seal the basil-wrapped ricotta inside. Twist each corner towards the centre to meet and form a ring and press together, then set aside. You need five pieces per portion and you should make 20 pieces from this mixture.

Bring a large pan of salted water to the boil, drop the tortellini in and cook for 3–4 minutes or until they float to the surface, drain and return to the pan. Add the pesto and toss to coat and finish cooking the pasta through, then toss in the pine nuts to serve.

Serve immediately with a generous grating of Parmesan and a few small basil leaves.

Tip

Filled tortellini freezes well. Use any leftover pasta to roll out again and make into tagliatelle.

Asparagus, cured ham, poached duck egg and hollandaise

I love duck's eggs. They are larger than hen's eggs, so need a few more minutes to cook. Hollandaise is a simple sauce that can go wrong very easily, but it needn't with just a few rules: melt the butter, cool it, then add it to the eggs slowly.

Serves 4 as a starter or light lunch

For the asparagus, ham and eggs

sea salt and freshly ground black pepper

2 tbsp white wine vinegar

4 duck's eggs

16 asparagus stalks, stems peeled and trimmed

8 slices air-cured ham, ideally British, or Serrano or Parma

For the hollandaise

125g unsalted butter

50ml white wine vinegar

1 shallot, finely chopped

½ tsp black peppercorns

2 large free-range (hen's) egg yolks

First, poach the eggs. Bring a wide pan of salted water to the boil and add the vinegar. Crack one egg into a small bowl. Whisk the water to create a whirlpool then carefully drop the egg into the vortex. Simmer for 3–4 minutes, then carefully lift the egg out and place into a bowl of iced water. Repeat with the remaining eggs. Set aside the pan and its water.

For the hollandaise, place the butter in a hot saucepan, then turn the heat off and set aside. Place the vinegar, shallot and peppercorns into a separate small pan and heat until just boiling, then simmer until reduced by half.

Place the egg yolks into a food processor with a pinch of salt and turn on. With the motor running, slowly add the melted butter – drip by drip at first – until it is all incorporated. Pour into a bowl, strain in the reduced vinegar (discarding the shallot and peppercorns), season to taste, then cover and keep warm in a bowl set over a pan of hot water.

Working quickly, return the wide pan of salted water to the boil, add the asparagus and simmer for 3–4 minutes, depending on the thickness of the asparagus, until tender when pierced with a knife. Lift out of the water and drain on kitchen paper.

Return the eggs and heat for 20–30 seconds, then drain on kitchen paper.

Divide the asparagus between four plates, top each with an egg and slivers of the ham, then spoon over some warm hollandaise. Sprinkle everything with salt and pepper and serve.

The team named these nuggets, but there isn't a fancier name really. Think of them as nuggets of gold, though, rather than the other famous fried nuggets… The chutney works so well with them, but bought stuff could be used, too.

Crispy cheese nuggets with grape chutney and pecan salad

Serves 4–6

For the grape chutney

100g light muscovado sugar
1 onion, finely chopped
100g sultanas
150ml sherry vinegar
2 tomatoes, roughly chopped
300g red grapes, halved
sea salt and freshly ground black pepper

For the pecan salad

100g caster sugar
100g pecan halves
2 heads little gem lettuce, leaves separated
2 tbsp 'house' dressing (see page 78)

For the cheese nuggets

flavourless vegetable oil, to deep-fry
125g plain flour
4 eggs, lightly beaten
150g fresh breadcrumbs
400g assorted cheese, cut into 3cm chunks

Heat a large frying pan until hot, add the muscovado sugar and heat until the sugar is just caramelising. Don't stir, but swirl the pan from time to time. Add the onion and sultanas, then pour in the sherry vinegar. Add the tomatoes and grapes and cook for 12–15 minutes, or until the grapes are tender and the mixture has thickened. Season with salt and pot into a sterilised jar (see page 232).

For the salad, pour 100ml of water into a saucepan and add the sugar. Bring to a boil and simmer until the sugar has dissolved and the syrup thickened slightly. Add the pecans and cook for 2–3 minutes, then transfer to a plate lined with greaseproof paper.

Heat a deep-fat fryer to 180°C/350°F or heat the oil for deep-frying in a deep heavy-based saucepan until a breadcrumb sizzles and turns brown when dropped in. (CAUTION: hot oil can be dangerous. Do not leave unattended.)

Carefully place the pecans, a few at a time, into the hot oil for a couple of minutes, or until golden-brown. Remove using a slotted spoon and transfer to a plate lined with greaseproof paper. Set aside to cool.

To make the cheese nuggets, tip the flour into a shallow bowl and put the egg and breadcrumbs into another two shallow bowls. Pass the chunks of cheese through the flour, turning to coat on all sides, then through the beaten egg. Finally roll each through the breadcrumbs to coat.

Carefully lower a batch into the hot fat and fry for 30–60 seconds until golden, softened and hot through. Drain on kitchen paper and keep warm while you cook the rest.

Place the little gem leaves in a bowl, drizzle the dressing over, then scatter in the cooled pecans and toss to coat.

Top with the crispy cheese nuggets and finish with a spoonful of chutney.

I know it's just a bacon sandwich… but this is the best I've ever had. Gran used to cook them on one of those old white enamel gas cooker grills with the red knobs. Choose the best bacon and use thick-sliced white bread. Gran bought hers from M&S. She sadly passed away 12 years ago. If I was 10% of what she was, I would be a 100% better person. Granny Smith was a legend, as were her bacon sarnies; she would be proud they are now in print.

Granny's bacon sarnie

Serves 1

4 rashers of dry-cured back bacon
50g salted butter, softened
1 tomato, quartered
2 thick slices of white bread

Put the bacon into a cold frying pan, then increase the heat and cook for a couple of minutes before adding a knob of the butter and the tomato.

Cook, turning once, until the bacon is just golden brown at the edges and cooked through and the tomatoes are softened (5–6 minutes).

Slather the bread with the remaining butter and place the tomatoes on to one slice. Press them down slightly, then layer on the bacon and top with the second slice of bread.

Press down lightly to squish it all together, then cut in half and eat, mopping up any spilled butter and juices with the sandwich as you go.

Sourdough cod cheeks with spicy pea salsa

Cod cheeks are solid lumps of meat with a membrane running through them, which needs to be removed. Cheeks mainly come from cod and monkfish and you can easily find them in good fishmongers or – frozen – online, but, if you can't get hold of them, fish fillets will do. It's easy to find cod cheeks in France; even village markets will sell them.

Serves 4

150g stale sourdough bread, chopped

finely grated zest of 1 unwaxed lemon, plus lemon wedges to serve

75g plain flour

3 eggs, lightly beaten

sea salt and freshly ground black pepper

20 cod cheeks, cleaned, membranes removed

flavourless vegetable oil and 100g beef dripping, to deep-fry

For the spicy pea salsa

300g frozen peas, defrosted

3 tbsp roughly chopped mint leaves

2 green chillies, deseeded and roughly chopped

juice of 2 limes

100g crème fraîche

Put the bread into a food processor and blitz until crumbs are formed, then add the lemon zest and blitz once more. Tip the lemon crumbs into a shallow bowl and put the flour and egg into another two shallow bowls. Season the flour, then dip the cod cheeks into the flour to coat, then into the egg and finally into the lemon crumbs until totally covered. Cover and set aside in the fridge until ready to serve (you can make these a day in advance).

Wash the food processor out, then make the salsa. Put in the peas, mint, chillies, lime juice and crème fraîche and blitz until chunky; you don't want it to be smooth. Tip out into a serving bowl; this can also be made a day ahead and kept, covered, in the fridge.

Heat a deep-fat fryer to 190°C/375°F, or heat the oil for deep-frying in a deep heavy-based saucepan, until a breadcrumb sizzles and turns brown when dropped into it. (CAUTION: hot oil can be dangerous. Do not leave unattended.)

Drop the cod cheeks into the hot fat in batches, and cook for 2–3 minutes until golden and cooked through. Drain on kitchen paper while you quickly cook the rest.

Pile the cod cheeks on to a serving plate and serve with lemon wedges and the spicy pea salsa.

Courgette and lemon arancini with deep-fried courgette flowers

Feed some of the risotto to the kids, then use the cold rice to make arancini later in the evening for the adults. The whole idea is that you only have to cook once to create two meals. It's not leftovers, it's two dishes in one.

For the risotto, pour the stock into a saucepan and set it over a medium-low heat. Heat a sauté pan until medium hot, add a knob of the butter, the shallots, garlic and thyme and cook for a couple of minutes without colour. Tip in the rice and stir well, then pour in the wine and cook until it has reduced to nothing.

Add a couple of ladlefuls of hot stock at a time, simmering and stirring until the rice has absorbed all the stock, then add more. After 7–8 minutes, add the courgettes and continue to cook until all the stock has been used and the rice is tender; it should take 15–18 minutes. Add the Parmesan, lemon zest and juice and season to taste. Serve one-third of it now as a risotto (it's a great meal for kids), with more Parmesan. Put the remaining two-thirds on a tray lined with cling film, cover and leave to cool.

Heat a deep fat fryer to 190°C/375°F or heat the oil for deep-frying in a deep heavy-based sauté pan until a breadcrumb sizzles and turns brown when dropped into it. (CAUTION: hot oil can be dangerous. Do not leave unattended.)

Add the chopped ham and Parmesan to the cold risotto and mix well, then form into balls, each about the size of a golf ball. Put 40g of the flour, the egg and breadcrumbs separately into three shallow dishes.

Pass the risotto balls through the flour, turning to coat on all sides, then through the beaten egg and finally through the breadcrumbs to coat totally. Carefully lower a batch into the hot fat and fry for 2–3 minutes until golden and hot through.

Drain on kitchen paper and set aside while you cook the rest – working quickly – in the same way.

For the courgette flowers, put the cornflour, remaining 50g of plain flour and sparkling water into a bowl and whisk quickly to combine to a smooth batter. Add the courgette flowers and gently mix until coated.

Place them into the fat and fry for 1–2 minutes until golden-brown, then drain on kitchen paper.

Serve the arancini with the courgette flowers, with lemon wedges alongside.

Tip

Make sure there is plenty of cheese in this as it will melt when cooked. Try stuffing mozzarella inside the arancini, too, before coating and frying.

Serves 4 (2 kids and 2 adults)

For the risotto

750ml chicken stock
25g unsalted butter
2 shallots, finely chopped
3 garlic cloves, finely chopped
leaves from 3 sprigs of thyme
200g risotto rice
200ml white wine
200g courgettes, cut into 1cm cubes
4 heaped tbsp grated Parmesan, plus more to serve
finely grated zest of 1 unwaxed lemon, plus 1 tbsp lemon juice
sea salt and freshly ground black pepper

For the arancini and deep-fried courgette flowers

flavourless vegetable oil, to deep-fry
50g Serrano or Parma ham, chopped
4 tbsp grated Parmesan
90g plain flour
2 eggs, lightly beaten
75g fresh breadcrumbs
50g cornflour
125ml sparkling water
4 courgette flowers
1 lemon, cut into wedges

Gruyère and pancetta brioche sandwich

This comes not from France – where brioche is from – but from the States. A baker friend of mine made this for us for breakfast. They have great streaky bacon out there; maple-cured stuff that gets nice and crispy. Here I use pancetta instead. It's a proper hangover cure and – trust me – I needed it that day.

Serves 4

12 rashers of thinly sliced pancetta
2 tbsp maple syrup
8 slices of brioche
4 large slices of gruyère
2 eggs, lightly beaten
1 tsp caster sugar
150ml whole milk
sea salt and freshly ground black pepper
50g unsalted butter

Heat a frying pan until hot, add the pancetta and cook on each side for 1–2 minutes until just crispy and cooked through. Add the maple syrup, then tip out on to a plate.

Lay four slices of the brioche on a board, top with the gruyère cheese and divide the pancetta and any of its juices between them, then top with the remaining four slices of brioche and press down lightly.

Place the eggs, sugar and milk into a shallow wide bowl, whisk to combine and season with salt and pepper, then dip the sandwiches into the mixture and to soak for a few seconds.

Heat a large frying pan until medium hot, add half the butter and, when it's just foaming, add two of the soaked sandwiches and fry gently on each side until golden and hot through.

Serve straightaway, or keep warm in a low oven while you cook the remaining sandwiches in the remaining butter.

Smoky chilli chicken wings, spiced potato wedges and Padrón peppers

A Spanish friend of mine taught me this. It's so simple too but, as he stresses, you must use the correct vinegar and paprika or it won't work. Padrón peppers are like Russian roulette; about one in 10 are hot, so have a cold beer to hand in case it's you that gets it.

Serves 4–6

For the wedges

1 tsp Szechuan peppercorns, ground

1 tbsp ground coriander

1 tbsp ground cumin

1 tbsp sweet smoked paprika

3 tbsp olive oil

1 tsp sea salt

4 large potatoes, scrubbed and cut into wedges

For the chicken wings and peppers

12 large, meaty chicken wings

sea salt and freshly ground black pepper

3 tbsp olive oil, plus more for the chicken

6 tbsp extra virgin olive oil

6 garlic cloves, finely sliced

2 tsp hot smoked paprika

2 tbsp sherry vinegar

juice of ½ lemon, or to taste

150g Padrón peppers

Preheat the oven to 220°C/425°F/gas mark 7.

For the wedges, mix the spices together in a bowl with the olive oil and salt, then add the potatoes and toss well to coat thoroughly.

Pour out on to a flat baking sheet and place in the oven for 25 minutes, turning halfway through, until they are golden, crunchy around the edges but tender when pierced with a knife.

Meanwhile, place the wings on a roasting tray, toss with salt, pepper and a little of the regular oil, then roast for 15–20 minutes until golden and cooked through.

Make the dressing: heat a frying pan until hot, add the virgin oil and garlic and cook for a couple of minutes over a gentle heat – you don't want to burn the garlic – then add the paprika and vinegar with a squeeze of lemon juice. Set aside.

When the wedges and wings are nearly ready, heat a frying pan until hot, add the 3 tbsp of regular oil and the peppers, then fry for 2–3 minutes until they are charred. Sprinkle with salt. Pile into a serving bowl and top with some more sea salt.

Put the wings in a serving bowl and drizzle with some of the warm garlic dressing. Serve with the wedges and Padrón peppers.

Tip

You can deep-fry the peppers if you prefer, in good olive oil not vegetable oil, as you want the taste.

Beetroot salad with buffalo curd cheese

I grow my own beetroots in the garden and think they pair really well with the curd cheese in this recipe. Buffalo milk is so rich and creamy, which means you get loads of curd, and it has an amazing flavour too. Give this salad a go, it's so easy to make and looks great.

Serves 4

5 raw beetroots, tops on
2 litres buffalo milk
50ml lemon juice
90ml extra virgin olive oil
½ baguette, cut into small chunks
2 sprigs of rosemary, leaves picked
2 sprigs of thyme, leaves picked
2 tbsp sherry vinegar
1 tsp cumin seeds
1 tbsp tarragon leaves
1 tbsp oregano leaves, plus extra to garnish
1 tbsp marjoram leaves
1 tbsp chopped flat-leaf parsley leaves
sea salt and freshly ground black pepper
4 sprigs of edible flowers or herbs
4 sprigs of dill

Cut the leaves from the tops of the beetroots and set aside. Place the beetroots in a saucepan half filled with water, bring to the boil, and simmer for 30–45 minutes until tender when pierced with a knife. Set aside to cool.

Place the buffalo milk in a saucepan and bring to the boil, without stirring. When it is just about to boil, whisk in the lemon juice – you will immediately see a reaction as the milk solidifies and separates into curds and whey. Carefully pour it through a sieve set over a bowl and allow to drain for 5 minutes. The longer you leave it to drain, the more solid a cheese you will get.

Heat a frying pan until hot, then add 50ml of the olive oil and the bread. Add the rosemary and thyme, and fry until golden brown and just crispy. Tip straight into a bowl, along with the oil from the pan and the sherry vinegar.

Add 2 tablespoons of the oil to the pan, then add the cumin seeds and beetroot tops, and cook until just wilted. Add to the croutons.

Peel the beetroot and cut into chunks, then add to the bowl along with the tarragon, oregano, marjoram and parsley, and mix well. Season with salt and pepper, then spoon onto serving plates.

Top with spoonfuls of the curd, a drizzle of olive oil, and the sprigs of oregano, edible flowers and dill.

I'm fortunate to have many great Indian chefs as mates, and this is one of the recipes I've picked up from them. It's simple but tasty. I've taken the heat down a bit, as they do like this dish to be spicy over there! This also works really well with monkfish and salmon if you don't fancy prawns.

Keralan prawns

Serves 4

2 tbsp vegetable oil
1 tsp black onion seeds
10 curry leaves
2 tsp ground cumin
½ tsp ground turmeric
½ tsp fenugreek seeds
1 onion, finely chopped
2 garlic cloves, finely chopped
2 green chillies, finely chopped
2 tsp finely chopped ginger
1 tbsp tamarind paste
160ml coconut cream
150ml chicken or vegetable stock
400g raw tiger prawns, peeled and
  deveined
1 lime, juiced
2 tbsp roughly chopped coriander leaves
sea salt and freshly ground black pepper
4 naan, roti or paratha breads, to serve

Preheat the oven to 200°C/400°F/gas mark 6.

Heat a large wok until just smoking. Add the vegetable oil, black onion seeds and curry leaves, and stir-fry until the seeds pop. Add the spices and fry for 1 minute, then add the onion, garlic, chillies and ginger, and fry over a medium heat for 10 minutes, until softened.

Add the tamarind, coconut cream and stock, and bring to the boil, then turn the heat down and simmer for another 10 minutes, until the onion is soft.

Toss in the prawns, coating them in the sauce, and cook for 3–4 minutes, until they have cooked through and changed colour.

While the prawns are cooking, place the breads in the oven to warm through.

Add the lime juice and coriander to the prawns, then taste and season with salt and pepper, if necessary. Cook for 1 minute, then serve on top of the warmed bread.

When I do get away, which to be fair isn't very often, one of the places I head to is Spain. I love their attitude towards food. Sure, the Italians are good, but they do like to shout about it, whereas I feel the Spanish just let the ingredients do the talking. One trip to the famous market of La Boqueria in Barcelona is proof of that. It's the best market I've been to, and in it are the best tapas bars. This dish comes from there.

Chicken and Serrano ham croquetas with Padrón peppers

Serves 4

75g unsalted butter
150g plain flour
450ml milk
sea salt and freshly ground black pepper
75g Serrano ham, roughly chopped
75g cooked chicken, chopped
1 small bunch of parsley, leaves picked and roughly chopped
25g flaked toasted almonds
2 eggs, beaten
75g fresh breadcrumbs
vegetable oil, for deep-frying

For the Padrón peppers

4 tbsp olive oil
200g Padrón peppers
½ tsp sea salt flakes

Melt the butter in a large saucepan, then whisk in 75g of the flour and cook for 30 seconds. Whisk in the milk slowly until you have a very thick sauce – almost the consistency of mashed potato. Season with salt and pepper.

Tip into a bowl and stir in the Serrano ham, chicken and parsley. Season with salt and pepper, then stir in the flaked almonds. Place in the fridge to chill for 10 minutes until just firm.

Wet your hands, then take spoonfuls of the mixture and roll them into balls.

Place the remaining 75g of flour, the eggs and breadcrumbs in separate bowls, and season with salt and pepper. Roll the balls first in the flour, then in the eggs, then in the breadcrumbs, then place on a work surface and roll gently into cylinder shapes. Set aside while you heat the oil and fry the peppers.

Heat a deep-fat fryer to 170°C/340°F, or heat the oil for deep-frying in a deep heavy-based frying pan until a breadcrumb sizzles and turns brown when dropped into it. (CAUTION: hot oil can be dangerous. Do not leave unattended.)

While the oil is heating up, heat a frying pan until hot, then add the olive oil, Padrón peppers and half the flaked salt, and fry for 2–3 minutes, until just golden and softened. Tip into a serving bowl and sprinkle with the last of the salt.

Deep-fry the croquetas in batches for 3–4 minutes, until golden-brown and hot through. Remove and drain on kitchen paper.

Serve the croquetas with the warm Padrón peppers.

Hot paper bag pastrami, fontina and pickled cucumber sarnie with parsnip and carrot crisps

The team thought I was going mad when I made this. I wanted an old army ammo tin to cook it in, but the producers of the show would only let me go so far. Pastrami is an amazing thing to see being made – the meat is coated in a rub to cure it, then smoked, then steamed to produce that fantastic flavour.

Preheat the oven to 200°C/400°F/gas mark 6.

Put the rice wine vinegar, sugar, salt and mustard seeds into a saucepan, and heat until simmering and the sugar has dissolved. Put the cucumber into a bowl and pour the hot vinegar mixture over the top, add the dill, then stir well and set aside to infuse.

Meanwhile, toast all the sourdough bread and spread with butter. Lay four slices on a board, butter-side up, and spread with a little mustard. Top with half the pastrami, then half the cheese and a layer of pickled cucumber. Place a second piece of bread on top of each sandwich, spread with mustard, and repeat the layers of pastrami, cheese and pickled cucumber. Top with the last piece of bread so you have four three-storey sandwiches.

Take four large sheets of baking parchment and wrap each sandwich individually in the parchment, then secure with string. Place the parcels on a baking sheet in the oven and bake for 10 minutes, until hot through.

Heat a deep-fat fryer to 160°C/320°F, or heat the oil for deep-frying in a deep heavy-based frying pan until a breadcrumb sizzles and turns brown when dropped into it. (CAUTION: hot oil can be dangerous. Do not leave unattended.)

Carefully lower the parsnip and carrot peelings into the oil in batches, and fry for 4–5 minutes, until crispy but not browned – you want to dry the peelings out, without letting them get burnt. Drain on kitchen paper and toss with salt.

Serve the hot sandwiches with a pile of parsnip and carrot crisps.

Serves 4

12 slices wheat 'n' rye sourdough bread
40g softened unsalted butter
1 tbsp Dijon mustard
300g thinly sliced pastrami
400g sliced fontina cheese
vegetable oil, for deep-frying
3 parsnips, peeled into ribbons
3 carrots, peeled into ribbons
sea salt

For the pickled cucumbers

150ml rice wine or cider vinegar
50g caster sugar
2 tsp sea salt
1 tsp yellow mustard seeds
1 cucumber, thinly sliced
1 small bunch of dill, roughly chopped

Tomato tarts with blowtorched salad

Simple flavours are always the best, and fresh tomatoes from the greenhouse are the epitome of this. Warming them gently with a blowtorch is a great way to serve them in a salad, just with a simple dressing. The great thing about these tomato tarts is that you can freeze them, wrapped in greaseproof paper, and cook them straight from frozen.

Serves 4

For the tarts

500g all-butter puff pastry
1 egg yolk, beaten
200g Gruyère cheese, grated
400g mixed heritage tomatoes, thickly sliced
sea salt and freshly ground black pepper
4 sprigs of thyme, leaves picked
1 tbsp rapeseed oil

For the salad

300g mixed heritage tomatoes
1 red onion, thickly sliced
2 heads of romaine lettuce, cut into thick slices
4 tbsp vegetable oil
1 tbsp white wine vinegar
1 tbsp Dijon mustard
1 egg yolk

Preheat the oven to 220°C/425°F/gas mark 7.

Roll the pastry into a large square, about 3mm thick, then cut out four 17.5cm circles and place on a baking tray. Mark a border with a knife about a little finger's width in from the edge, then brush with the beaten egg yolk.

Pile the grated cheese in the centre of each disc, leaving the border free of cheese. Lay the tomatoes in a circle on top of the cheese. Season the tarts with salt and pepper, then scatter the thyme leaves over the top, drizzle with rapeseed oil and bake for 15 minutes, until golden brown and cooked through.

Meanwhile, make the salad. Place the tomatoes, red onion and lettuce in a roasting tray and drizzle over a little of the vegetable oil. Toss to combine, then char with a blowtorch or under a hot grill until caramelised – about 4–5 minutes.

Put the vinegar, mustard, egg yolk and the rest of the vegetable oil into a jam jar with a lid and shake well until emulsified. Season with salt and pepper. Drizzle just enough of the dressing over the salad to coat.

Pile the salad into a bowl and serve alongside the tarts. The remaining dressing will keep in the sealed jar in the fridge for up to a week.

Scotch egg with homemade vegetable crisps

These are not the Scotch eggs you find in service stations all over the country – dry ones with overcooked eggs; the eggs inside these are lovely and soft-boiled. You have to be very careful and work delicately when moulding, as you don't want to break the creamy egg.

Serves 4

vegetable oil, for deep-frying

6 eggs

400g Lincolnshire sausages, skin discarded

50g plain flour, seasoned

salt and freshly ground black pepper

100g fresh breadcrumbs

1 large sweet potato, peeled and finely sliced on a mandolin

2 medium potatoes, peeled and finely sliced on a mandolin

2 raw beetroots, finely sliced on a mandolin

2 carrots, cut into fine slices with a peeler

1 jar of piccalilli, to serve

Heat a deep-fat fryer to 160°C/320°F, or heat the oil for deep-frying in a deep heavy-based frying pan until a breadcrumb sizzles and turns brown when dropped into it. (CAUTION: hot oil can be dangerous. Do not leave unattended.)

Put 4 eggs into a pan of boiling water and simmer for 5 minutes until soft-boiled. Drain and place in a bowl of iced water for 10 minutes until cold. Crack the shells, then peel.

Crack the remaining 2 eggs into a bowl and beat lightly.

Divide the sausage meat into four equal portions and wrap each piece around a soft-boiled egg, pressing gently but firmly to ensure the meat covers the egg completely. Roll first in the seasoned flour, then in the beaten egg and finally in the breadcrumbs. Set aside in the fridge for 30 minutes to chill, then reshape slightly to ensure the meat clings tightly around the egg.

Drop them into the fat fryer and cook for 7–8 minutes until golden and the meat is cooked through. Drain on kitchen paper and set aside while you cook the crisps.

Drop the sliced vegetables into the fryer in batches and cook for 2–3 minutes until cooked through and golden. Drain on kitchen paper and season with salt and pepper.

Cut the Scotch eggs in half and serve with piccalilli and the vegetable crisps.

Comforting Family Favourites

Classic prawn cocktail with langoustines

The 1970s are back… well, they should be, as people seem to love stuff like this when I have dinners at home. If you like you could push the boat out and make melba toast but, for heaven's sake, stop at a melon boat. There is only so much us 70s children can cope with.

Serves 4 as a starter

600g raw tiger prawns, shell on
600g raw langoustines, shell on
3 Little Gems, leaves separated
2 tbsp 'house' dressing (see page 78)
2 tbsp mustard cress
½ tsp cayenne pepper
1 lemon, cut into 4 wedges, to serve
buttered brown bread, to serve

For the sauce

2 egg yolks
1 tsp Dijon mustard
300ml vegetable oil
1 tsp Worcestershire sauce
4 dashes of Tabasco sauce
25ml brandy
50ml tomato ketchup
sea salt and freshly ground black pepper
a squeeze of lemon juice

Place the prawns into a steamer set over a pan of boiling water. Cover and cook for 2½ minutes, then add the langoustines and cook for a further 1½ minutes until the prawns and langoustines turn pink and are just cooked through.

Remove and allow to cool on a plate for 10 minutes before peeling and deveining if necessary.

Meanwhile, place the egg yolks and mustard into a food processor and blend until pale and creamy. With the motor running, pour in enough oil, in a very thin stream, until the mayonnaise is thick. You may not need all the oil.

Place the mayonnaise into a bowl, then add the Worcestershire sauce, Tabasco, brandy and tomato ketchup. Check the seasoning, add a squeeze of lemon juice and mix well. Cut the remaining lemon into four wedges.

Place the Little Gem leaves into a bowl and toss with the dressing, then layer into a cocktail glass.

Lay the peeled langoustines and prawns over the top, then spoon over the sauce and finish with a scattering of mustard cress, a pinch of cayenne pepper and a wedge of lemon. Serve with the buttered brown bread.

Chicken fricassee

Dishes such as this are where I cut my teeth as a chef and learned the true art of great cooking and flavour. This is a classic of French bistro food and it should be cooked at home all the time. Just be careful at the end of the process when adding the yolks to thicken the sauce: watch the pot doesn't boil, or you will have chicken and scrambled eggs. You can use just cream instead, but it works and tastes better with eggs.

Serves 4

For the fricassee

500ml chicken stock

200ml white wine

125g pearl onions

leaves from 3 sprigs of thyme, plus more to serve (optional)

1.5kg whole chicken, cut into 8 pieces, with the rest of its carcass (get a butcher to do this if you prefer)

200g baby button mushrooms

4 egg yolks

150ml double cream

salt and freshly ground black pepper

2 tbsp finely chopped flat-leaf parsley

For the mash

1kg floury potatoes, peeled and cut into chunks

150g unsalted butter

150ml double cream

Place a large casserole over a high heat, add the stock, white wine, onions and thyme and bring to a simmer. Add the chicken, including the carcass, return to a simmer, then tip in the mushrooms. Cover and cook for 15–20 minutes, or until the chicken is cooked through.

Remove the casserole from the heat and lift out the chicken, discarding the carcass. Keep it warm. Let the sauce cool slightly.

Whisk the egg yolks and cream together in a bowl then gradually add to the casserole, whisking constantly as you pour; if the pan is too hot, the eggs will cook too quickly and curdle the sauce.

Return the chicken to the pan, then adjust the seasoning and finally stir in the parsley.

Meanwhile, place the potatoes into a pan of cold, salted water and bring to the boil. Reduce the heat and simmer for 12–15 minutes, or until tender. Make the mash as on page 154.

Spoon the mash into bowls, then top with two pieces of chicken and a ladleful of sauce. Sprinkle with more thyme, if you like.

Penne carbonara

One of my go-to recipes, this is quick and simple but – because it's so pared-down – you must use good-quality ingredients, such as pancetta that will get nice and crisp. Adding the hot drained pasta straight into the sauce cooks the egg yolks, melts the cheese and produces a sauce that coats the pasta really well.

Serves 2–4

1 tbsp olive oil
300g thinly sliced pancetta, cut into strips
3 egg yolks
100ml double cream
50g grated Parmesan, plus more to serve
3 tbsp roughly chopped flat-leaf parsley leaves
sea salt and freshly ground black pepper
350g fresh or dried penne

Heat a frying pan until hot, add the olive oil and pancetta and cook until crispy; this should take 3–5 minutes. Drain on kitchen paper, then roughly chop.

Place the egg yolks, cream, Parmesan, pancetta and parsley in a bowl and season to taste with salt and pepper.

Bring a pan of salted water to the boil, add the pasta and cook according to the packet instructions. Drain and immediately add the pasta to the cream mixture. Mix well; the heat of the pasta will cook the egg.

Spoon into warmed bowls and grate over some more Parmesan.

Chicken and wild mushroom frying pan pie

Many chefs, when asked how they dreamt up a recipe, will relate a romantic story: perhaps they thought of it while climbing K2 and it was like an epiphany. Truth be told, this dish came about because I'm not one for washing up, I couldn't be bothered to find a dish and I was in a rush. Not K2, I know, but the truth. And it works.

Serves 3–4

For the rough puff pastry

250g plain flour, plus more to dust

250g very cold unsalted butter, cut into small cubes

½ tsp salt

For the filling

25g unsalted butter

1 banana shallot, finely chopped

1 garlic clove, finely sliced

2 large skinless boneless chicken breasts, cut into 1cm-thick slices

150g mixed mushrooms, such as chanterelle, girolle and chestnut, sliced if necessary

50ml Madeira

150ml chicken stock

2 tbsp chopped tarragon leaves

200ml double cream

sea salt and freshly ground black pepper

2 egg yolks, lightly beaten

For the pastry, place the flour in a mound on a clean work surface and make a well in the centre.

Place the butter and salt in the well and work them together with the fingertips of one hand, gradually drawing the flour into the centre with the other hand. When the cubes of butter have become small pieces and the dough is grainy, gradually add 125ml of ice-cold water and mix until it is all incorporated. But don't overwork the dough; the butter should give a marbled effect to the pastry and not be mixed in fully.

Roll the mixture out on a lightly floured surface into a 2.5cm-thick rectangle, wrap in cling film and refrigerate for 20 minutes.

Flour the work surface and roll out the pastry into a 40 x 20cm rectangle. Fold one short side over by one-third, then the other short side on top of it, as though you were folding a business letter. Turn 90°. Roll the block of pastry into a 40 x 20cm rectangle as before and fold it into three again. These are the first two turns. Repeat twice more to make four turns in total.

Wrap the pastry in cling film and refrigerate for at least 30 minutes before using.

Meanwhile, make the filling. Heat a large (24cm) ovenproof frying pan until hot, add the butter and, when it foams, add the shallot and garlic and fry for 1 minute, then add the chicken and fry until just coloured. Add the mushrooms and fry over a high heat for 2–3 minutes until just softened, then add the Madeira and set the mixture alight with a match, standing well back.

When the flames subside, pour in the stock and bring to a simmer, then add the tarragon and cream and simmer for 5 minutes. Check the seasoning, then set aside to cool.

Preheat the oven to 200°C/400°F/gas mark 6.

Roll out the pastry on a lightly floured work surface until it is 5cm wider than the frying pan and 4–5mm thick. Brush the edges of the frying pan with the egg. Lay the pastry over the filling and crimp at the edges. Trim away any excess pastry and brush the top of the pie with the remaining egg. Decorate with any pastry trimmings, if you like.

Bake in the oven for 25 minutes, or until the pastry is crisp and golden and the filling is bubbling.

Classic chicken Kiev with bean ragoût

There are a few dishes in this book which hark back to the 1970s. I'm not so old that I was cooking back then, but my mum's cooking dates back that far. This, together with the rest of the Johnny Mathis collection of recipes in this book, is down to her. It's proper home-cooked grub and for that I thank you, mother: for showing me the way at a young age. Garlic scapes are the stalks and buds of young garlic plants and you can often find them on sale at markets.

Serves 4

175g softened unsalted butter

1 garlic bulb, cloves peeled and crushed

4 tbsp chopped flat-leaf parsley leaves

sea salt and freshly ground black pepper

flavourless vegetable oil, to deep-fry

4 French-trimmed skinless chicken breasts (wing bones attached)

75g plain flour

3 eggs, lightly beaten

90g panko crumbs

For the bean ragoût

125g runner beans, trimmed and cut into 4cm pieces

50g unsalted butter

125g garden peas

4 spring onions, roughly chopped

125g broad beans, skins removed

6 garlic scapes, blanched, cut into 4cm pieces (optional)

Put the 175g of butter, all but one clove of the garlic and half the parsley into a bowl and beat together, then season with salt and black pepper. Spoon in a line on to a sheet of cling film and roll up into a log, then twist the end to secure and place in the fridge for 1 hour to set.

Heat a deep-fat fryer to 160°C/320°F or heat the oil for deep-frying in a deep heavy-based saucepan until a breadcrumb sizzles and turns brown when dropped into it. (CAUTION: hot oil can be dangerous. Do not leave unattended.)

Insert a knife horizontally into the bone end of the chicken breast, just next to the bone, and carefully move the knife from side to side, creating a pocket in the centre of the breast.

Slice the garlic butter into 1cm-thick fingers and place a few in each pocket, pressing in as far as possible.

Put the flour, eggs and panko crumbs into three separate shallow dishes. Season the flour. Pass the chicken through the flour, turning to coat all sides, then through the egg. Repeat, so each chicken breast has two coats of flour and egg. Finally roll each through the breadcrumbs to coat totally.

Carefully lower two at a time into the hot fat and fry for 8–10 minutes until golden and the chicken has cooked through. Drain on kitchen paper and set aside to keep warm while you cook the rest.

Meanwhile, heat a sauté pan until medium hot, add the runner beans, 275ml of water and 25g of the butter and bring to the boil Add the peas, spring onions, garlic and broad beans and simmer for 3–4 minutes until all the vegetables are tender. Add the rest of the butter and parsley and the garlic scapes (if using) and heat through, then check the seasoning.

Spoon the vegetables into the centre of four plates, top with a chicken kiev and serve.

My gran's old recipe from her gran. Yes, it really does use eight eggs. This is the best Yorkshire pudding recipe there is. End of.

Gran's toad-in-the-hole with my mum's onion gravy

Serves 4–6

225g plain flour
8 eggs, lightly beaten
1 tbsp grainy mustard
570ml whole milk
75g beef dripping or lard
6 good-quality sausages

For the gravy

2 onions, finely sliced
1–2 tbsp yeast extract
75ml red wine
1 tbsp gravy granules
200ml beef stock
sea salt and freshly ground black pepper
knob of unsalted butter

Place the plain flour into a bowl and make a well in the centre.

Whisk in the eggs and mustard until just smooth, then gradually add the milk and a pinch of salt, whisking to a smooth batter.

Place in the fridge for at least 4 hours, preferably overnight.

Preheat the oven to 220°C/425°F/gas mark 7. Place three-quarters of the beef dripping into a roasting tin and place in the oven.

Heat a frying pan until hot, then add the remaining dripping and, when it's melted, add the sausages and cook, turning, until brown on each side.

Remove the batter from the fridge and whisk once more to combine.

Place the sausages in the roasting tin and pour over the batter.

Place in the oven for 30 minutes, then open the door and allow the steam to escape, then shut the door once more and cook for a final 10 minutes.

Meanwhile, make the gravy using the same pan that the sausages were cooked in. Place the pan back on the heat, add the onions and cook over a high heat for 10 minutes until just softened and browned.

Add the yeast extract and cook for 1 minute, then add the wine and cook until reduced by half. Whisk the gravy granules with a little water until smooth, then add 250ml of water and whisk once more.

Pour into the pan and cook for a few minutes, then add the stock and simmer for 5 minutes. Season to taste and keep warm until the toad is cooked, then whisk in the knob of butter to make it glossy.

Remove the toad from the oven and let it stand for a few minutes. Serve a large spoonful with a ladleful of gravy and some buttered peas.

Making your own mustard is so easy to do and mixing in other flavours such as whiskey gives it a different appeal. If you blend it for longer, the mixture will turn as smooth as French mustard. You do have to start it the day before, ideally, and the Yorkshire batter will benefit from being rested overnight, too.

Roast peppered beef with bourbon mustard and all the trimmings

Serves 6–8

For the Yorkshire puddings

225g plain flour
sea salt and freshly ground black pepper
8 eggs
600ml whole milk
50g beef dripping or lard

For the beef

100ml cider vinegar
75g light soft brown sugar
1 tbsp runny honey
50g yellow mustard seeds
50g brown mustard seeds
75ml bourbon whiskey
4kg 3-bone forerib of 28-day-aged beef, at room temperature
a little flavourless vegetable oil
300ml beef stock

For the roast potatoes

10 King Edward potatoes, peeled and cut into 2 or 3
50g lard, beef dripping or vegetable oil

For the Yorkshire puddings, place the flour into a bowl and season. Add the eggs and whisk to a batter. Pour in the milk and whisk until smooth, then place in the fridge for at least 1 hour, but preferably overnight.

Place the vinegar, sugar and honey into a saucepan and bring to a simmer. Turn the heat off and allow to cool. Put the mustard seeds into a bowl, then tip the vinegar over, stir, cover and set aside for at least 4 hours, preferably overnight. The mustard seeds will absorb all the liquid. Pour everything into a blender with the bourbon and blitz until the mustard becomes creamy, but leave it slightly grainy. Season.

For the beef, preheat the oven to 200°C/400°F/gas mark 6. Season the beef with plenty of pepper. Heat a large frying pan until very hot, then add a little oil and fry the beef on all sides until browned. Put it in a roasting dish, then spread some of the mustard all over the beef and season with salt. Roast for 1½ hours.

Place the potatoes into a large saucepan, cover with water, add a pinch of salt and bring to the boil. Simmer for 1 minute. Drain into a colander and shake around a little to rough up the edges. Set a deep roasting tray on a medium heat and add the fat. Add the potatoes and fry on each side until they start to brown. Sprinkle with salt and place in the oven with the beef for the last 30 minutes of cooking time, until starting to turn golden and crispy.

Remove the beef from the oven, cover with foil and rest for 30 minutes. Turn the potatoes, increase the oven temperature to 220°C/425°F/gas mark 7 and cook for a further 20–30 minutes, while the beef rests.

Set the beef roasting pan over a medium heat until bubbling, then add the stock and cook until reduced by half, then season.

At the same time, divide the dripping or lard between 2 x 12 hole muffin tins or Yorkshire tins. Place in the oven for 10 minutes until smoking hot. Whisk the batter, then carefully pour it into the tins, filling each hole two-thirds full. Place into the oven for 20 minutes (do not open the door during this time). If the roast potatoes are done, take them out and keep them warm.

After 20 minutes, open the oven door to allow any steam to escape, then reduce the temperature to 190°C/375°F/gas mark 5. Cook for 15 minutes until golden and crispy.

Carve the beef. Pile everything on to platters so everyone helps themselves.

Burgers are about great meat, seasoning and nothing else… well, that's what I learned while in America. I worked in one of the oldest diners in the US; the menu was the size of the Bible and it ended up being a bit of a joke trying to pick something to eat! But the burger was the reason the diner was still there after all that time. Served in a brioche bun with home-made mayo, this is the business. Proper home comfort food. And a quick note to the blokes: if you're considering this recipe, don't burn it on the bloody barbecue like you do everything else.

The ultimate burger

Serves 4

800g minced beef steak
sea salt and freshly ground black pepper
3 egg yolks
1 tbsp Dijon mustard
300ml rapeseed oil
25g beer or wholegrain mustard
juice of ½ lemon
2 tbsp vegetable oil
4 brioche rolls, halved
4 tbsp mild chilli relish
½ round lettuce, leaves separated
2 tomatoes, sliced
200g cheese slices, preferably Monterey Jack
8 gherkins, sliced
1 red onion, sliced

Put the minced meat in a large bowl and season with salt and pepper, then divide into four and form into patties. Set on a plate, cover and place in the fridge for 1 hour to firm up.

Meanwhile, prepare your barbecue (if using) so the flames have died down and the coals are just glowing.

Whisk together the egg yolks and mustard then, still whisking, start adding the rapeseed oil in a very thin trickle to make a mayonnaise; the mixture should be thick yet light once all the oil is incorporated. Stir in the beer mustard and lemon juice and season to taste with salt and pepper.

Rub the patties with the vegetable oil, then place on the barbecue and chargrill on each side for 3–4 minutes. (Alternatively cook over a high heat on a griddle pan.) Place each brioche cut side down on to the barbecue and cook for 1 minute, then set aside.

To assemble the burger, place some relish on the base of each bun, top with lettuce, tomatoes, the burger, cheese, mustard mayo, gherkins and red onion, then top with the bun lids.

Place the burgers on serving plates and secure with wooden skewers to keep them together, if you like.

Chicken chasseur with creamy mash

This is an old school dish that has fallen out of fashion, but who cares about that? It should be on every restaurant menu as it tastes so good. And it can easily be made at home. The vital thing is to use fresh tarragon – it tastes miles better than dried.

Serves 4

For the chicken

1.5kg whole chicken, jointed into 8

sea salt and freshly ground black and white pepper

1 tbsp plain flour

2 tbsp olive oil

110g unsalted butter

110g smoked streaky bacon, sliced into lardons

125g shallots, thickly sliced

150g chestnut mushrooms, halved if large

2 tbsp tomato purée

175ml white wine

400ml chicken stock

leaves from a small bunch of tarragon

3 tomatoes, skinned, deseeded and finely chopped (see page 184)

2 tbsp finely chopped flat-leaf parsley leaves

For the creamy mash

1kg floury potatoes, peeled and cut into chunks

150g unsalted butter

150ml double cream

Season the chicken with salt and pepper then toss in the flour to coat.

Heat a large sauté pan until hot, add the oil, a knob of the butter and half the chicken pieces and fry skin side down for 3–4 minutes until golden. Turn and fry on the other side for another 1–2 minutes, then remove from the pan. Repeat with another knob of butter and the remaining chicken.

Add another knob of butter and the bacon and fry until golden brown, then add the shallots, mushrooms and tomato purée and fry for another couple of minutes.

Pour in the wine and bring to a simmer, stirring to deglaze the pan. Add the stock, then return the chicken to the pan with half the tarragon and bring to the boil.

Reduce the heat to a simmer, cover and cook for 30–40 minutes until the chicken is tender and the liquid slightly reduced.

Roughly chop the remaining tarragon. Add the tomatoes, parsley and tarragon to the pan, then check the seasoning and adjust it if needed.

Meanwhile, place the potatoes into a pan of salted water and bring to the boil. Reduce the heat and simmer for 12–15 minutes until tender. Make the mash as on page 154.

Serve each person with two pieces of chicken, with the sauce spooned over and a dollop of mash.

HRH the Prince of Wales is one of the biggest supporters of mutton in the UK. I've even done a dinner at his place using it. Mutton is one of those meats that people need to try and, when you do, you will realise how good it tastes. Like most things in this chapter it needs long cooking and is even better reheated on the second day.

Mutton hotpot with heritage carrots

Serves 4

2 mutton kidneys, fat on

1kg boneless leg of mutton, cut into 2.5cm pieces

2 tbsp plain flour

2 large onions, thickly sliced

2 bay leaves

2 tsp Worcestershire sauce

600ml beef stock

900g potatoes, peeled and cut into 5mm-thick slices

sea salt and freshly ground black pepper

100g unsalted butter, plus more to glaze (optional)

300g carrots, ideally heritage carrots, cleaned and trimmed

Preheat the oven to 180°C/350°F/gas mark 4.

Trim the kidneys of fat, then chop them into largish pieces. Place the kidney fat into a large ovenproof casserole pan and heat over a medium heat until it has rendered down. Meanwhile, toss the kidneys and mutton in the flour and shake off any excess. Add half the mutton leg and kidneys to the casserole and cook until browned on each side, then remove and set aside.

Add the remaining meat and cook again until browned on each side, then set aside. Now layer in half the onions and a bay leaf. Make another layer with all the mutton, then the last of the onions and the remaining bay leaf. Add the Worcestershire sauce and stock and bring to a simmer.

Arrange the potato slices on top in an overlapping pattern. Season the potatoes and add a few dots of butter over the surface. Cover with a tight-fitting lid and cook for two hours.

At the end of cooking, you can remove the lid, brush the potatoes with a little more butter, then place under the grill to glaze up if you like. Otherwise, just remove the lid and increase the oven temperature during the last 30 minutes of cooking time.

When it is cooked, bring a pan of salted water to the boil, add the carrots and simmer until just tender, three to five minutes. Drain and toss with the remaining butter, salt and pepper.

Serve a helping of hotpot with some carrots alongside.

If there is one dish that got eaten up more quickly than any on the shoot, it was this one. The idea is that the lamb fat and juices drip on to the dish of potatoes cooking below it at the same time. The name of these potatoes comes from the baker's oven in which they were once cooked in villages all over France. The locals would use the oven heat leftover from bread baking to cook the spuds.

Weeping lamb with boulangère potatoes and home-made mint sauce

Serves 8

2.7kg leg of lamb
3–4 garlic cloves, cut into slivers
3 big sprigs of rosemary
1 tbsp olive oil
sea salt and freshly ground black pepper
6 large potatoes, peeled and thinly sliced
4 onions, thinly sliced
75g unsalted butter
500ml chicken stock
750ml good red wine
1 litre beef stock

For the mint sauce

75ml malt vinegar
pinch of caster sugar
leaves from a large bunch of mint, finely chopped

Preheat the oven to 200°C/400°F/gas mark 6. Using a small sharp knife, make a series of small deep slits about 4cm apart all over the leg of lamb and insert a sliver of garlic and a spriglet of rosemary into each one, pressing right down.

Drizzle with the olive oil, add a good sprinkling of salt, then set aside while you build the potato dish.

Layer the potatoes and onions into a large ovenproof tray, seasoning each layer with salt and black pepper and finishing with potatoes. Dot with 50g of the butter, then pour over the chicken stock and press down lightly.

Put the roasting dish into the bottom of the oven and place the lamb on a small trivet on the oven rack directly above the potatoes.

Leave to roast for 1½ hours until the potatoes are cooked through, pressing the potatoes down into the cooking liquid every 30 minutes as it cooks.

Meanwhile, make the gravy: pour the red wine and beef stock into a sauté pan and set over a medium heat, bring to a simmer and cook for 30–45 minutes until reduced by three-quarters, thickened and glossy. Whisk in the last 25g of butter, check the seasoning and adjust it if needed.

Heat the malt vinegar and sugar in a pan until just simmering, then add the mint and stir until wilted. Taste and add salt, if you want.

Remove the meat from the oven and rest for 15 minutes before carving.

Carve the lamb and serve with the potatoes, gravy and mint sauce.

Lamb shanks pie

When I was younger and worked in London, we used to buy lamb shanks for 15p each. But, thanks to us chefs using them more, the price has gone up. They are still cheap given the amount of meat on them, but they need to be well cooked so it falls off the bone. They can also be bought in most supermarkets nowadays, which is an added bonus.

Serves 4

4 lamb shanks

sea salt and freshly ground black pepper

1 tbsp rapeseed oil

2 onions, roughly chopped

4 garlic cloves, crushed

2 tbsp plain flour, plus more to dust

250ml white wine

750ml chicken stock

600g potatoes, peeled and cut into 2.5cm chunks

3 large carrots, peeled and cut into 2.5cm chunks

4 celery sticks, cut into 2.5cm chunks

2 bay leaves

2 sprigs of rosemary

4 sprigs of thyme

400g can of haricot beans, drained

1 egg and 1 egg yolk, lightly beaten

400g rough puff pastry (for home-made, see page 49)

300g peas

Preheat the oven to 170°C/340°F/gas mark 3½.

Season the lamb shanks with salt and pepper. Heat a large casserole dish until hot, add the rapeseed oil and the lamb shanks and seal, turning, until golden brown on all sides. Remove and set aside, then add the onions. Cook for 2–3 minutes until softened, then add the garlic and cook for another minute. Add the flour, stir well and cook out for another minute before adding the white wine, stock, potatoes, carrots, celery, bay leaves, rosemary and thyme to the casserole. Bring to a simmer.

Stir in the beans, then return the lamb shanks to the pan and return to a gentle simmer. Cover and place in the oven for 2 hours, or simmer over a low heat on the hob if you prefer, until the lamb shanks are tender.

Remove from the oven. The lamb should be totally tender, but not quite falling off the bone. Place them upright in a baking dish with the vegetables around them, then set aside to cool completely. The lamb must be cold before you put the pastry on.

Preheat the oven to 180°C/350°F/gas mark 4.

Brush the sides of a pie dish with egg wash, inside and out. Roll the pastry out on a floured surface to 5cm bigger than the pie dish and 5mm thick.

Lay the sheet of pastry over the lamb shanks. Make four small slits with a sharp knife where the bones are and press gently down so that the bones stick out through the pastry. Crimp the pastry around the rim of the dish; this will help it stay attached and not slide off the dish. Brush with the egg and season with a little salt, then place in the oven and bake for 45–60 minutes until the pastry is golden brown and cooked through and the filling hot.

Bring a pan of salted water to the boil, add the peas and cook for 3–4 minutes until tender. Drain and serve with the pie.

Tip

The key is make sure the shanks are cooked well and cooled before making the pie, that way the meat will just fall apart.

Braised hogget pie

Wherever possible and whenever the season allows, I always try to buy hogget or mutton. Hogget is a sheep that is between one and two years of age, and it has a much deeper and more intense flavour than young lamb. It lends itself well to this kind of braising or slow cooking to make it nice and tender.

Serves 6–8

1.5kg boneless shoulder of hogget
sea salt and freshly ground black pepper
6 shallots, thickly sliced
2 tbsp tomato purée
2 garlic cloves, crushed
4 carrots, cut into large dice
2 celery sticks, thickly sliced
1 small bunch of thyme
1 bottle of red wine
500ml beef stock
1kg waxy potatoes, peeled and thickly sliced
50g butter

Preheat the oven to 200°C/400°F/gas mark 6.

Season the hogget well with salt and pepper. Heat a large casserole dish until hot, then add the hogget and seal on each side until browned. Remove and set aside. Add the shallots and tomato purée, and cook for a couple of minutes. Add the garlic, carrots and celery, and sweat for a few minutes.

Place the hogget on top and add the thyme and red wine. Bring to the boil, add the stock, return to a simmer, then place in the oven and cook for 2 hours.

Lift the hogget out of the dish and set on a board to cool slightly. Adjust the seasoning of the sauce, then tear the meat into strips and return them to the pan, mixing them well with the sauce and vegetables.

Layer the sliced potatoes over the meat in the casserole dish, then dot over the butter and season with salt and pepper. Return to the oven and cook for another 30 minutes until hot, golden and bubbling.

I'm a massive fan of moussaka and lasagne. So often vegetarian food can be a bit boring, but it doesn't need to be that way, as ingredients like aubergine and lentils can taste amazing when cooked properly.

Aubergine and lentil lasagne

Serves 4–6

For the filling

3 tbsp olive oil
1 onion, roughly chopped
2 garlic cloves, finely chopped
2 aubergines, roughly chopped
1 tbsp tomato purée
200g Puy lentils, rinsed
3 sprigs of thyme, leaves picked
150ml white wine
400g tin chopped tomatoes
500ml vegetable stock
sea salt and freshly ground black pepper
9 lasagne sheets

For the white sauce

25g unsalted butter
25g plain flour
500ml milk
275g Cheddar cheese, grated
a pinch of freshly grated nutmeg

Preheat the oven to 200°C/400°F/gas mark 6.

Heat a large sauté pan until hot. Add the olive oil, onion and garlic, and sweat gently for 5 minutes until softened. Turn the heat up, add the aubergines and fry until just golden.

Add the tomato purée and cook for 1 minute, then add the Puy lentils, thyme and white wine, stirring well. Add the tinned tomatoes and stock, and bring to the boil, then turn the heat down, cover and simmer for 30 minutes until the lentils are tender and the mixture has thickened. Season with salt and pepper, and set aside.

While the lentils cook, make the white sauce. Melt the butter in a saucepan, then whisk in the flour and cook for 1 minute. Whisk in the milk slowly, then continue to cook for 5 minutes, until thickened and silky smooth. Stir in 200g of the cheese and season with the nutmeg, salt and pepper.

Spoon one-third of the lentil mixture into the bottom of a medium ovenproof dish. Top with enough lasagne sheets to cover, then spoon over one-third of the white sauce. Repeat the layers of lentils, pasta and sauce until all have been used.

Top with the last of the cheese and then bake for 30 minutes, until golden brown and bubbling.

I've been privileged in my time to work with some of the best and most influential chefs and cooks that Britain has ever produced. One of these was the late, great Marguerite Patten, not only a wonderful person but a highly knowledgeable cook with thousands of books and leaflets sold. She was one of the people who gave people something to look forward to at the dinner table after the Second World War. Marguerite was an inspiration to so many and will be sadly missed. This simple fish pie is a tribute to her.

Fish pie with peas

Serves 6–8

8 baking potatoes

1 tbsp vegetable oil

rock salt

1 onion, thinly sliced

½ tsp black peppercorns

2 bay leaves

500g smoked haddock, boneless and skinless

400g haddock, boneless and skinless

400g cod, boneless and skinless

200g unsalted butter

3 heaped tbsp plain flour

475ml milk

1 lemon, zested and juiced

sea salt and freshly ground black pepper

1 small bunch of flat-leaf parsley, roughly chopped

250g frozen cooked peeled prawns, defrosted and drained

200g frozen peas

Preheat the oven to 180°C/350°F/gas mark 4.

Prick the potatoes all over with a fork, then rub with a little oil and set on a bed of rock salt in a tray and bake for 1–1½ hours, or until tender.

Half fill a deep sauté pan with 1 litre of water and set over a high heat, then add the onion, black peppercorns and bay leaves. When it's simmering, add the smoked haddock, haddock and cod, return to the boil, then gently simmer for 3–4 minutes.

Lift the fish out with a slotted spoon into a colander set over a large bowl, then place the colander on a plate to catch any other juices. Place a fine sieve over the bowl and strain the cooking liquor into it, discarding the onion, peppercorns and bay leaves.

Clean the pan out and return to the heat. Add 100g of the butter and when it's melted, add the flour and cook for 1 minute until light golden-brown. Add 50ml of the milk and mix to a paste, then add another 350ml of the milk and cook until thickened.

Add 750ml of the reserved stock to the pan and cook for 5 minutes until the sauce is smooth and just thick enough to coat the back of a spoon. Discard the rest of the stock, or chill it and use in another dish. Add the lemon zest and juice, season to taste with salt and pepper, then remove from the heat.

Flake the fish into the sauce, keeping it in reasonably large pieces, then add the parsley and lightly mix together. Add the prawns and stir through, then spoon into a large ovenproof dish. Turn the oven up to 220°C/425°F/gas mark 7.

When the potatoes are cooked and just cool enough to handle, cut them in half, scoop out the flesh and pass through a potato ricer into a sauté pan. Warm up with 75g of the butter and the last 75ml of milk – it needs to be a smooth thick mash, not too soft – beating until smooth. Spoon the mash into a piping bag fitted with a large star nozzle and pipe over the top of the fish.

Place on a baking sheet in the oven and bake for 5–10 minutes until golden and hot through. (Or, if preparing in advance and chilling, bake for 30 minutes until piping hot.)

While the pie heats through, bring a pan of salted water to the boil, add the peas and cook for 2–3 minutes until tender. Drain and return to the pan, add the remaining butter and season to taste.

Serve the pie with the peas.

Cauliflower cheese with crispy maple syrup pancetta

To be honest, I wasn't sure whether cauliflower cheese should make it into this book, as it's left many people scarred for life – overcooked cauliflower with lumpy cheese sauce. When it's made properly (so easily done: blanching cauliflower, then dipping it into iced water, then reheating it in the oven), it can be a fantastic dish. The crispy maple pancetta turns it into a certain favourite in my house.

Serves 4

1 cauliflower, cut into florets
100g unsalted butter
40g flour
500ml milk
1 tbsp Dijon mustard
300g extra-mature Cheddar cheese, grated
sea salt and freshly ground black pepper
3 slices of brioche, blitzed to crumbs
20 rashers of pancetta or streaky bacon
2 tbsp maple syrup

Preheat the grill to high. Bring a large pan of salted water to the boil, add the cauliflower and cook for 5–6 minutes until tender.

While the cauliflower cooks, melt 50g of the butter in a large saucepan, then whisk in the flour and cook for 1–2 minutes. Whisk in the milk slowly until you have a thick sauce, then add the mustard and half the grated cheese, and whisk until smooth. Season with salt and pepper.

Drain the cauliflower and place it in a bowl of ice-cold water to stop it cooking. Drain again and tip into an ovenproof dish. Pour the sauce over the cauliflower, top with the rest of the grated cheese, then place under the grill for 5 minutes until golden and bubbling.

While it's under the grill, heat a frying pan until hot, add the last 50g of butter, and when it's foaming, add the brioche crumbs and fry, tossing occasionally until golden-brown and crispy. Tip out into a bowl, then wipe out the pan and add all the pancetta. Fry until golden brown and crispy, then add the maple syrup and toss until sticky.

Scatter the breadcrumbs over the top of the cauliflower cheese and top with the pancetta and any remaining drizzles of maple syrup. Serve straight away.

Cottage pie

If you asked me for one dish aside from steak and chips that I'd be happy cooking for any big-name chef who ventures into my kitchen at home, this would be it. The key is in its simplicity: good-quality slow-cooked beef, fantastic mashed potato, cooked with care and attention, and fresh peas. Life just does not get any better. All chefs love the crispy edges, so don't clean the dish before serving! Those are the best bits.

Serves 4

8 medium baking potatoes

1 tbsp vegetable oil, plus extra for rubbing

rock salt

600g minced beef

2 onions, finely chopped

3 garlic cloves, finely chopped

4 sprigs of thyme, leaves picked and finely chopped

1 celery stick, finely diced

2 tbsp tomato purée

Worcestershire sauce, to taste

9 carrots, unpeeled

100ml red wine

500ml beef stock

salt and freshly ground black pepper

50g caster sugar

125g unsalted butter

150ml milk

Preheat the oven to 190°C/375°F/gas mark 5.

Prick the potatoes all over with a fork, then rub with a little oil. Set them on a bed of rock salt in a tray and bake for 1–1½ hours, or until tender.

Heat a large sauté pan until hot. Add the vegetable oil and fry the beef until just browned. Add the onions, garlic, thyme and celery, and fry for a couple of minutes until softened. Add the tomato purée and cook for 1–2 minutes, then add the Worcestershire sauce and one of the carrots, finely diced. Add the red wine and cook until reduced by one-third, then add the beef stock and bring to a simmer, stirring occasionally. Cook for 30 minutes until the beef is tender and the sauce has thickened. Tip the mince into a bowl and season to taste with salt and pepper, and as much Worcestershire sauce as you like. Set aside in the fridge to cool while you make the mash.

While the beef cools, top and tail the remaining carrots and place them in a pan half filled with water. Add a pinch of salt, the sugar and a knob of butter, bring to the boil, then reduce to a gentle simmer and cook for 30–40 minutes until soft. The liquid should evaporate, leaving a lovely glaze to the carrots.

When the potatoes are cooked and just cool enough to handle, slice them in half, scoop out the flesh and pass through a potato ricer into a bowl. Turn the oven up to 220°C/425°F/gas mark 7. Add almost all the remaining butter to the potatoes and warm the milk in a saucepan until just simmering. Pour onto the potatoes and beat until the mash is smooth and creamy. Season to taste with salt and pepper.

Pour the cooled mince into a baking dish and spoon the hot mash over the top, fluffing the top with a fork. Scatter over a few dots of butter, then place in the oven for 10–15 minutes, until golden-brown and piping hot throughout.

Serve with the carrots.

Comforting
Weekends

This to me is a lazy dish: marinate it the day before in a beery brine, then slam it in the oven while watching football on the box. But it tastes great. The idea of the chard gratin came about because I had masses of the stuff I planted in the garden by mistake. Jeff, my gardener, has since taught me that one pack of seeds doesn't make just one row of veg. Thanks Jeff! This dish is now named after you.

Beer-marinated rack of pork with Jeff's chard gratin

Pour 100ml of cold water into a saucepan, add the sea salt and sugar and heat until the sugar dissolves. Remove from the heat. Now mix in 400ml of cold water, the peppercorns, garlic, bay, unsoaked yellow mustard seeds, thyme, parsley and beer.

Put the pork into a large bowl or sealable bag then pour in the liquid and cover. Place in the fridge for 24 hours, turning occasionally.

When ready to cook, preheat the oven to 150°C/300°F/gas mark 2. Remove the pork from the bag and pat dry. Heat a large frying pan over a medium heat, then add the butter and heat until foaming. Carefully seal the pork on each side until light golden brown, then transfer to a roasting tray. Roast for 25 minutes.

Put the brioche, mustard powder and soaked yellow and brown mustard seeds into a food processor and blitz to a paste, then season. Set aside.

Meanwhile, make the gratin: layer half the chard and potatoes into an ovenproof dish, scatter over the onion, then place the rest of the chard and potatoes on top.

Put the butter in a saucepan and melt, then add the flour and cook for a couple of minutes until light golden brown. Add the milk gradually, whisking until you have a smooth white sauce, then whisk in the stock and half the cheese and cook until melted. Season with salt and pepper, then pour the sauce over the chard and potatoes and top with the remaining cheese.

After the pork has been cooking for 15 minutes, spread the brioche paste over the top. Increase the oven temperature to 200°C/400°F/gas mark 6, then return it to the oven for 15 minutes to crisp the crumb and finish cooking the pork through. Place the gratin in the oven at the same time.

Remove the pork from the oven and allow to rest for 15 minutes, while the gratin finishes cooking.

Carve the pork and serve with the hot chard gratin.

Serves 6

For the pork

2 tbsp sea salt

2 tbsp dark brown sugar

1 tsp black peppercorns

4 garlic cloves, lightly crushed

2 bay leaves

2 tbsp yellow mustard seeds, 1 tbsp soaked in water overnight

4 sprigs of thyme

4 sprigs of flat-leaf parsley

500ml beer, preferably a good ale

2 x 6-rib pork loin racks, French-trimmed

50g unsalted butter

100g brioche, roughly torn

1 tsp English mustard powder

1 tbsp brown mustard seeds, soaked in water overnight

sea salt and freshly ground black pepper

For the gratin

700g chard, chopped into 2cm pieces

2 large potatoes, peeled and cut into 1–1.5cm chunks

1 onion, sliced

50g unsalted butter

50g plain flour

400ml whole milk

200ml chicken stock

100g gruyère cheese, grated

When I was growing up on the farm, proper grilled pork chops were what we lived on. That and butter, of course. We never served chops like this — it would be frozen croquettes, if anything — but making your own croquettes makes the potatoes more of a treat and adding the almonds works really well.

Grilled pork chops with almond croquettes and house salad

Serves 2

vegetable or sunflower oil, for deep-frying

2 pork loin chops

1 apple, cored and cut into wedges

1 tbsp finely chopped flat-leaf parsley leaves

500g mashed potatoes (see page 154)

50g plain flour

1 egg, lightly beaten

75g flaked almonds

1 Little Gem, roughly chopped

2 handfuls lamb's lettuce

For the 'house' dressing

1 egg yolk

1 tsp English mustard

2 tsp runny honey

2 tbsp cider vinegar

150ml vegetable or sunflower oil

1 banana shallot, finely chopped

1 garlic clove, finely chopped

1 tbsp finely chopped flat-leaf parsley leaves

1 tbsp finely chopped mint leaves

1 tbsp finely chopped basil leaves

1 tbsp finely chopped thyme leaves

sea salt and freshly ground black pepper

Preheat the grill to high and heat the oil for deep-frying in a deep-fat fryer or large saucepan to 180°C/350°F. (CAUTION: hot oil can be dangerous. Never leave the pan unattended.)

Place the pork chops into an ovenproof frying pan along with the apple wedges, then season the pork fat with salt and place under the grill for 10 minutes, turning halfway through.

Meanwhile, make my 'house dressing'. Place the egg yolk into a bowl along with the mustard and honey. Add the cider vinegar and whisk, then gradually add the 150ml of vegetable oil, whisking all the time until thick and creamy.

Add the shallot, garlic, 1 tbsp parsley, mint, basil and thyme and whisk once more, then check the seasoning and set aside.

Check the seasoning of the mashed potatoes, then add the remaining 1 tbsp parsley and mix well. Take a small handful of potato and roll into a sausage shape. Repeat to shape all the mash into croquettes.

Place the flour, beaten egg and almonds in three shallow dishes.

Roll the potato sausages in the flour, then the egg and finally in the flaked almonds to coat.

Fry in batches for 2–3 minutes until golden, crispy and hot through, then drain on kitchen paper while you cook the rest.

Place the salad leaves in a bowl and add enough dressing to just coat the leaves, then serve alongside the croquettes, pork chops and apples.

This is what I cook for myself: it is packed full of flavour and colour and – using chicken thighs – relatively cheap to make, too. Chorizo comes in many guises but look for the word 'picante' which means spicy. It will be full of paprika and perfect for this dish.

Chicken with chorizo and bean stew

Serves 2

3 tbsp olive oil

40g unsalted butter

2 whole skin-on chicken legs, divided into drumsticks and thighs

2 shallots

1 lemon, halved

1 garlic bulb, halved horizontally

2 sprigs of rosemary

4 sprigs of thyme

200g chorizo, cut into small chunks

2 tomatoes, peeled, deseeded and finely chopped (see page 184)

1 x 660g jar of white haricot beans, drained and rinsed

250ml chicken stock

2 tbsp roughly chopped flat-leaf parsley leaves

sea salt and freshly ground black pepper

Preheat the oven to 220°C/425°F/gas mark 7.

Heat an ovenproof frying pan until hot, add half of both the olive oil and butter and, when it's foaming, add the chicken and fry until just golden on both sides.

Cut one shallot in half lengthways and add to the pan with the lemon and garlic, reserving 2 garlic cloves. Add half the sprigs of herbs. Place in the oven and roast for 15 minutes until golden and the chicken is cooked through. (Cut through the thickest piece to check: the juices should run clear with no trace of pink. If there is, cook for a few minutes longer, then check again.)

Meanwhile, finely chop the remaining shallot, reserved garlic cloves and the leaves from the remaining sprigs of herbs. Heat a sauté pan until medium hot, add the remaining olive oil and the chorizo and cook for 5 minutes, until the oil has changed colour and the chorizo is crispy around the edges. Add the tomatoes, chopped garlic and shallot and cook without colour for 1 minute. Add the beans, rosemary and thyme and sauté for 2 minutes.

Pour in the stock and bring to a simmer, then cook for 4–5 minutes until softened and the stock has slightly reduced.

Stir in the remaining butter and the parsley, seasoning to taste, especially with plenty of pepper.

Ladle the beans into the middle of soup plates, top with some chicken, then place a sautéed lemon half, shallot half and garlic bulb half alongside.

Barbecue baby back ribs with celeriac slaw

The crew couldn't wait to get stuck into these… but all good things come to those who wait and this recipe is the prime example, because the ribs are cooked for a long time. Some recipes tell you to cook ribs in sauce in the oven from raw. I find, cooked that way, they end up tough. The best way is to poach them first, so the meat just falls off the bones.

Serves 2–4

For the ribs

2kg racks of baby back pork ribs
2 celery sticks, halved
1 onion, thickly sliced
2 red chillies, split lengthways
1 garlic bulb, halved horizontally
250ml apple juice
125ml tomato ketchup
150g dark muscovado sugar
2 tbsp Worcestershire sauce
1 tsp smoked hot paprika
1 tsp smoked sweet paprika
75ml white wine vinegar
50ml bourbon whiskey

For the slaw

3 egg yolks
1 tbsp Dijon mustard
2 tbsp cider vinegar
150ml rapeseed oil
150ml vegetable oil
1 celeriac, peeled and julienned
2 tbsp roughly chopped flat-leaf parsley leaves
sea salt and freshly ground black pepper

Place the ribs into a large, wide saucepan, add the celery, onion, chillies, garlic and apple juice, then pour in enough water just to cover. Bring to the boil, then reduce the heat and simmer very gently for 1–1½ hours until tender, skimming off any scum from time to time.

Meanwhile, make the sauce. Heat a frying pan until hot, add the ketchup and muscovado sugar and cook for 2–3 minutes until it liquefies. Add the Worcestershire sauce, smoked paprikas and vinegar. Bring to the boil, then reduce the heat and simmer for 5 minutes until thickened. Add the bourbon, mix well, then set aside.

To make the slaw, whisk together the egg yolks, mustard and vinegar in a bowl or small processor. Still whisking, start adding the oils in a very thin trickle to make a mayonnaise; the mixture should be thick and light once the oils are incorporated.

Pour into a bowl, then stir in the celeriac and parsley and mix well. Season with salt and pepper.

When the ribs are done, preheat the oven to 240°C/475°F/gas mark 9, or as hot as it will go.

Lift the ribs out of the poaching liquor and place on a tray, then brush with the sauce on all sides. Roast the oven for 10–15 minutes, until charred around the edges and sticky, turning occasionally.

Pile on to a platter and serve the celeriac slaw and remaining sauce alongside.

Southern-fried buttermilk chicken with tomato and sweetcorn salsa

Go on, you know you want to try it. Proper TV food: just pile it up in the centre of the table and watch everyone dive in. Once you have cooked it, you can change the spices to make it hotter if you want. Make sure the frying oil isn't too hot, or the coating will burn rather than turn deliciously brown.

Put the buttermilk and salt into a bowl and whisk to combine, then add the chicken and stir to coat. Cover and place in the fridge to marinate for at least 4 hours, preferably overnight.

Remove from the fridge and allow to come to room temperature. Preheat the oven to 180°C/350°F/gas mark 4.

Place the flour, lemon zest and all the spices into a bowl and toss together until well combined. Lift the chicken out of the buttermilk, scraping off as much of it as you can, then place into the spiced flour, tossing really well to coat all the pieces.

Heat a large ovenproof frying pan until hot, add enough oil to coat the bottom of the pan by 1cm, then add half the chicken, skin side down, and cook for 5 minutes on either side until golden. Place the whole pan in the oven for 15 minutes until the chicken is cooked through and the skin crispy. Cook the second batch, repeating the process. Take from the oven and place on kitchen paper to remove excess oil.

Meanwhile, for the salsa, heat a frying pan until hot, add the caster sugar and, without stirring, wait until it's a light golden caramel, swirling the pan occasionally. Add the chopped tomatoes and cook for 1 minute until just softened.

Add the chillies, sweetcorn, red wine vinegar, lime juice and parsley and cook for 6–8 minutes until thickened and the tomato is all broken down. Season well with salt and pepper.

Pile the chicken on to a platter and serve the salsa alongside.

Serves 3–4

For the chicken

400ml buttermilk

1 tsp sea salt

1 medium chicken, cut into 10 portions

125g plain flour

finely grated zest of 1 unwaxed lemon

1½ tsp smoked hot paprika

1½ tsp mustard powder

1½ tsp celery salt

1½ tsp dried thyme

1½ tsp dried oregano

2 tsp cracked black pepper

flavourless vegetable oil, to shallow-fry

For the salsa

90g caster sugar

300g tomatoes, finely chopped

2 red chillies, finely chopped

300g canned sweetcorn, drained and rinsed

2 tbsp red wine vinegar

juice of 1 lime

2 tbsp roughly chopped flat-leaf parsley leaves

Most of the time, 'ribs' means pork ribs but, every once in a while, you can find beef ribs at a butcher. Buy them. They are off the scale in terms of flavour and appearance. We use them in the restaurant, but they are simple to prepare and eat, with one big bone and tons of meat. I make these when my mates are over watching the Grand Prix.

Beef ribs with barbecue sauce, jacket potatoes and chive cream

Serves 4–6

For the beef ribs and jacket potatoes

4 'Jacob's ladder' beef ribs, sometimes known as short ribs

1 onion, chopped

1 garlic bulb, halved horizontally

1 tsp fennel seeds

2 star anise

4 baking potatoes

a little olive oil

sea salt and freshly ground black pepper

For the barbecue sauce

25g unsalted butter, plus more for the potatoes

1 onion, roughly chopped

2 red chillies, finely sliced, deseeded or not, to taste (leaving the seeds in makes it hotter)

1 tsp fennel seeds, crushed

2 star anise

150g light muscovado sugar

300g tomato ketchup

150g chipotle chilli ketchup

150ml dark soy sauce

For the chive cream

200ml double cream

juice of 1 lemon

2 tbsp finely chopped chives

Place the ribs into a large, wide saucepan. Just-cover with water and add the onion, garlic, fennel seeds and star anise. Bring to the boil, then reduce the heat and simmer very gently for 3 hours until tender, skimming off any scum occasionally. Remove with a slotted spoon and pat dry with kitchen paper.

When the meat has been simmering for 2 hours, preheat the oven to 200°C/400°F/gas mark 6. Rub the baking potatoes with a little oil then place on a small pile of sea salt on a baking tray. Bake in the oven for 1½ hours, or until tender.

Meanwhile, make the sauce. Heat a sauté pan until hot, add the butter and onion and fry for 4–5 minutes until softened.

Add the chillies, fennel seeds, star anise and sugar and cook for a further 3–4 minutes, until the sugar has dissolved. Add both ketchups and the soy sauce and bring to the boil, then reduce the heat and simmer for 5 minutes until thickened.

Remove from the heat and cool slightly, then place in a blender and purée until nicely smooth.

Dip the ribs into the sauce, then place into a baking tray and spoon some more sauce over the top.

Bake in the oven alongside the potatoes for their last 15–20 minutes of cooking time, until sticky.

While the ribs cook, put the double cream, lemon juice, chives and a pinch of salt into a large bowl and whisk until thickened.

Serve the ribs with the jacket potatoes topped with a dollop of butter and the chive cream.

Wild boar are amazing creatures and, with my background on a pig farm, they are very interesting to me. Jody Scheckter at Laverstoke Park introduced me to the joys of eating wild boar, as he produces them. He barbecues all year round, even in the depths of winter – you have to forgive him as he's South African and that's what they do – and serves these sausage rolls. They are delicious with a cold beer. Double the recipe if you're having a big party.

Home-made puff pastry wild boar sausage rolls

Serves 4–6

For the puff pastry

250g plain flour, plus more to dust
pinch of fine salt
300g unsalted butter, 50g cut into cubes, the rest left in a block

For the filling

25g unsalted butter
1 onion, chopped
3 garlic cloves, chopped
50ml brandy
500g minced wild boar
leaves from 6 sprigs of tarragon, roughly chopped
sea salt and freshly ground black pepper
2 egg yolks, lightly beaten

Start with the puff pastry. Put the flour and salt into a bowl with the cubes of butter and rub together with your fingertips to form crumbs, then stir in 150ml of cold water and mix to form a soft dough. Pat out to form a 2cm-thick rectangle.

Put the block of butter between two pieces of greaseproof paper and bash out with a rolling pin to a rectangle measuring about 15 x 10cm.

Lightly flour a work surface, roll the dough out to form another rectangle, this time 30 x 20cm, then remove the butter from the papers and place in the centre of the dough. Fold one side of the dough over the butter, then fold the other side over to meet it, covering the butter. Pinch together the dough at the top and bottom to seal the butter inside, then fold it in half lengthways.

Turn 90°, then roll out again to a 30 x 20cm rectangle. Fold one-quarter of the dough across to the centre, then fold the other side over to meet it. Fold in half lengthways, then repeat the process one more time. Cover and place in the fridge to chill for 1 hour.

Meanwhile, make the filling. Heat a frying pan until medium hot, add the butter, onion and garlic and sweat for 5 minutes, until softened. Add the brandy, then stand back while you set light to the pan. When the flames die down, tip the mixture into a large bowl to cool.

When the onions are cold, add the minced wild boar and tarragon and mix, then season generously.

Preheat the oven to 230°C/450°F/gas mark 8. Line a baking tray with baking parchment.

Lightly flour a work surface, then roll out the pastry into a 40 x 30cm rectangle about 5mm thick. Cut the rectangle in half so you have two 40 x 15cm rectangles of pastry.

Divide the sausage mixture into two and place in a line lengthways down each sheet of pastry towards one side. Brush the long edges of the pastry with the beaten egg. Fold the pastry over to cover the filling, crimp the edge, then trim to straighten. Place on the prepared baking tray, seam sides down, then brush once more with egg.

Place the rolls in the oven and cook for 20–30 minutes until golden brown and cooked through.

Cut each sausage roll into pieces, pile on to a plate and serve hot or cold.

Roasted sardines and mackerel with radishes

I love my wood-fired oven, but this also can be done on a tray in a barbecue with a lid. The idea is to get it really hot and to get a nice smoky taste going on in the fish.

Serves 4

6 ripe tomatoes, cut into chunks
4 sprigs of thyme, leaves picked
3 garlic cloves, crushed
1 baguette, torn into pieces
125ml extra virgin olive oil
sea salt and freshly ground black pepper
8 sardines, gutted and cleaned
4 mackerel, gutted and cleaned, cut into large chunks
2 bunches of radishes, trimmed
1 tsp cumin seeds
2 tbsp clear honey
1 small bunch of basil, leaves picked

Preheat the oven to 200°C/400°F/gas mark 6.

Place the tomatoes, thyme, garlic and baguette pieces in a roasting tray and drizzle with 75ml of the oil. Season with salt and pepper, then roast until the bread is charred around the edges.

Meanwhile, place the sardines stomach-down on a board and press gently down the length of the fish. Flip over and cut through the backbone at the tail and head, then, using your fingers, peel the bones out, leaving the fish boneless.

Remove the tomatoes from the oven, then turn the heat up as high as it will go and lightly oil a baking tray. Lay the mackerel, sardines and radishes on the tray, scatter the cumin seeds over, then drizzle the honey and 2 tbsp of the olive oil over the top. Roast for 5–10 minutes, until the fish is cooked through.

Tear the basil leaves and scatter over the roasted tomatoes and bread. Crush the tomatoes lightly.

Pile the roasted tomatoes and bread on to serving plates and top with the fish and radishes. Drizzle over the last of the olive oil.

Cooking on a beer can is nothing new: in Australia they've been doing it for years. The secret is that the beer keeps the inside of the chicken nice and moist while it's cooking on the barbecue. You'll need a barbecue with a lid, and you can cook the jacket potatoes in foil alongside. With added garlic butter at the end, this makes a truly delicious summertime meal.

Beer can piri piri chicken with garlic butter jacket potatoes

Serves 4

1½ tbsp sweet smoked paprika
½ tbsp hot smoked paprika
½ tsp chilli flakes
2 tbsp Dijon mustard
1 tbsp red wine vinegar
3 limes
3 lemons
5 tbsp olive oil, plus extra to drizzle
1 x 2kg whole chicken
4 baking potatoes, scrubbed
sea salt and freshly ground black pepper
2 garlic bulbs
1 can of beer, half full
3 tbsp finely chopped chives
250g unsalted butter, softened
1 head of lettuce, root removed and leaves separated
4 ripe tomatoes, cut into chunks
¼ cucumber, cut in half lengthways, then into slices
2 tbsp extra virgin olive oil

Put both the paprikas, chilli flakes, Dijon mustard, red wine vinegar, the juice of 1 lime and of 1 lemon into a bowl and mix to a paste. Pour the paste into a large plastic bag, then add the olive oil and the chicken. Seal at the end and shake around so that the chicken is covered in spices.

Prick the potatoes, then rub with a little oil, salt and black pepper, and wrap each one in foil. Place 1 garlic bulb on another sheet of foil and drizzle with oil, then twist tight.

Cut the second garlic bulb in half and place inside the chicken, then manoeuvre the half-full beer can into the bottom of the chicken too. The beer will bubble up and create steam inside the chicken, keeping it moist as it cooks, but you only need the can to be half full otherwise it will spill over.

Put the potatoes and garlic on a barbecue, then place the chicken upright, standing on the beer can in the centre. Make a silver foil collar for the base of the chicken to protect it slightly, then cover with a lid and roast for 15 minutes. Remove the garlic bulb and roast for another 30 minutes, until the chicken is cooked through and the potatoes are tender. If you want to cook this in a roasting tray in the oven, you will probably need to place the chicken on a low shelf to fit it in. Cook the garlic for 15 minutes and the chicken and potatoes for 45–60 minutes, at 200°C/400°F/gas mark 6.

Take the cooked garlic out of the foil and allow to cool. Cut the top off the bulb and squeeze the cooked garlic out into a bowl. Add the chives and the softened butter, and mix together.

Toss the lettuce, tomatoes and cucumber together in a large serving bowl, and drizzle with a little extra virgin olive oil. Cut the remaining limes and lemons into chunks.

Place the cooked chicken on the beer can in the centre of a serving platter. Loosen the foil from the potatoes, cut a cross in the top of them, squeeze gently and spoon the garlic butter on top. Place them around the chicken and garnish with the lemons and limes.

Lamb belly with bbq sauce and pickled red onions

While filming TV shows and on my travels I've found that there are ingredients that are a bit harder to get hold of. Lamb belly is one such cut of meat, but it's worth seeking out. You can order it in advance from a butcher; it's inexpensive and makes for one of the tastiest dishes in this book. You can also add a quarter of a cucumber, finely sliced, to the red onion pickle to give it a fresher crunch.

Put the carrot, onion, star anise, garlic, parsley and chipotle chilli into a large saucepan, half fill with cold water, then lay the lamb belly on top and pour over more water if necessary, to cover. Bring to the boil, then turn the heat down and simmer for 1 hour, until really tender. Drain and place on a board until cool enough to handle.

Preheat the oven to 200°C/400°F/gas mark 6.

While the lamb cooks, pickle the red onions. Put the sliced red onions into a bowl, then heat the cider vinegar, caster sugar, mustard seeds and salt until just simmering and the sugar has dissolved. Pour over the onions, stir well and leave to cool.

Meanwhile, make the barbecue sauce. Heat a frying pan until hot, add the chipotle paste and fry for a couple of minutes, then add the ketchup and maple syrup and cook for 2–3 minutes until it's bubbling up. Add the Worcestershire sauce, cider vinegar and soy sauce, bring to the boil, then reduce the heat and simmer for 5–6 minutes until thickened.

Put the naan bread or pides into the oven for a few minutes to warm through.

Shred the lamb into thick pieces and fold them into the warm barbecue sauce. Serve the lamb on top of the hot bread, with the pickled red onions and coriander leaves scattered over the top.

Serves 4–6

For the lamb

1 carrot, roughly chopped
1 onion, roughly chopped
2 star anise
1 head of garlic, cut in half
1 small bunch of parsley
1 dried smoked chipotle chilli
1 x 1.75kg lamb belly, bones removed

For the pickled red onions

2 red onions, finely sliced
200ml cider vinegar
2 tbsp caster sugar
½ tsp black mustard seeds
½ tsp sea salt

For the barbecue sauce

75g chipotle paste
275ml tomato ketchup
175ml maple syrup
1 tbsp Worcestershire sauce
1 tbsp cider vinegar
75ml light soy sauce

To serve

8–12 pitta breads or pides
1 small bunch of coriander

Tandoori chicken lollipop drumsticks with raita

The key to this is in the preparation. Making the lollipops is simple enough, but you do need to get yourself some pliers and remove the tendons from the drumsticks, otherwise they are awkward to eat.

Serves 4

For the drumsticks

12 chicken drumsticks
300ml natural yoghurt
1 tsp garam masala
1 tsp ground cumin
1 tbsp chilli powder
½ tsp ground turmeric
½ tsp ground cinnamon
5cm piece of ginger, unpeeled, finely grated
1 garlic clove, finely chopped
1 lemon, juiced

For the raita dip

1 green chilli, finely chopped
1 garlic clove, finely chopped
½ cucumber, finely diced
½ tsp ground cumin
2 tbsp finely chopped mint leaves
2 tbsp finely chopped coriander leaves
200ml natural yoghurt
1 lime, juiced
sea salt and freshly ground black pepper

Using the heel of a heavy knife, chop through the top of each drumstick, taking the knuckle off. Turn upside down and chop the bottom of the bone off, then press the meat down towards the bottom of the bone so that it looks like a little ball at the bottom of the drumstick. Using a pair of tweezers, pull the tendons out and discard. Repeat with all the drumsticks, then set aside.

Place one-third of the yoghurt in a bowl with the remaining drumstick ingredients and mix to a paste, then mix in the rest of the yoghurt. Put the drumsticks into the marinade and wriggle them around so that they are coated properly. Cover and place in the fridge to marinate for at least 4 hours, preferably overnight.

Preheat the oven to 200°C/400°F/gas mark 6. Remove the drumsticks from the fridge and place on a baking tray, bones upright. Roast for 12–15 minutes until browned and cooked through.

While the drumsticks roast, make the raita. Put the chilli, garlic and cucumber in a bowl and mix together, then add the cumin, mint and coriander, and mix once more. Add the yoghurt and lime juice, season to taste with salt and pepper, then place in the fridge until the chicken is ready.

Pile the drumsticks onto a plate, spoon the raita into a bowl and serve the two together.

Baked potato with bacon, tallegio and leek

Taleggio is a wonderful Italian soft cheese that looks like creamy Brie when it melts. Its flavour goes really well with potato and leek. This dish can very easily be transformed into a vegetarian one by simply omitting the bacon.

Serves 4

4 large baking potatoes, washed
1 tbsp olive oil
sea salt and freshly ground black pepper
25g unsalted butter
1 shallot, finely diced
1 garlic clove, finely sliced
2 leeks, sliced lengthways, then across into slices
75ml white wine
300ml double cream
150g Taleggio cheese, roughly chopped
8 slices of streaky bacon

Preheat the oven to 200°C/400°F/gas mark 6.

Rub the baking potatoes with the olive oil, prick all over with a fork and place each one on a little pile of sea salt on a baking sheet. Place on the top shelf of the oven and bake for 1 hour, or until the potatoes are tender (allow more time for larger ones). Remove from the oven and leave to cool until you're able to handle them.

Meanwhile, heat a frying pan until it is medium hot. Add the butter, shallot and garlic, and cook for 2–3 minutes, then add the leeks and cook for another 2 minutes. Add the white wine and cook until reduced by half, then add the cream and cook for 3–4 minutes, until thickened. Season with salt and pepper.

When the potatoes are cool enough, cut them into quarters, place in an ovenproof dish and pour the leek sauce over the top. Slice the Taleggio and tear into pieces over the top of the sauce.

Heat a frying pan until hot. Add the bacon and cook until golden-brown, then remove, roughly chop and scatter over the top of the cheese. Place in the oven and bake for 10 minutes until golden and bubbling.

Hot tinned Serrano, mozzarella and rocket pesto sandwich

I don't know where this idea came from – maybe it was watching Bear Grylls on TV as he was climbing a mountain with his food in a tin box! This is a simple sandwich that can be reheated using a disposable barbecue. If you don't want to make your own bread, just use a good bought loaf.

Serves 4–6

For the bread sponge

50g very strong flour
50g durum wheat semolina flour
6g fresh yeast
¼ tsp caster sugar
90ml tepid water

For the bread

450g very strong flour
450g durum wheat semolina flour
2½ tsp sea salt
475ml tepid water

For the hot tinned sandwich

unsalted butter, for greasing
150g rocket leaves
a large bunch of basil
1 garlic clove, peeled
50g Parmesan cheese, grated
125ml extra virgin olive oil
50g pine nuts, toasted
freshly ground black pepper
3 balls of mozzarella cheese, drained and thinly sliced
150g sliced Serrano ham

To make the bread sponge, put the flour, semolina flour, yeast and sugar into a bowl and mix well. Add the water and whisk to form a thick batter. Cover and set aside to ferment for 1½ hours.

To make the bread, put the fermented sponge into a kitchen mixer fitted with a dough hook, add the flour, semolina flour and salt, then start the machine running. Add about two-thirds of the water to start the dough, then add the remainder of the water a little at a time until a soft dough forms. Tip the dough onto a floured work surface and knead for a few minutes until smooth, then put back into the bowl and leave to prove for 1½ hours.

Knock the air out of the dough and divide in half, then knead lightly and form into a long sausage with pointed ends. Transfer to a baking sheet and cut slashes along the top. Repeat with the other half of the dough, then set aside to prove for 1 hour.

Preheat the oven to 220°C/425°F/gas mark 7. Bake the bread for 45 minutes, then set aside to cool before slicing.

To make your hot tinned sandwich, preheat the oven to 200°C/400°F/gas mark 6, or light a barbecue and leave until the coals are glowing. Line a 1kg loaf tin with buttered silver foil.

Place three-quarters of the rocket, half the basil, the garlic, Parmesan and olive oil in a food processor or a pestle and mortar and blitz to a fine purée. Add the pine nuts and black pepper to taste, and blitz again until well combined.

Lay two slices of bread out on a work surface and spread with some of the pesto. Layer on the rest of the rocket and basil, the mozzarella and Serrano ham, then top with another slice of bread. Spread with pesto, then repeat, layering up with the remaining ingredients until you have two piles.

Place the two piles of sandwiches along the length of the lined loaf tin, squeezing them together slightly so that they fit snugly. Fold the foil over the top so that everything is enclosed, then place in the oven or on the barbecue for 30 minutes, until hot through.

To serve, simply unwrap the tin and pull the sandwiches out.

Corned beef hash with beer-battered onion rings

I don't understand why so many chefs sneer at tinned produce – corned beef is a stalwart of my larder. With crispy onion rings on top, corned beef is always a favourite in my house.

Serves 6

4 medium potatoes, peeled and diced into cubes

50g unsalted butter

1 onion, chopped

1 garlic clove, crushed

4 tomatoes

340g tinned corned beef, roughly chopped

1 tbsp Worcestershire sauce

4–5 drops of Tabasco sauce

For the onion rings

vegetable oil, for deep-frying

100g plain flour

1 tbsp caster sugar

sea salt and freshly ground black pepper

2 tbsp cider vinegar

150–200ml beer

1 onion, sliced into 1cm thick rings

Heat a deep-fat fryer to 190°C/375°F, or heat the oil for deep-frying in a deep heavy-based saucepan until a breadcrumb sizzles and turns brown when dropped into it. (CAUTION: hot oil can be dangerous. Do not leave unattended.)

Put the potatoes into a saucepan and cover with water. Bring to the boil, then simmer for 8–10 minutes until just tender. Drain and set aside.

While the potatoes are cooking, make the onion rings. Put the flour, sugar, a pinch of salt, the vinegar and 100ml of the beer into a bowl and whisk to a thick batter, then gradually add more beer until the batter is the consistency of double cream. Drop the sliced onions into the batter, tossing to coat, then carefully place in batches in the hot oil and cook for 3–4 minutes. Drain on kitchen paper.

Heat a frying pan until medium hot. Add half the butter and the chopped onion and cook for 2–3 minutes until softened. Add the garlic, the drained potatoes and the rest of the butter and fry for 2–3 minutes.

Chop two of the tomatoes, then add them to the pan with the corned beef and stir-fry until softened and hot through. Add the Worcestershire sauce and Tabasco and season to taste with salt and pepper.

Slice the last two tomatoes and lay on serving plates, then spoon the hash alongside and finish with a pile of onion rings on top.

I'm lucky enough to live near the home of river trout, the River Test in Hampshire, and I've fished on the river a few times in search of the prize – the great brown trout. When I do catch one – and it doesn't happen often – this is one of the dishes I make. Smoked trout has a milder flavour and to me is less strong than salmon. Home-smoking is actually very easy and gives a wonderful flavour that you can't get in the bought stuff.

Home-smoked trout with feta salad

Serves 4–6

For the smoked trout

100g caster sugar
200g sea salt
1 large trout, cleaned, filleted and
 pin-boned

For the salad

1 tbsp white balsamic vinegar
3 tbsp extra virgin olive oil
sea salt and freshly ground black pepper
2 shallots, cut into rings
200g cooked beetroots, roughly chopped
200g feta cheese, roughly chopped
100g watercress

Mix the sugar and sea salt together in a bowl. Place a couple of pieces of clingfilm on top of each other on a work surface, then sprinkle a quarter of the salt sugar mixture onto the centre in a line. Place one trout fillet, skin-side down, on the salt sugar and cover with one-third of the remaining mixture, then cover with the clingfilm. Repeat with the other fillet and the rest of the salt sugar. Place on a tray in the fridge for 12–24 hours.

Remove the trout from the clingfilm and brush off the salt sugar mixture. Rinse the fish thoroughly under cold running water, then pat dry.

Place three lit candles underneath a bucket barbecue with holes at the bottom. Cover the base with foil, then sprinkle over a generous handful of oak chips. Drizzle with a little water, then place a grate over the top and lay the trout, skin-side down, in the centre. Cover with a lid and leave to smoke for 1½ hours, checking that the chips are smouldering, not burning. Remove and allow to cool.

Whisk the vinegar and olive oil together, and season with salt and pepper.

Place the shallot rings, beetroots and feta on a plate, and flake the smoked trout over the top. Finish with the watercress leaves and a drizzle of dressing.

Seaweed is one of the joys of cooking, and it can be a great way to season and reduce the amount of salt you add to your diet. And dulse is amazing – added to food like this the taste is simple and clean. I've been to harvest the stuff off the south Welsh coast, but it's found all over the British Isles and you can buy it, mainly dried.

Grilled mackerel with dulse butter and summer veg stew

Serves 2

20g dulse seaweed
175g unsalted butter, softened
½ lemon, juiced
2 mackerel, gutted
1 shallot, finely sliced
75g podded broad beans
100g fresh peas, half podded, half opened but left in the pod
12 asparagus spears, trimmed
4 sprigs of tarragon, leaves picked
freshly ground black pepper

Preheat the grill to high.

Soak the dulse in cold water for about 10 seconds, then drain and roughly chop. Place in a food processor and blitz until finely chopped, then add the softened butter and blitz again until totally combined. Add the lemon juice and blitz once more. You can keep this in the freezer if you don't use it all here.

Open up the belly of the mackerel and slide a sharp knife in under the rib cage, flicking the bones away from the flesh. Snip the bones at the head end and tail end, then lift out the whole rib cage and any bones. Open the mackerel out slightly, then spoon the dulse butter down the centre, reserving just one large spoonful.

Cut two double-thickness rectangles of foil a little larger than each mackerel and place on a heavy baking tray. Turn up the edges all the way round to make foil trays. Lay the mackerel on the foil and place under the grill to cook while you cook the vegetables – the turned-up edge stops any of the butter running away.

Pour 100ml of water into a sauté pan and bring to the boil. Add the shallot and broad beans, and simmer for 2 minutes. Add the peas and podded peas, and simmer for 1 minute, then add the asparagus and tarragon, and return to a simmer.

Add the last spoonful of dulse butter and cook for 2 minutes, until all the vegetables are tender and the butter is emulsified. Season with a little pepper.

Lift the mackerel out of the trays onto serving plates, pouring any excess butter over the top, and spoon the vegetable stew alongside.

Lavender leg of lamb in hay

Unusual I know, but pet shop hay is best for this, as what it produces is an earthy flavour. It's great with lamb and chicken. If you like, you can use a shoulder of lamb rather than a leg, but it will need longer, slower cooking at a lower temperature.

Serves 6–8

1 x 2.7kg whole long leg of lamb
small handful of fresh picked lavender
½ bag of eating hay (from a pet shop)
50g softened unsalted butter
sea salt and freshly ground black pepper
10 King Edward potatoes, peeled and cut into 2 or 3 pieces
75g beef dripping or vegetable oil
75ml malt vinegar
25g caster sugar
1 large bunch of mint, leaves picked, finely chopped
400g purple-stemmed broccoli

Preheat the oven to 180°C/350°F/gas mark 4. Pierce the leg of lamb about 10–12 times with the point of a knife, then push pieces of lavender into the holes.

Put the hay into a large deep-sided roasting tray, big enough to take the lamb, and sprinkle the rest of the lavender over the top. Place the lamb on the hay, then smear the softened butter over the top, and season with salt and pepper. Cover with foil and place in the oven for 2–3 hours, until cooked to your liking. Remove and leave to rest for at least 30 minutes.

Meanwhile, put the potatoes into a large saucepan, cover with water, add a pinch of salt and bring to the boil. Reduce the heat and simmer for 2 minutes, then drain in a colander and shake around to fluff up the edges.

When the lamb has about an hour left to cook, put the beef dripping into a large roasting tray and tip the potatoes on top. Sprinkle with salt and place in the oven for 30 minutes, until starting to turn golden-brown and crisp. Turn the potatoes and return them to the oven for a further 20–30 minutes.

Heat the vinegar and sugar in a saucepan until simmering, then remove from the heat and stir in the chopped mint.

When ready to serve, bring a pan of salted water to the boil, add the broccoli and simmer for 2–3 minutes until just tender. Drain, and season with salt and pepper and a knob of butter.

Lift the lamb from the hay, then carve and serve with the roast potatoes, mint sauce and broccoli.

Shellfish cassoulet

You can make this with a mixture of any shellfish, and you can include oily fish or fresh tuna. If you're adding shellfish like mussels and clams, add them in the last 5 minutes to avoid overcooking. I cook this in a wood-fired pizza oven, but any heavy-based pot in a hot oven will do fine. You can even make it on a barbecue with a lid, which gives it an added smokiness. The combination of bread, fish and tomatoes tastes superb.

Serves 4

1 onion, roughly chopped
6 garlic cloves, crushed
200ml extra virgin olive oil
1 head of fennel, roughly chopped
1 tsp fennel seeds
4 star anise
300ml white wine
2 x 400g tins chopped tomatoes
a handful of torn basil leaves
200g puréed brown crabmeat
1 small sourdough loaf, cut into small chunks
1 cooked small lobster, cut into pieces
3 x 75g cod or pollock fillets, skin on
1 mackerel, cut into large chunks
12 raw tiger prawns, shells on
1kg mussels
freshly ground black pepper

Preheat the oven to as high as it will go.

Put the onion, garlic, 75ml of the olive oil, the fennel, fennel seeds, star anise and half the white wine into a large ovenproof sauté pan. Stir well, then place in the oven for 5–6 minutes until just softened. Remove and stir well, then mix in the tomatoes, half the basil and the crabmeat, and return to the oven for another 5 minutes.

Meanwhile, put the chunks of bread into a roasting tray, drizzle with 50ml of the olive oil, toss to coat, then take the sauce out of the oven and put the bread in to roast for a few minutes until just browned.

Add the lobster, cod or pollock, mackerel, prawns, mussels and the rest of the wine to the pan of sauce, then add lots of black pepper. Return to the oven for 8–10 minutes, or until the fish is cooked through.

Scatter the croutons on top of the fish, then sprinkle the remainder of the basil over the top, and finish with the last of the olive oil.

Serve in the cooking pot at the table.

Lemon grass poussin with red cabbage salad

This is one of my all-time favourite meals, and it was great cooking it with my great friend Pierre Koffmann on the show – thanks to all his help, the dressing is off the scale!

Soak a clean wooden broomstick in cold water, overnight preferably. Set a barbecue going and wait until the flames have died down.

Place the lemon grass, coriander, garlic, chillies, ginger and lime juice in a bowl with the 50ml of vegetable oil, and mix to combine. Toss the poussins in this marinade, scooping some inside too. Slide them onto the centre of the soaked broomstick and tie each one with string to secure them onto the stick.

Set the broomstick over the barbecue, about 30cm above the coals, and cook for 30 minutes, turning every so often to cook each side all the way through. If you want to cook the poussins in the oven, put them in a roasting tray and roast for 30–40 minutes at 200°C/400°F/gas mark 6.

While the poussins cook, make the salad. Whisk the egg yolk, Dijon mustard, vinegar and 250ml of water together in a bowl until combined. Add the oil gradually, whisking all the time until emulsified. Season well with salt and pepper.

Place the red cabbage in a bowl, add 100ml of the dressing and toss to combine. Check the seasoning, then set aside until ready to serve. This salad can be made up to a day in advance. The remainder of the dressing can be kept in a sealed container in the fridge for up to a week.

To check that the poussins are cooked through, insert the point of a knife or the prongs of a carving fork into the thigh and check that they're hot all the way through. If not, keep roasting for another 5 minutes and check again.

Serve with a pile of red cabbage salad.

Serves 4

For the poussin

2 lemon grass stems, finely chopped
2 tbsp roughly chopped coriander leaves
4 garlic cloves, finely chopped
2 red chillies, finely chopped
5cm piece of ginger, peeled and grated
2 limes, juiced
50ml vegetable oil
4 poussins

For the salad

1 egg yolk
2 tsp Dijon mustard
2 tsp red wine vinegar or walnut vinegar
250ml vegetable oil
sea salt and freshly ground black pepper
1 small red cabbage, very finely sliced

Comforting
Spice Suppers

Vanilla-cured salmon with cucumber ketchup, charred cucumber and home-pickled ginger

It's so easy to make cured salmon: all it needs is salt, sugar and a bit of time in the fridge. The ketchup doesn't need any cooking. It uses xantham gum (buy that from health food shops) which thickens the mixture while in the blender.

Serves 8–10

For the salmon

2 whole vanilla pods, roughly chopped
200g caster sugar
200g sea salt
1.5g salmon fillet, skin on, pin-boned, rinsed and patted dry
bunch of breakfast radishes, halved lengthways
punnet of mustard cress

For the cucumber (ketchup and charred)

2 cucumbers
100ml rice wine vinegar
1 tsp caster sugar
1 tsp sea salt
2–3 tsp xantham gum
a little rapeseed oil

For the pickled ginger

100ml rice wine vinegar
pinch of caster sugar
pinch of sea salt
5cm piece of ginger, peeled and finely julienned

Start with the salmon. Put the vanilla and sugar in a food processor and blitz to a fine purée, then stir in the salt.

Place four pieces of cling film, slightly overlapping, on a clean work surface, then put half the sugar mixture in a line down the centre.

Place the salmon fillet on top, skin-side down, then sprinkle the rest of the mixture over the top to cover the salmon. Wrap the salmon up loosely in the cling film, then place it on a tray in the fridge for 24 hours.

Remove the salmon from the cling film, brush off the salt mixture and rinse the fish thoroughly under cold water, then pat dry and wrap in cling film until ready to serve.

For the cucumber ketchup, trim the outer edges of the cucumbers off so that you are left with two long 2cm square rectangles. Set those aside. Roughly chop the trimmings of the cucumber, then put into a food processor with the rice wine vinegar, sugar and salt. Blitz to a fine purée, then add the xanthan gum 1 tsp at a time until it thickens.

For the charred cucumber, chop the long rectangles of cucumber into batons, discarding the central seedy bits. Heat a griddle pan until hot, drizzle the batons with a little rapeseed oil, then cook on each side until charred and hot through. Remove from the heat and cut into small cubes.

To make the pickled ginger, place the vinegar, sugar and salt into a medium saucepan and heat until the sugar has dissolved. Add the ginger and simmer for 1–2 minutes until the ginger has wilted down. Remove from the heat and leave to cool.

Slice the salmon finely as you would smoked salmon: take a long sharp knife and cut thin slices on the diagonal, cutting the fish away from the skin. Lay on plates, top with pieces of the charred cucumber, blobs of the cucumber ketchup and the halved radishes. Scatter the pickled ginger and mustard cress over the top to finish.

Chicken tagine with pistachio tabbouleh

I know the ingredients list may be long, but the end result will be worth it all. The spices are so important, as is the mix of fruit in this dish. Tabbouleh can't have enough stuff added to it as far as I'm concerned; you need to pack it in to make it taste good. You can make the tabbouleh with couscous, but I think it's better with bulgar.

Serves 3–6

For the tagine

2 tbsp olive oil

6 large skin-on bone-in chicken thighs

1 onion, finely chopped

2 garlic cloves, finely chopped

5cm piece of root ginger, grated

½ tsp saffron strands

1 tsp turmeric

1 tsp ground coriander

1 tbsp ras el hanout

½ long cinnamon stick

500ml chicken stock

1 red chilli, finely sliced

2 tomatoes, roughly chopped

2 tbsp runny honey

2 tbsp roughly chopped mint leaves

2 tbsp roughly chopped coriander leaves

25g unsalted butter

sea salt and freshly ground black pepper

For the tabbouleh

150g bulgar wheat, soaked in water overnight

3 tbsp roughly chopped mint leaves

3 tbsp roughly chopped coriander leaves

½ red onion, finely chopped

50g pistachio nuts, roughly chopped

100g whole blanched almonds

100g dried apricots, roughly chopped

juice of 2 lemons

seeds from 1 pomegranate, to serve

Start with the tagine. Heat a large, heavy-based saucepan until hot, add the olive oil and chicken thighs skin side down and fry until golden brown, then flip over and seal on the other side before removing to a plate.

Add the onion, garlic and ginger to the pan and sweat for 2–3 minutes. Add all the ground spices and the cinnamon stick and cook for 1 minute, then return the chicken to the pan and stir well to coat.

Add the stock, chilli, tomatoes and honey and bring to the boil. Reduce the heat to a simmer, cover and cook for 20 minutes until the chicken is cooked through. Add the herbs, whisk in the butter, then check the seasoning.

Meanwhile, make the tabbouleh. Drain the bulgar wheat well, pressing down lightly to ensure all the water is removed, then place into a large bowl. Add all the other ingredients and mix well, then check the seasoning.

Pile the tabbouleh on plates and serve with the chicken and some sauce, with the pomegranate seeds sprinkled over.

Thai crab risotto with lemon grass and kaffir lime

Coriander cress is a micro-herb, the first young shoots of the growing herbs. You can of course grow it yourself, cutting it when it just starts to sprout, but micro-herbs are now available in some supermarkets.

Preheat the oven to 200°C/400°F/gas mark 6.

Place half the crab shell into a saucepan with the chicken stock, lemon grass and one of the kaffir lime leaves and heat through.

Place the rest of the crab shell into a deep oven dish, then add the chilli and garlic. Roughly chop one of the shallots and add it with the tomato purée. Pour over all the vegetable oil then place in the oven for 30 minutes until the shell is roasted. Mix well, then carefully strain the oil into a sterilised jar (see page 232) and set aside.

Heat a sauté pan until medium hot, then add the butter. Finely chop the remaining shallot and add along with the last kaffir lime leaf. Tip in the rice and stir well to coat in the buttery mix, then add the Thai green curry paste and wine and cook until nearly dry.

Add a couple of ladlefuls of crab stock at a time, simmering and stirring until the rice has absorbed all the stock, then add some more and continue to cook. Repeat until all the stock has been used and the rice is tender; it should take 15–18 minutes.

When the rice is tender, stir in the cream and fold in the picked crab. Add the Parmesan, mascarpone, green chilli and coriander and finish with the lime juice, then check the seasoning.

Spoon on to a plate, then scatter with a little of the coriander cress (if using) and finish with a drizzle of the roasted, spiced crab oil from the jar.

Tip

Don't use too much Thai curry paste, because the flavour gets stronger as you cook and you can't take it out.

Serves 3–4

1 crab shell, broken up

300ml chicken stock

1 lemon grass stalk, tough outer layers removed, finely chopped

2 kaffir lime leaves, shredded

1 long red chilli, deseeded and roughly chopped

1 garlic clove

2 shallots

1 tbsp tomato purée

300ml vegetable oil

50g unsalted butter

75g arborio rice

1 tsp Thai green curry paste

75ml muscat wine

50ml double cream

50g picked brown crab meat

110g picked white crab meat

2 tbsp grated Parmesan

1 tbsp mascarpone

1 green chilli, deseeded and finely chopped

1 tbsp roughly chopped coriander leaves

juice of 1 lime

sea salt and freshly ground black pepper

1 tbsp coriander cress (optional)

Thai lamb salad with spicy dressing

I love this dish. Frying the cold lamb until crisp on the edges gives it a great texture, then adding the brilliant dressing means you get masses of flavours in. You really need all the dressing ingredients sadly; it won't work with normal sugar or without the fish sauce. It doesn't need poncing around, just whack it on the plate and put it on the table. Simple. This is one of the dishes I do all the time at home.

Serves 4

2 red chillies, 1 chopped, 1 finely sliced

4 garlic cloves, crushed

90g root ginger, peeled and roughly chopped

2 tbsp palm sugar

6 tbsp soy sauce

4 tbsp fish sauce

300g cooked lamb, cut into thick slices, with the fat left on

½ cucumber, halved lengthways, sliced thinly on the diagonal

100g fresh podded peas, some in the pods if really fresh

100g sugar snap peas, sliced lengthways

75g beansprouts

6 spring onions, sliced on the diagonal

3 tbsp roughly chopped mint leaves

small handful of coriander sprigs

juice of 2 limes

25g pea shoots

Place the chopped chilli, garlic, ginger and palm sugar into a food processor or mortar and pestle and blitz or grind to a fine paste. Add the soy and fish sauce then blitz once more. Taste and adjust if necessary.

Heat a frying pan until hot, add the fatty lamb and fry for 2–3 minutes until crispy on one side. Add half the dressing and heat through until sticky and coating the lamb nicely, then remove from the heat and set aside.

Place the cucumber, peas, sugar snaps, beansprouts, spring onions, mint and coriander into a bowl and toss to combine. Add some dressing and lime juice to the bowl then add the pea shoots and toss once more.

Divide the salad between the plates then top with the crispy lamb. Finish with more of the dressing, sprinkle on the finely sliced chilli and serve straight away.

Chilli tomato pizza and lobster calzone

Lobster pizza is a bit flash but you can make this with crab or prawns, or even with salmon. Whatever you use, make sure the fish filling is cooked beforehand as the pizza cooks so quickly that there is no time to cook the filling. The semolina flour will give both the pizza and the calzone a nice crust.

Serves 4–6

For the pizza dough

800g '00' flour, plus more to dust

200g semolina flour

1 tsp salt

1 tbsp caster sugar

2 x 7g sachets fast-action yeast

For the topping

2 x 400g cans of San Marzano tomatoes (see page 10)

2 large balls of cow's milk mozzarella, roughly torn

50g finely grated pecorino cheese

2 chillies, deseeded and finely sliced

4 tbsp peanut oil

large handful of basil leaves

sea salt and freshly ground black pepper

1 small cooked lobster

bottle of mango chilli sauce

To make the dough, place the flour, semolina, salt, sugar and yeast into a large bowl and stir. Make a well in the centre of the flour and pour in 650ml of water, gradually mixing with the flour to form a soft dough.

Tip out and knead on a lightly floured work surface until smooth and elastic. Divide into four and roll each into a ball, then place on a tray, cover and leave to rise for 24 hours.

Preheat the oven to as high as it will go. Place a heavy baking tray or pizza stone in the oven and allow to heat.

Roll each piece of dough out until about 5mm thick, then place on to an upturned floured tray.

Make the topping. Place the tomatoes in a food processor and blitz to a purée. Spoon thinly over two of the pizzas, just to the edges.

Scatter over half the mozzarella and pecorino and all the chillies, then drizzle over half the peanut oil. Finish with a few basil leaves and season with salt and black pepper.

Scoot into the oven – pushing the pizza from the tray on to the heated tray or pizza stone – and cook for 5–8 minutes until cooked through and bubbling. Serve immediately.

Meanwhile, cover half of each of the other pizzas with the tomato sauce, then place pieces of lobster over that half, with the remaining mozzarella, pecorino, a drizzle of mango chilli sauce, the remaining peanut oil and a scattering of basil. Season with salt and pepper.

Fold the empty halves of the pizzas over the filled halves, then crimp the edges and place on the heated pizza tray or stone.

Cook for 5–10 minutes until golden and crispy. Serve immediately.

Tip

For best results, you need a pizza stone in your oven; and get the oven as hot as possible.

Lots of my mates are Indian and I've learned a few tips from them over the years. I have had to, as they've come for dinner a few times! This is my go-to recipe: you just stick it in the oven and forget about it. Using a lamb shoulder means you have to cook it for a while, but the taste will be worth it in the end.

Indian-spiced lamb shoulder with Bombay potatoes

Serves 4–6

For the spice mix

1 tbsp coriander seeds

1½ tsp each cumin seeds, chilli flakes and turmeric

1 cinnamon stick, broken up

½ tsp each fennel seeds, peppercorns and fenugreek

¼ tsp cloves

For the lamb

1 lamb shoulder

sea salt and freshly ground black pepper

2 tbsp vegetable oil

2 onions, finely chopped

2 green finger chillies, split lengthways

4 garlic cloves, finely chopped

5cm piece of root ginger, finely chopped

1 tsp cardamom pods, lightly crushed

8 curry leaves

2 tbsp tamarind pulp

400g can of chopped tomatoes

500ml beef stock

2 tbsp chopped coriander leaves

2 tbsp chopped mint leaves

For the Bombay potatoes

750g potatoes, cut into 3cm cubes

4 tbsp flavourless vegetable oil

1 onion, finely chopped

1 garlic clove, finely chopped

1 tsp each mustard seeds, chilli powder, ground coriander and cumin

½ tsp turmeric

400g can of chopped tomatoes

1 tbsp each chopped coriander and mint leaves

To make the spice mix, place the coriander and cumin seeds into a dry frying pan and heat for 1–2 minutes until just browning and aromatic. Pour into a spice grinder or a mortar and pestle with the rest of the spices and blitz to a powder.

For the lamb, preheat the oven to 150°C/300°F/gas mark 2. Season the lamb with plenty of salt and pepper. Heat the vegetable oil in a large non-stick casserole pan and sear the lamb for 2 minutes on each side until golden-brown all over, then remove from the pan and set aside.

Add the onions and chillies and cook for 4–5 minutes until softened and just coloured. Add the spice mix, garlic and ginger, mix well and cook for another 2 minutes, then add the cardamom, curry leaves and tamarind.

Add the chopped tomatoes and stock and bring to the boil, then reduce the heat to a simmer and cover. Cook in the oven for three to 4 hours, until the lamb is virtually falling off the bone. Remove the lid, baste the lamb with the sauce and cook for another 5 minutes. Season to taste with salt and black pepper, then stir in the herbs.

Meanwhile, make the Bombay potatoes. Place the potatoes in cold water, bring to the boil and cook for 12–15 minutes, then drain.

Heat a large sauté pan and add the oil. Once it is hot, add the onion, garlic, mustard seeds, chilli powder, ground coriander and cumin and turmeric. Tip in the tomatoes, mix really well and bring to a gentle simmer, then add the potatoes and cook for another 3–5 minutes until they absorb the spices and are very tender. Season to taste, then stir in the herbs.

Pile chunks of the lamb carefully on to each plate, then spoon the sauce over and serve with a pile of potatoes.

All the components here are simple, but it requires back-timing so everything is ready at the same time. The solution is this: don't be afraid to ask for help in the kitchen. Ken Hom showed me this one and it's fantastic. He really is the master at this stuff. Enjoy it! The usual warnings about using cold cooked rice apply (see page 4). If you prefer, you can pair it with a sticky rice omelette (see page 238) instead of egg-fried rice.

Sweet-and-sour pork and pineapple with egg-fried rice

Serves 4

For the pork

450g pork fillet, cut into 5cm-long strips

2 tsp light soy sauce

2 tsp Shaoxing rice wine or dry sherry

1 tsp sesame oil

2 tsp cornflour

1½ tbsp groundnut oil

3 tbsp coarsely chopped garlic

225g fresh or canned pineapple, chopped

2 tbsp finely chopped coriander leaves, plus a large handful of sprigs of coriander

1 tbsp dark soy sauce

2 tsp caster sugar

For the egg-fried rice

2 eggs, lightly beaten

2 tsp sesame oil

1 tsp salt

2 tbsp groundnut or vegetable oil

400g long-grain rice, cooked, drained and chilled

½ tsp freshly ground black pepper

2 tbsp spring onions, finely chopped

Put the pork in a bowl with the light soy sauce, rice wine or sherry, sesame oil and cornflour and set aside.

Heat a wok over high heat until it is hot, add the oil and, when it is very hot and slightly smoking, add the garlic and stir-fry for 15 seconds or until golden brown. Then add the pork and stir-fry for 3 minutes.

Add the pineapple, coriander leaves, dark soy sauce and sugar and continue to stir-fry for another 3 minutes. Spoon on to a platter and garnish with the sprigs of coriander.

Meanwhile, to cook the egg-fried rice, mix the eggs, sesame oil and a pinch of the salt in a small bowl and set aside.

Heat a wok or large frying pan over high heat until it is hot. Add the groundnut or vegetable oil and, when it is very hot and slightly smoking, add the cooked rice and stir-fry for 3 minutes or until it is thoroughly warmed through.

Drizzle the egg mixture over the rice and continue to stir-fry for 2–3 minutes or until the eggs have set and the mixture is dry. Add the remaining salt and the pepper, stir-fry for 2 more minutes, then toss in the spring onions. Stir several times and turn on to a serving plate.

Indian soft shell crabs with home-made lime pickle

Soft shell crabs will more often than not be bought frozen; they can be found online or from good fishmongers. So buy plenty at a time, as you can keep them in the freezer at home. You need hot oil to fry them and you'll need an oil thermometer to get the right temperature; don't guess for this as you need to get the inside cooked and the outside nice and crisp to get the contrasting textures right.

Serves 4 as a starter

For the lime pickle

500g limes, cut into wedges
2 tbsp fine sea salt
1 tbsp vegetable oil
1 tbsp mustard seeds
4 garlic cloves, finely chopped
5cm piece of root ginger, peeled and finely chopped
1 tbsp ground cumin
1 tbsp ground coriander
½ tsp asafoetida
1½ tsp mild chilli powder
300g soft light brown sugar
50ml white wine vinegar

For the crab

5cm piece of root ginger, peeled and grated
4 garlic cloves, crushed
1 tbsp ground coriander
2 tsp ground cumin
1 tsp chilli powder
4 tbsp chopped coriander leaves and roots
4 tbsp gram flour
finely grated zest and juice of 2 limes
4 tbsp groundnut oil
8 small soft shell crabs
flavourless vegetable oil, to deep-fry

First, make the lime pickle; it's best to make it a week or so before. Place the limes and salt into a bowl and toss to combine, then cover and place in the fridge to cure for 48 hours, stirring occasionally.

Heat a large sauté pan over a high heat, then add the oil and mustard seeds. As soon as they start popping, add the garlic and ginger and stir for 1 minute. Add the cumin, coriander, asafoetida and chilli powder and stir for another minute, then add the sugar and cook, without stirring, until it liquefies, shaking the pan occasionally. Now tip in the salted limes and the juices from the bowl, the vinegar and 200ml of water.

Bring to the boil, then reduce the heat, cover and simmer for 1½ hours over a gentle heat, until thickened and the limes are very soft. Cool slightly before pulsing in a food processor for 20 seconds until the pieces of lime are quite small. Spoon into sterilised jars (see page 232) and ideally leave for a few days to mature.

For the crab, place all the ingredients except the crabs and the oil for deep-frying into a bowl and mix to a thick paste, then add the crabs and mix well so the crabs are coated in the mixture. Cover and place in the fridge for at least 2 hours. Remove from the fridge and bring to room temperature before you want to cook them.

Heat a deep fat fryer to 160°C/320°F or heat the oil for deep-frying in a deep heavy-based sauté pan until a breadcrumb sizzles and turns brown when dropped into it. (CAUTION: hot oil can be dangerous. Do not leave unattended.)

Carefully lay the crabs one at a time into the oil and cook for 1–2 minutes until cooked through. Drain on kitchen paper and season with a little salt.

Serve the crabs with generous dollops of lime pickle.

It used to be that you were advised to only buy mussels when there was an 'r' in the month. I never really knew where that came from, as I've been to loads of farms around the country producing mussels all year round; they're cheap and packed full of flavour. Stuff such as lemon grass and ginger are commonplace in supermarkets nowadays and the flavours here with the coconut make it really tasty. Try not to reduce the liquid too much, as you will want to mop up the liquor left in the bowl with plenty of bread. Add a squeeze of lime juice if you want it, too.

Lemon grass and ginger mussels

Serves 4

2kg mussels, scrubbed, beards removed

50g unsalted butter

2 shallots, finely chopped

2 lemon grass stalks, outer layers discarded, finely chopped

2 garlic cloves, finely chopped

10cm piece of root ginger, peeled and finely chopped

1–2 red chillies (depending on their heat), finely sliced

200ml white wine

150ml coconut water

160ml coconut cream

2 tbsp olive oil

1 loaf sourdough bread, thickly sliced

2 tbsp roughly chopped coriander leaves

Wash the mussels in a colander to remove any dirt or grit and discard any of the beards (the tufty bits on the mussels). If you want to be fussy, scrape off any little barnacles with an old butter knife, too. Throw away any mussels that are not firmly closed, and don't shut when tapped firmly on the side of the sink.

Place the butter in a large pan and, when it's foaming, add the shallots, lemon grass, garlic, ginger and chilli(es) and cook without colour for 5 minutes until soft.

Increase the heat to high and add the wine, coconut water and coconut cream, bring to the boil, then add the mussels. Cover and cook for 4–5 minutes until the mussels open.

Meanwhile, heat a griddle pan until hot. Drizzle the olive oil over the bread and char on each side until golden.

Add the coriander leaves to the mussels and stir through, then check the seasoning.

Serve the mussels with the charred bread, discarding any shellfish that have refused to open and warning your guests to do the same.

Tempura squid and prawns with Asian 'pesto'

This 'pesto' has tonnes of flavour and works well with most meat and fish. I love squid now. If I'm honest I never used to but, like most things, it's wasted on the young! Fry the squid in oil that is as hot as you dare, as you don't want it to overcook.

Serves 4

For the tempura

flavourless vegetable oil, to deep-fry

500g squid, cleaned and cut into strips

500g raw king prawns, shelled and deveined

2 tbsp light soy sauce

2 tbsp Shaoxing rice wine or dry sherry

2 tbsp sesame oil

2 limes

100g cornflour

3 spring onions, finely sliced

1 long red chilli, roughly chopped

For the pesto

small handful of coriander leaves, roughly chopped

small handful of mint leaves, roughly chopped

1 garlic clove, sliced

1 long red chilli, sliced

2 tbsp palm sugar

1 tbsp fish sauce

1 tbsp soy sauce

1 tbsp sesame oil

1 tbsp Shaoxing rice wine or dry sherry

juice of 1 lime

Heat a deep-fat fryer to 180°C/350°F, or heat the oil for deep-frying in a deep heavy-based saucepan until a breadcrumb sizzles and turns brown when dropped into it. (CAUTION: hot oil can be dangerous. Do not leave unattended.)

While it heats up, put the squid and prawns into a bowl and mix them with the soy sauce, rice wine or sherry, sesame oil and the juice of 1 lime.

To make the pesto, put half the herbs and all the other ingredients into a small food processor and blitz well to make a fine purée.

Add the cornflour to the squid and prawns and mix well to coat; it will be very sticky.

Carefully place the seafood into the fat fryer in batches and fry for 2 minutes, until just cooked through and crispy. Drain on kitchen paper to blot off excess fat while you quickly cook the rest.

Lay the cooked seafood on a platter then drizzle over the pesto, scatter over the reserved herbs and finish with the spring onions and chopped chilli.

Cut the remaining lime into wedges and place alongside.

Lemon chicken, black bean squid and stir-fried rice

These are my favourites among the dishes that I order from my local Chinese restaurant. They make them properly, without MSG or any other unnecessary stuff, just simple clean flavours – that's the essence of Chinese cooking for me.

Place the chicken in a bowl, then mix the soy sauce, honey and cornflour together in a separate bowl and pour over the chicken. Toss to coat, then set aside while you prepare all the vegetables and herbs. Mix the lemon zest and juice and chicken stock together.

Mix the squid, sesame oil, soy sauce and mirin together in a bowl and set aside for 5 minutes.

To cook the lemon chicken, heat a wok or frying pan until hot and add the groundnut oil. Add the sherry to the chicken and stir through, then put into the hot wok and stir-fry for 2 minutes, until just sealed. Add the chilli, garlic and ginger, and the lemon and chicken stock, and bring to the boil, stirring well. Reduce the heat to a simmer and cook for 4–5 minutes, until the chicken is cooked through and the sauce has thickened. Remove from the wok and transfer to a bowl. Cover with clingfilm, and keep warm.

To make the stir-fried rice, clean the wok or frying pan and reheat until hot. Add the groundnut oil and when it's shimmering, add the rice and stir-fry for 1 minute before adding the spring onions, coriander, soy sauce and sesame oil. Stir-fry for 2–3 minutes until piping hot right through, then tip into a serving bowl, cover with clingfilm, and keep warm.

To cook the black bean squid, clean the wok or frying pan again, then reheat until hot. Add the groundnut oil, and when it's shimmering add the ginger, garlic and chillies and stir-fry for 2 minutes, until just softened. Add the marinated squid and the black beans and stir-fry for 2–3 minutes over a high heat. Add the chicken stock, sherry, spring onions and coriander, stir well, then simmer for another couple of minutes until the squid is cooked through.

Add the spring onions to the chicken, and serve with the black bean squid and stir-fried rice.

Serves 4

For the chicken

400g boneless skinless chicken breast, cut into strips

2 tbsp light soy sauce

1 tbsp clear honey

2 tbsp cornflour

2 lemons, zested and juiced

75ml chicken stock

1 tsp groundnut oil

1 tbsp dry sherry

1 red chilli, finely chopped

3 garlic cloves, finely sliced

2cm piece of ginger, peeled and finely grated

3 spring onions, finely sliced

For the squid

300g squid, cleaned and cut into strips

1 tsp sesame oil

1 tbsp soy sauce

1 tbsp mirin

2 tbsp groundnut oil

3cm piece of ginger, peeled and finely chopped

2 garlic cloves, finely chopped

2 red chillies, finely chopped

40g black beans, rinsed, drained and roughly chopped

50–75ml chicken stock

2 tbsp dry sherry or Shaoxing rice wine

3 spring onions, finely sliced

2–3 tbsp roughly chopped coriander

For the stir-fried rice

1 tbsp groundnut oil

300g cooked and cooled basmati rice

2 spring onions, sliced

2 tbsp coriander leaves, roughly chopped

2 tbsp soy sauce

1 tsp sesame oil

Pan-fried black pudding with scallops and ginger purée

As there are so few ingredients here, you need to make sure you get really good-quality black pudding and scallops. Be careful with the ginger purée, as it can pack a pretty hot and spicy punch!

Serves 4

200g root ginger, peeled and thinly sliced
4 curry leaves
75g palm sugar
50g tamarind paste
a pinch of sea salt
25g caster sugar
1 apple, cut into 12 thin slices
10g unsalted butter
8 thin slices of pancetta
8 x 1cm thick slices of black pudding
4 large scallops, with roe
1 tsp olive oil
½ lemon, juiced
4 tsp extra virgin olive oil

Put 500ml of water into a sauté pan and set on the heat. Add the ginger, curry leaves, palm sugar, tamarind and salt, and bring to the boil, then simmer for 10 minutes. Cool slightly, then place in a blender and blitz to a fine purée.

Put the caster sugar into a frying pan and heat until just golden, then add the apple slices and cook in the caramel for a few seconds before adding the butter. Add a splash of water and swirl around so that the apple is coated with a light caramel.

Heat a non-stick frying pan until very hot, then add the pancetta and cook on both sides until crispy. Remove from the pan and set aside, then add the black pudding to the pan. Fry on each side for 30 seconds only, until just crispy but still soft on the inside. Remove and set aside.

Drizzle the scallops with the olive oil and sear for 1½ minutes on each side until golden and just cooked. Squeeze the lemon juice over the top and remove from the pan.

Cut the scallops in half widthways. Place a piece of caramelised apple in the centre of each plate. Top with a small spoonful of ginger purée, then a piece of black pudding, then half a scallop, and repeat with another piece of apple, the purée, black pudding, scallop and apple, finishing with a final spoonful of the purée.

Finally, add a couple of pieces of crispy pancetta and drizzle with the extra virgin olive oil.

Salmon and charred sweetcorn salsa

It's taken ten years to master the art of growing sweetcorn in my garden, and all we really did was move the plants round from year to year to see where it grew best. We now have the perfect site. The problem now is that the dog has got a taste for it too, so he's forever pulling the plants up.

Serves 4

4 whole corn on the cob, outer husks removed

6 spring onions, trimmed

2 red chillies

3 limes, cut in half

2 tbsp roughly chopped coriander, stems and leaves

5 tbsp extra virgin olive oil

sea salt and freshly ground black pepper

4 x 100g salmon fillets, boneless and skinless

Put the corn on the cob into a large pan of water, set over a high heat and bring to the boil, then turn the heat down and simmer for 15 minutes until tender.

Meanwhile, heat a griddle pan until hot. Add the spring onions and chillies, and char on each side for a couple of minutes, until just blackened. Remove and roughly chop.

Add the limes to the griddle pan, cut-side down, and char for 1 minute until just blackened. Remove and set aside.

When the corn is tender, drain and set on the griddle pan to char – keep an eye on it as you don't want one side very black! Turn every couple of minutes so that it is evenly charred. Remove from the griddle, then cut 2 cobs in half and set aside.

Remove the kernels from the other 2 cobs and place in a food processor along with the chopped spring onions, chillies and coriander. Squeeze in the juice from 1 lime and add 2 tbsp of the olive oil, then pulse until everything is roughly chopped. Season to taste with salt and pepper.

Rub each side of the salmon fillets with a little of the olive oil, then place on the griddle pan and char on each side for 1 minute until just cooked through.

Place on plates with a spoonful of the salsa, half a charred corn on the cob and a piece of lime. Finish with the last of the olive oil, drizzled over.

Singapore chilli crab with egg noodles

The aptly named Crab Under the Bridge, in Singapore, is where I tried this for the first time, and I loved it as much then as I do now. It's not food for a fancy dinner party – it's food for getting messy, and you need a bib and tea towels as you pick the meat from the shells. The keys to it are the spices and the stickiness, and to spend as much time eating the crab as you do licking your fingers.

Serves 2–3

2 tbsp vegetable oil

10cm piece of ginger, peeled and finely chopped

3 garlic cloves, chopped

3 red bird's-eye chillies, finely chopped

4 spring onions, roughly chopped, tops and bottoms kept separate

225ml tomato ketchup

125ml sweet chilli sauce

125ml hoisin sauce

1½ tbsp fish sauce

3 tbsp soy sauce

2 tbsp caster sugar

200g fine egg noodles

1kg whole crab

2 tbsp roughly chopped mint leaves

2 tbsp roughly chopped coriander leaves

Heat a wok until hot, then add the vegetable oil, ginger, garlic and chillies, and stir-fry for 2 minutes. Add the chopped tops of the spring onions and stir-fry for another minute. Add the tomato, sweet chilli, hoisin, fish and soy sauces and the sugar, then bring to the boil. Reduce the heat to a simmer and cook for 5 minutes. Transfer three ladlefuls of the sauce to a bowl and set aside.

Meanwhile, cook the noodles according to the packet instructions and drain in a sieve.

Chop the crab into large pieces. Remove and discard the dead men's fingers, then crack the claws lightly. Add the crab to the wok of simmering sauce and toss to coat thoroughly, then simmer for 5 minutes. Transfer to a serving bowl, cover with clingfilm and keep warm.

Clean the wok or frying pan and return to the heat. Add the reserved three ladlefuls of sauce, and when it's simmering, add the cooked drained noodles, three-quarters of the remaining chopped spring onions, the mint and coriander, and toss to combine and heat through.

Serve the crab in a large bowl, garnished with the rest of the spring onions and with the noodles in a separate bowl.

This is better than any takeaway, and ready in less time than it would take to get one delivered! I'm fortunate to work with some amazing Indian chefs, and this is my adaption of one of their most popular recipes.

Chicken curry with basmati rice

Serves 4

200g basmati rice

40g unsalted butter

1 tbsp vegetable oil

1 onion, finely sliced

50g medium curry paste

4 small chicken breasts, cut into 2cm thick slices

200g tinned chopped tomatoes

300ml coconut milk

2 tbsp roughly chopped coriander leaves

2 tbsp roughly chopped mint leaves

1 lime, juiced

sea salt and freshly ground black pepper

3 tbsp desiccated coconut, lightly toasted

Place the basmati rice in a medium saucepan, then pour on 400ml of cold water and add a knob of butter. Cover with a lid, then set over a high heat and bring to a simmer. Reduce the heat to low and cook for 12–15 minutes, while you make the curry.

Heat a large sauté pan or wok until hot. Add the vegetable oil and onion, and stir-fry for 2–3 minutes, until just softening, then add the curry paste and stir-fry for 1 minute. Add the chicken and stir to coat in the sauce, then add the tomatoes and coconut milk, and bring to the boil. Reduce the heat and simmer for 10 minutes until the chicken is cooked through and the sauce has thickened slightly. Stir in the chopped coriander and mint, then add the lime juice and the rest of the butter, and season to taste with salt and pepper.

The rice should be cooked by now – lift the lid and see if all the water has been absorbed. The rice should have little pockmarks all over it and be light and fluffy, in separate grains.

Serve the rice with a ladleful of chicken curry and the toasted desiccated coconut.

Quinoa – one of the great superfoods – is a type of seed originating from Peru. It comes from the same family as beetroot, spinach and tumbleweed, and is really high in protein, making it popular in vegetarian cooking. Once you've tried it you will appreciate its unique texture and flavour.

Spiced quinoa, cauliflower, pine nut and blue cheese salad

Serves 4

70g quinoa

2 tbsp olive oil

½ small cauliflower, cut into florets, then into thick slices

4 shallots, finely chopped

1 tsp medium curry powder

4 tbsp red wine vinegar

100ml maple syrup

4 tbsp extra virgin olive oil

sea salt and freshly ground black pepper

4 heads of baby gem lettuce, cut into quarters

50g pine nuts

2 tbsp finely chopped chives

150g Gorgonzola dolce or soft blue cheese

Cook the quinoa according to the packet instructions, then drain and set aside.

Meanwhile, heat a frying pan until hot. Add 1 tbsp of the olive oil and the cauliflower florets, and cook until lightly browned on each side, then remove and place in a large bowl.

Add the rest of the olive oil to the frying pan with the shallots and fry for a couple of minutes until just softened, then add the curry powder and cook for 2 more minutes, stirring well.

Add the red wine vinegar and turn the heat down to a simmer, then stir in the maple syrup and extra virgin olive oil. Simmer the dressing for 1 minute, then remove from the heat.

Pour half the dressing into the cooked drained quinoa, season with salt and pepper, and toss well so that it is coated thoroughly. Pour the remaining dressing into the bowl with the cooked cauliflower, add the baby gems, pine nuts and half the chives, season and toss together. Add the dressed quinoa and toss lightly together, then divide between four plates. Place the small pieces of blue cheese over the salad, finish with a scattering of chives and serve straight away.

Piperade is a mixture of onions, peppers and tomatoes, with the addition of espelette pepper. The dish originates from the Basque region, on the French/Spanish border. The espelette pepper is traditional in the northern part of the region and can be bought dried, puréed or pickled in jars, but most commonly it's found as ground pepper. Once the veg are cooked you can add egg, garlic or a meat such as ham, but I love it with chicken and simply cooked pilau rice. It's also a dish that gets better the second time you cook it.

Chicken piperade with pilau rice

Serves 4–6

For the chicken

1 x 1.5kg chicken, giblets removed, cut into 8 pieces

1 tbsp plain flour

sea salt and freshly ground black pepper

25ml olive oil

2 onions, thickly sliced

2 garlic cloves, lightly crushed

4 red peppers, seeded and thickly sliced

1 tbsp tomato purée

75ml dry sherry

75ml white wine

400g tin chopped tomatoes

2 tsp ground espelette pepper

1–2 tsp caster sugar, to taste

2 tbsp finely chopped flat-leaf parsley

For the pilau rice

2 tbsp vegetable oil

1 onion, finely diced

6 cloves

1 cinnamon stick

200g basmati rice

2 bay leaves

1 lemon

Preheat the oven to 180°C/350°F/gas mark 4.

Heat a large sauté pan until hot. Dust the chicken pieces with the flour and season with salt and pepper. Heat a little of the olive oil in a sauté pan and seal the chicken on each side, in batches, until golden-brown. Remove from the pan and place in an ovenproof casserole.

Add the rest of the olive oil to the sauté pan, then add the onions, garlic and peppers, and cook for 5 minutes until just softening. Add the tomato purée and sauté for 1 minute, then add the sherry and white wine, and bring to a simmer.

Add the tinned tomatoes, espelette pepper and sugar, and stir well to combine, then pour over the chicken. Cover with a lid and bake for 1–1½ hours, until the chicken is cooked through, the peppers are tender and the sauce has reduced slightly.

While the chicken cooks, make the rice. Heat a wide sauté pan until hot, then add the oil and onion and sweat for 2 minutes. Add the cloves and cinnamon, and cook for another minute.

Add the rice and stir well to combine, coating all the grains in the onion mixture, then add 600ml water and stir once more. Add the bay leaves and 2 slices of the lemon, then cover with a lid and reduce to a gentle simmer. Cook for 15–20 minutes until the rice is tender and all the liquid is absorbed. Taste and add the rest of the lemon if necessary.

Season the chicken to taste with salt and pepper, then stir in the parsley. Serve with the pilau rice.

Tandoori king prawns with butter sauce

Cooked on the barbecue or under the grill, there can be few dishes better than this for cooking outside at home. So many people are used to burnt sausages and dry Frisbee burgers, but try these and you won't go back.

Place all the ingredients for the prawns, except the prawns and lemon, into a bowl and whisk to combine. Stir the prawns carefully into the mixture, then cover and place in the fridge to marinate for at least 20 minutes, preferably overnight.

Meanwhile, get a barbecue ready so that the coals are glowing, and make the sauce. Heat a sauté pan until hot, add the butter and red onion, cook for a couple of minutes until softened, then add the garlic, cumin and chilli, and cook for another minute.

Add the tomatoes, cream and ginger, and bring to the boil, then reduce the heat to a simmer and cook for 4–5 minutes until the sauce has thickened slightly and the tomatoes have broken down. Stir in the coriander and season to taste with salt and pepper.

Remove the prawns from the fridge and thread onto four metal skewers.

Cook on the barbecue for 2 minutes on each side until cooked through. Alternatively, preheat the grill to high and place the skewers on a baking tray. Cook for 2–3 minutes, then turn over and cook for a further 2 minutes until cooked through.

Serve the prawns on the skewers, with lemon halves and a dollop of sauce.

Serves 4

For the prawns

1 tsp garam masala

½ tsp ground cinnamon

1 tsp chilli powder

1 tsp ground cumin

2 garlic cloves, crushed

5cm piece of ginger, peeled and finely grated

200ml natural yoghurt

500g large tiger prawns, peeled but tails left on

2 lemons, cut in half

For the butter sauce

50g unsalted butter

1 red onion, finely chopped

2 garlic cloves, finely chopped

1 tsp ground cumin

1 red chilli, finely chopped

3 ripe tomatoes, roughly chopped

200ml double cream

5cm piece of ginger, peeled and roughly chopped

2 tbsp roughly chopped coriander leaves

sea salt and freshly ground pepper

Dahl chicken, chilli paneer and naan

I'm fortunate to count some top Indian chefs among my mates and I cooked this dish with Cyrus Todiwala on the show who is not only a true gentleman but also a hugely talented cook. Thanks for the advice and tips – I think it's one of my favourite recipes in the book!

Start with the naan. Place the flour in a food mixer fitted with a dough hook, or a large bowl, with the yeast and baking powder, and add the egg, sugar and salt. Mix together, then add the yoghurt and milk, and mix to a soft dough. Set aside to rise for 1 hour, then knead briefly until smooth and divide into six equal balls. Cover and set aside to rise in a warm place for another hour.

To make the dahl, rinse the lentils and soak them in 500ml water for 20 minutes.

Heat a large sauté pan until hot. Add half the oil and the dried chillies, and fry for 1 minute, then add the green chillies and onions, and sauté for 3–4 minutes until lightly coloured. Add the curry leaves, ginger, and garlic and continue to fry.

Mix the chilli powder, ground cumin, coriander and turmeric together in a small bowl with 150ml of the chicken stock to form a paste. Add to the pan and cook until you see the oil separate out – another 2–3 minutes. Add the lentils and their soaking water, and bring to the boil, then add the salt, cover with a lid and simmer for 5 minutes. Add the butter, cover, and simmer while you cook the chicken.

Chop the chicken into chunks. Heat a separate sauté pan until hot, add the rest of the oil and the chicken, and sauté for 3–4 minutes until coloured and nearly cooked.

Add the lentils to the chicken along with the tinned tomatoes and the rest of the chicken stock. Cook for another 15–20 minutes until the chicken is cooked through and the lentils are tender. Stir in the tamarind, brown sugar, coriander and mint, and check the seasoning. Add a little more stock if it becomes too thick. Leave to simmer gently on a very low heat.

While the chicken is cooking, make the chilli paneer. Cut the paneer into strips about 1cm wide and 3cm long. Heat a wok until hot, then add enough oil to cover the base by 2.5cm. Heat until shimmering, then fry the paneer in batches until golden brown. Drain into a sieve set over a bowl.

Discard the majority of the oil, leaving enough to just coat the bottom of the wok. Add the pine nuts, chillies, ginger and garlic, and stir-fry for 2 minutes. Add the red onion and both peppers, and stir-fry for 2 minutes, then add the vinegar, soy sauce and chicken stock, and bring to a simmer. Add the spring onions and simmer for 1 minute. Mix the cornflour with 3 tbsp of cold water to make a paste, then whisk into the peppers and onion, and cook until just thickened. Stir in the paneer and leave to simmer on a very low heat.

To cook the naan, preheat the oven as high as it will go. Place a heavy baking tray or pizza stone in the oven and allow to heat. Stretch the dough to an oval shape, then place on the tray or stone and bake for 4–5 minutes, until risen and golden brown. Brush with the melted butter.

Finish the chilli paneer with the coriander, and serve with the dahl chicken and naan.

Serves 4

For the dahl chicken

250g red lentils
4 tbsp vegetable oil
2 dried red chillies, torn, seeds removed
2 long green chillies, finely chopped
2 onions, finely chopped
1 tbsp chopped curry leaves
5cm piece of ginger, peeled, finely chopped
6 garlic cloves, finely chopped
1 tsp hot red chilli powder
1 tsp ground cumin
2 tsp ground coriander
1 tsp turmeric
300ml chicken stock
1 tsp sea salt
40g unsalted butter
6 boneless skinless chicken thighs
200g tinned chopped tomatoes
1 tbsp tamarind paste
1 tbsp dark brown soft sugar
1 small bunch of coriander, chopped
2 tbsp chopped mint leaves

For the chilli paneer

450g paneer
vegetable oil, for shallow-frying
50g pine nuts
4 long green finger chillies, finely sliced
5cm piece of ginger, peeled, finely chopped
8 garlic cloves, finely chopped
1 red onion, finely sliced
1 green pepper, finely sliced
1 long red pepper, finely sliced
50ml white wine vinegar
75ml light soy sauce
250ml chicken stock
3 spring onions, finely sliced
1 tbsp cornflour
2 tbsp chopped coriander

For the naan

450g plain flour
2 tsp fast-action dried yeast
1 tsp baking powder
1 egg
1 tsp caster sugar
a pinch of sea salt
150ml natural yoghurt
150ml milk
50g melted unsalted butter

Spiced pork and pomegranate tabbouleh

Many people think that tabbouleh is made with couscous, but for me it should always be made with bulghur wheat – a traditional Middle Eastern cracked grain. The spiced pork and pomegranate molasses go so well together, but you could also make this dish with chicken or fish.

Put a small handful of the chopped coriander and mint into a bowl with the juice of 1 of the lemons and the ground coriander, cumin, sumac and half the za'atar. Add 50ml of the olive oil and mix well. Add the pork and stir to coat, then set aside while you make the tabbouleh.

Put the pomegranate seeds, tomatoes, spring onions, all the remaining herbs and the soaked and drained bulghur wheat into a large bowl, and mix together.

Mix the remaining lemon juice, honey, pomegranate molasses and 50ml of the olive oil together in a separate bowl, and season well with salt and pepper. Add to the salad, season generously with more salt and pepper, then stir in the flaked almonds.

Heat a frying pan until hot, then add the last of the olive oil and the pork, and fry in batches for 2–3 minutes, until golden-brown and cooked through. Tip into a serving bowl with all the cooking oil, and serve with the tabbouleh.

Serves 4

1 large bunch of coriander, roughly chopped

1 large bunch of mint, roughly chopped

3 lemons, juiced

1 tsp ground coriander

1 tsp ground cumin

½ tsp sumac

2 tbsp za'atar

150ml extra virgin olive oil

450g pork tenderloin, trimmed of sinew and thickly sliced

1 pomegranate, seeded

3 tomatoes, chopped

8 spring onions, roughly chopped

1 large bunch of flat-leaf parsley, roughly chopped

125g bulghur wheat, soaked in cold water for 2 hours, then drained

2 tbsp clear honey

2 tbsp pomegranate molasses

sea salt and freshly ground black pepper

50g flaked toasted almonds

Spiced duck breast with umeboshi sauce and steamed bok choi

A simple dish, but it's the umeboshi plums that make it – sour to taste, they cut through the fat in the duck. They are available online but can also be bought in some supermarkets.

Serves 4

1 tsp curry powder

1 tsp ground ginger

1 tsp five-spice powder

2 tsp sansho pepper

4 x 175g duck breasts

4 tbsp clear honey

1 bok choi, root removed and leaves separated

3cm piece of ginger, peeled and finely chopped

1 garlic clove, crushed

1 red chilli, finely sliced

½ red onion, finely sliced

200g umeboshi plums, stoned

Preheat the oven to 200°C/400°F/gas mark 6.

Mix the curry powder, ground ginger, five-spice and sansho pepper together in a bowl, then sprinkle half the mixture over the skin and flesh of the duck breasts.

Place the duck skin-side down in a cold non-stick frying pan and set over a high heat for 3–4 minutes until the fat renders out. Turn the duck over, then drizzle 2 tbsp of the honey over the skin and place in the oven for 8–10 minutes. When the duck is cooked, remove from the pan and leave on a plate for 8–10 minutes while you prepare the rest of the dish.

Lay the bok choi in a steamer set over a pan of simmering water. Add the ginger, garlic, chilli and red onion, then cover and steam for 5–6 minutes.

Put the plums into a small blender with 1 tsp of the remaining spice mix and the remaining 2 tbsp of honey. Blitz to a fine purée, then pour into a pan and warm through, adding the resting juices from the duck – taste to see if more honey is needed.

Lay the steamed veg on a plate, carve the duck into thick slices and lay alongside, and finish with a dollop of the umeboshi sauce.

Comforting
Food with
Friends

Double-baked old Winchester soufflé with dandelion and walnut salad

Together with the salad, these fluffy delights make a full meal. I came across Old Winchester cheese while making the TV show; it proves you can always make delicious discoveries on your own doorstep.

Serves 4 as a starter or light lunch

For the soufflés

40g softened unsalted butter, plus more for the ramekins

40g plain flour, plus more to dust

350ml whole milk

125g Old Winchester or other mature hard cheese, grated

1 tsp Dijon mustard

3 eggs, separated

sea salt and freshly ground black pepper

For the salad

110g caster sugar

110g walnut halves

flavourless vegetable oil, to deep-fry

110g dandelion leaves

chopped chives, to serve

3 tbsp 'house' dressing (see page 78)

For the glaze

250ml double cream

4 tbsp kirsch

100g Old Winchester or other mature hard cheese, grated

To make the soufflés, preheat the oven to 180°C/350°F/gas mark 4. Rub the inside of four 150ml ramekins with the softened butter, then dust with flour and place in a high-sided oven tray.

Melt the butter in a large saucepan over a medium heat, then add the flour and mix well. Cook over a low heat for 2–3 minutes, stirring with a wooden spoon. Gradually whisk in the milk, a little at a time, stirring constantly to avoid any lumps forming. Continue until all the milk has been added, then reduce the heat to very low and cook for a further 2–3 minutes.

Add the cheese and mustard, then take off the heat and beat the egg yolks into the mixture. Season with salt and black pepper.

In a clean, dry bowl, whisk the egg whites until they hold medium peaks, then fold the egg whites into the soufflé mixture. Divide the mixture between the soufflé dishes and put the ramekins in a roasting tin.

Pour enough hot water from the kettle into the tin to reach halfway up the sides of the ramekins. Bake the soufflés for 15–20 minutes, or until they are risen and evenly coloured.

Remove the ramekins from the tin and set aside for a few minutes, then run a knife around the edges of the soufflés and turn them out on to individual ovenproof dishes.

Make the salad. Pour 110ml of water into a saucepan, add the sugar and bring to the boil. Simmer until the sugar has dissolved and the syrup has thickened slightly. Add the walnuts and cook for 2–3 minutes. Empty the pan on to a sheet of baking parchment placed on a baking sheet.

Pour enough vegetable oil into a sauté pan to cover the bottom by 2cm and heat until just shimmering. Carefully place the walnuts a few at a time into the hot oil for a couple of minutes until golden brown. Drain on a sheet of baking parchment and leave to cool.

For the glaze, preheat the grill to medium-high. Whisk the cream and kirsch until combined. Coat the tops of the soufflés with the cream, then scatter over the cheese and place under the grill until golden. Serve in their dishes, or transfer to plates.

Put the dandelion leaves and chives into a bowl and toss in the dressing and nuts. Pile the salad on top of the soufflé and serve immediately.

Tip

These soufflés freeze really well and can be cooked from frozen with the sauce and the cheese on top (give them an extra 5 minutes in the oven).

This dish has travelled a fair bit; it came from when I was in the southern Indian ocean cooking with a Spanish chef. He had worked in some amazing places and this is an idea he had. It's cheffy, I know, but not that hard. The main thing is the quality of the mushrooms. Red mullet works with it, but you can serve it with any fish, or without. A common mistake people make with risotto is to make it too thick and heavy; keep it loose and add more stock if needed. You've been told…

Teriyaki mushroom risotto with red mullet and lime foam

Serves 4

250g mixed oyster and shiitake mushrooms
600ml chicken stock, plus more if needed
25g unsalted butter
2 shallots, finely chopped
2 garlic cloves, finely chopped
100g risotto rice
100ml white wine
sea salt and freshly ground black pepper
2 tbsp olive oil
4 tbsp teriyaki sauce
2 tbsp mascarpone
2 tbsp grated Parmesan
200ml whole milk
4 kaffir lime leaves, very finely chopped
1 tsp lecithin
4 x red mullet fillets

Prepare the mushrooms, brushing off any dirt, then trimming off the stems and tearing any large ones in half. Pour the stock into a saucepan with the trimmings and stalks from the mushrooms and warm through.

Heat a sauté pan until medium hot, add a knob of the butter, the shallots and garlic and cook for a couple of minutes without colouring, then add the rice and stir well. Pour in the wine and cook until it has disappeared.

Strain the stock into a clean saucepan, discarding any grit at the bottom, and place over a gentle heat. Add a couple of ladlefuls of stock at a time, simmering and stirring until the rice has absorbed all the stock, then add some more and continue to cook. Repeat until all the stock has been used and the rice is tender; it should take 15–18 minutes. Season well.

Heat a non-stick frying pan until hot, add the remaining butter and 1 tbsp of the olive oil, then tip in the mushrooms and cook over a high heat until just golden and tender. Any moisture they release into the pan should have evaporated.

Toss straight into the risotto, then fold in the teriyaki sauce, mascarpone and Parmesan. At this point adjust the texture of the risotto if needed. It shouldn't be too thick or heavy, so add a bit more stock to loosen the texture, if necessary.

Pour the milk into a saucepan with the lime leaves and lecithin and bring just to a simmer. Blitz with a stick blender to create a foam.

Put a frying pan on a high heat, add the remaining 1 tbsp of olive oil, then the red mullet, skin-side down. Cook for 1 minute, then turn and cook for another 30 seconds on the flesh side.

Spoon the risotto into bowls, top with the fish, skin side up, and finish with a spoonful of lime leaf foam.

Spoil-yourself Yorkshire wagyu fillet steak with fries and béarnaise sauce

I came across Yorkshire Wagyu when we set up my Manchester restaurant and it's ace. It is grown just like the amazing Japanese beef and we can't get enough of it (but a good fillet steak is fine here). Béarnaise sauce is the best with chips or beef. This is my treat when I'm home alone. Obviously, scale up the recipe to serve more people.

Serves 1

flavourless vegetable oil, to deep-fry

125g unsalted butter

3 tbsp tarragon vinegar

3 tbsp white wine

¼ tsp white peppercorns

½ small banana shallot, finely chopped

3 egg yolks

sea salt and freshly ground black pepper

1 tbsp chopped tarragon leaves

juice of ½ lemon (optional)

1 tbsp olive oil

1 x 200g good fillet steak (I love Yorkshire wagyu for a special occasion)

100g frozen chips

Preheat the oven to 200°C/400°F/gas mark 6.

Heat a deep-fat fryer to 190°C/375°F, or heat the oil for deep-frying in a deep heavy-based frying pan until a breadcrumb sizzles and turns brown when dropped into it. (CAUTION: hot oil can be dangerous. Do not leave unattended.)

Put 100g of the butter into a small saucepan and set over a medium heat to melt fairly gently. Wait until it is liquid and all the impurities have risen to the top in a foam. Skim off all the foam. Leave until just tepid.

Place the vinegar, white wine, peppercorns and shallot into a separate small saucepan and bring to the boil. Simmer until the liquid nearly disappears, leaving only about 1 tbsp.

Put the egg yolks into a bowl, then set over a pan of simmering water and whisk until thickened and light in colour.

Gradually add the melted butter, drop by drop, whisking constantly. Once the mixture has emulsified, add it in a thin stream. You want a sauce that is about the same thickness as mayonnaise. Stop adding the butter just before you get to the white milky

solids at the bottom of the pan (discard these). Season the sauce with salt and pepper, add the cooled vinegar reduction and the chopped tarragon leaves and mix well. Taste and see if you want to add lemon juice. Turn off the heat and leave the bowl over the pan until ready to use. Don't leave it too long, and work quickly.

Heat an ovenproof frying pan until searing hot, add the oil and steak then leave to cook on one side for 2–3 minutes before turning over and placing in the oven for 2–3 minutes more.

While the steak is in the oven, carefully lower the chips into the fat fryer and cook for 3–4 minutes until golden brown and cooked through.

Remove the steak from the oven (make sure you wear an oven glove to protect y our hands from the frying pan handle) and add the remaining butter to the pan, then spoon over the steak repeatedly for at least 2–3 minutes while the steak rests; this will give a lovely shine and add to the flavour.

Place the steak on a plate, pile the chips alongside then finish with a dollop of the béarnaise.

Salt baked sea bass with warm artichoke and bacon salad

Salt baking produces a wonderful taste and keeps the flesh of the fish nice and moist. You do need good sea salt for the job, though – mixed with the egg whites it creates a cocoon around the fish so that it steams inside.

Serves 4–6

4 egg whites

3 lemons

2 bunches of fresh basil, leaves torn

1.25kg sea salt

1 x 2kg whole sea bass, scaled, gutted and cleaned

1 tbsp vegetable oil

200g smoked back bacon, cut into lardons

600g cooked new potatoes

½ red onion, finely sliced

280g jar of roasted artichokes in olive oil

sea salt and freshly ground black pepper

Preheat the oven to 200°C/400°F/gas mark 6 and line a large baking tray (big enough for the fish) with silicone paper.

Whisk the egg whites in a large bowl until foamy, then add the zest of 2 of the lemons. Chop half the basil and add to the mixture, then add the salt and mix really well to combine.

Slice one of the zested lemons and place in the cavity of the fish along with half of the remaining the basil.

Take one-third of the salt mixture and lay it over the centre of the baking tray, then place the fish on top. Cover with the remaining salt mixture to cover the fish totally. Bake for 30 minutes, or until the crust is golden-brown and the fish is cooked. Push the tip of a knife into the centre to see if the fish is cooked – it should be hot through. Remove and leave to rest for 15 minutes while you make the salad.

Heat a frying pan until hot, add the vegetable oil and bacon, and fry for 3–4 minutes until golden brown and just crispy at the edges. Tip into a serving bowl, then add the potatoes to the pan and fry until hot through and browned at the edges. Add to the bowl, then add the red onion, artichokes and all their oil, and the last of the basil. Season well with plenty of pepper and toss together.

Carefully remove the salt crust from the sea bass and brush any excess salt away from the skin, then carefully lift some of the fish onto each serving plate. Serve with lemon wedges and a spoonful of salad.

Whole roast trout with salsa verde, roast lemons and new potatoes

One of my favourite recipes in the book. I made it up thanks to the great watercress and trout I have around my village. I eat this with spuds from the garden roasted in the wood-fired oven… what more do you want? Fresh trout is so underrated and is one fish we should all be eating more of.

Serves 4

sea salt and freshly ground black pepper
400g new potatoes
1 quantity salsa verde (see page 182)
1.5kg whole trout, cleaned
3 lemons, halved
herb stalks left over from the salsa verde (mint, dill, tarragon, parsley, watercress and basil)
olive oil

Bring a large pan of salted water to the boil, add the new potatoes and return to the boil. Simmer for 10 minutes, then drain and set aside.

Preheat the oven to 220°C/425°F/gas mark 7.

Make the salsa verde as on page 182.

Put the trout on to a large roasting tray along with the halved lemons and the potatoes. Put a couple of spoonfuls of salsa verde into the cavity of the trout, along with the herb stalks, then drizzle with olive oil and season well with salt and pepper.

Put in the oven and roast for 15–20 minutes until just cooked through.

Serve the trout with the roasted potatoes and lemon halves and an extra drizzle of salsa verde.

Sirloin steak with red wine and snail sauce

'Snails, you say? Snails?' But in the UK we have snail farmers and on the TV show you might have seen one. Don't go fetching snails from the veg patch, they're not the same thing! And don't diss this recipe until you at least try snails. I was on the snail section once at a restaurant in Paris, so I learned to love them.

Serves 4

2 quantities of mashed potatoes (see page 154)

sea salt and freshly ground black pepper

4 x 250g sirloin steaks, at room temperature

75g unsalted butter

1 tbsp olive oil

4 banana shallots, 2 with skin on and cut lengthways in half, 2 peeled and finely chopped

1 garlic clove, finely chopped

25g caster sugar

250ml red wine

175ml veal stock

12 cooked snails, chopped

2 tbsp finely chopped tarragon leaves

2 tbsp chopped flat-leaf parsley leaves

Prepare the mashed potatoes as on page 154. Cover and set aside while you cook the steaks.

Season the steaks with salt. Heat a large frying pan until very hot, add 25g of the butter, the olive oil, steaks and halved shallots, cut sides down. Fry the steaks for 3–4 minutes on each side, basting with the butter, but leave the shallots cut side down without turning them. Remove everything from the pan and leave to rest on a plate.

Now, working quickly, return the frying pan to the heat, add 25g more of the butter, the chopped shallots and garlic and cook without colour for 2–3 minutes until softened. Increase the heat to high, add the sugar and, when it's caramelised, add the wine and cook until reduced by half. Add the stock, bring to a simmer and cook for 2 minutes, then add the snails and heat through.

Whisk in the last 25g of the butter, then season and stir in the herbs.

Lay the steaks on serving plates, take the halved shallots out of their skins and fan the layers over the top of the steak, then spoon the snail sauce over the top. Spoon some mash alongside.

Duck confit is around in cans in the supermarkets, so it's easy to add to this. Don't be afraid to add some of the duck fat it sits in; that's pure flavour. And calories, of course, but what the hell… If you prefer, you can just cook the first bit of the recipe up to when the sausages and beans have been combined and cooked through; that is a good family meal and kids love it.

Confit duck cassoulet with mash

Serves 4–5

3 tbsp olive oil

6 good-quality Yorkshire pork sausages

2 shallots, finely chopped

2 garlic cloves, finely chopped

2 tsp tomato purée

2 tsp roughly chopped rosemary leaves

1 tsp thyme leaves

400ml chicken stock

400g can of flageolet beans, drained and rinsed

400g can of tomatoes

2 tbsp chopped flat-leaf parsley leaves

sea salt and freshly ground black pepper

4–5 thick slices of sourdough bread

50g pancetta lardons

2 confit duck legs, boned and roughly chopped

150ml white wine

For the mashed potatoes

500g King Edward potatoes, peeled and chopped

50g unsalted butter

75–90ml double cream

Heat a frying pan until hot, add 1 tbsp of the regular oil, then the sausages and cook over a medium heat, turning, until golden brown on each side.

Meanwhile, heat a sauté pan until medium hot, add 1 tbsp of the olive oil and the shallots and sweat for 2 minutes, then add the garlic, tomato purée, half the rosemary and all the thyme and sweat for another minute before adding the half the stock and the flageolet beans. Bring to a simmer.

Meanwhile, place the canned tomatoes in a blender (or use a stick blender), and blitz to a fine purée, then add to the pan. Return to a simmer, then add the sausages to the bean mixture, reduce the heat and simmer for 15 minutes until the sausages are cooked through and the sauce has thickened. Add half the parsley and season with salt and black pepper.

This is a fine meal for kids and you can stop here if you want. To serve, heat a griddle pan until hot, drizzle the last 1 tbsp of the olive oil over two slices of sourdough bread and toast on each side. Place a slice of bread on to two serving plates, divide half the bean mixture between the two, then top each with a sausage and serve.

To make the cassoulet, preheat the oven to 180°C/350°F/gas mark 4. Return the frying pan that was used for the sausages to the heat and, when it's hot, add the pancetta and duck and fry until golden.

Put the remaining cooked sausages into the sauté pan with the remaining bean mixture, then add the white wine and remaining stock and bring to a simmer. Add the remaining rosemary and parsley and the duck and pancetta and season to taste. Bring to a simmer.

Place the remaining slices of toasted sourdough into a food processor and blitz to fine crumbs. Top the cassoulet with the sourdough crumbs and place into the oven for 5–10 minutes.

Meanwhile, place the potatoes into a pan of salted water and bring to the boil. Reduce the heat and simmer for 12–15 minutes until the potatoes are tender. Drain and return to the pan, then place over the heat for 1 minute to drive off any excess moisture. Pass through a potato ricer back into the pan, then add the butter and cream, beating to form a smooth mash. Season with salt and pepper.

Serve the cassoulet with some mash.

This classic combination is one that I first did in France as a young apprentice chef. The flavour of sorrel is amazing – slightly bitter but fresh and lemony. This dish is all about the sorrel – overcook it and it can become a little too bitter. It's easy to grow, and you can find it in most garden centres in the herb section. It's great raw, just ripped or chopped into salads.

Salmon and sorrel with vermouth

Serves 2

40g unsalted butter, for greasing
sea salt and freshly ground black pepper
200g salmon fillet, cut into 8 thin slices
1 shallot, finely sliced
75ml vermouth
75ml white wine
150ml double cream
75g sorrel leaves, deveined and very finely sliced
1 bag of salad leaves
50ml house dressing (see page 78)

Preheat the grill to high. Butter an oven tray all over the base, then season with salt and pepper. Lay the salmon slices on the tray in two batches of four overlapping slices, then set aside.

Heat a frying pan until hot. Add the shallot, vermouth and white wine, and cook for about 5 minutes, until reduced by half. Add the double cream and cook the sauce for 2–3 minutes until reduced and thickened.

Meanwhile, put the salmon under the grill for 3 minutes until just cooked through.

Season the sauce to taste with salt and pepper, then remove from the heat and stir in the sorrel. Spoon onto a serving plate and carefully lay the salmon slices on top.

Toss the salad leaves with some of the house dressing and serve alongside.

A bit poncey calling this a terrine – that was the editor of the book as she lives in London – to you and me, it's a pâté, but a nice one at that. Once you've made it you will see how easy it is and, on the table for a party or lunch, it's a hit. I have it in the fridge and keep picking at it with bread and pickles (yeah, I know, kitchen pickers wear big knickers, but it's lovely).

Venison, chicken liver and Armagnac terrine

Serves 6–8

350g venison fillet, cut into 2cm-wide strips

350g chicken livers

sea salt and freshly ground black pepper

2 tbsp rapeseed oil, plus more for the foil

2 tbsp Armagnac

550g rashers of streaky bacon

300g skinless boneless chicken breasts, roughly chopped

200ml double cream

50g toasted chopped hazelnuts

50g dried cranberries

2 tbsp finely chopped tarragon leaves

Season the venison and chicken livers with salt and pepper, then heat a large frying pan and add the rapeseed oil. When the oil is hot, add the venison a few pieces at a time and seal on each side, then set aside. Repeat with the chicken livers, then – standing well back and protecting your forearms – pour in the Armagnac and set it on fire with a match. When the flames die down, set aside.

While these cool, use the bacon to line a 1kg loaf tin, overlapping the rashers in the base a little and leaving about 5cm of their lengths falling over the edge of the tin on each side. Preheat the oven to 180°C/350°F/gas mark 4.

Place the chicken breast into a food processor and blitz to a fine purée, then add the double cream and blitz to combine. Season with plenty of salt and pepper, then tip into a bowl and fold in the hazelnuts and cranberries.

Scoop one-third of the chicken mixture into the prepared tin, then top with the venison. Layer on another one-third of the chicken mixture, then the tarragon, chicken livers and their juices. Finish with the remaining chicken mixture, then fold the bacon over the top to cover all the filling.

Oil a piece of foil and place over the top of the tin, then seal tightly around the edges and place into a deep tray. Half fill the tray with hot water then place into the oven for 1¼–1½ hours.

To check that the terrine is cooked, insert a skewer into the centre, then run it against the inside of your wrist: if it's piping hot, it's cooked through. If not, return it to the oven and cook for another 10 minutes, then check again.

Remove from the oven and allow to cool completely before placing in the fridge to chill.

To serve, turn out of the mould and cut into slices. Serve with gherkins and some charred bread.

This stuffing comes from my time with the Roux Brothers. It's a great recipe and, with the lamb, makes a wonderful combination. I cook it on the barbecue at home, but 30–40 minutes in a hot oven will do the trick.

Tarragon-stuffed crown of lamb with duchess potatoes

Serves 4–6

For the lamb

1 small onion
25g unsalted butter, plus more for the foil
300g button mushrooms
leaves from 1 small bunch of tarragon, finely chopped
50g fresh white breadcrumbs
75g minced lamb
sea salt and freshly ground black pepper
2 x 7-bone French-trimmed racks of lamb

For the duchess potatoes

4 large baking potatoes
25g unsalted butter
3 egg yolks

Preheat the oven to 200°C/400°F/gas mark 6. Bake the potatoes for 1–1¼ hours, until tender when pierced with a knife. When they're ready, blitz the onion in a food processor until very finely chopped. Heat a frying pan until warm, add the butter and onion and sweat for a couple of minutes.

Add the mushrooms to the processor and blitz to a really fine purée, then add them to the frying pan and increase the heat to high. Fry for 2–3 minutes until all the moisture has been driven off.

Tip into a bowl and add the tarragon, breadcrumbs and minced lamb. Season with salt and plenty of pepper.

Rub some butter over a sheet of foil and place it on a baking sheet. Make nicks in each rack of lamb, between each chop, on the opposite side to the fat of the chops. The cuts should be only 1–2cm deep. Stand both racks of lamb upright, bones in the air, fat sides together. Curve them around; the nicks you made should open slightly to allow you to form a circle with the two racks, fat-side inwards. Tie with kitchen string, fairly firmly. Pile the stuffing in the centre, packing it well.

Cook in the oven for 30–40 minutes, then remove and rest for 10 minutes before carving.

Meanwhile, when the potatoes are cool enough to handle, scoop out the flesh and pass it through a fine sieve into a bowl. Beat to a smooth and fluffy purée, then add the butter and egg yolks and check the seasoning.

Spoon into a piping bag, then pipe little pyramids on to a baking tray. When the lamb comes out of the oven to rest, place the duchess potatoes in the oven and bake for 5–10 minutes until golden brown,

Carve the lamb and serve with the stuffing and duchess potatoes.

Spelt bread-crusted ham

I had this idea while in the States. They served something similar in a smaller portion – which is unlike them – but I've made it with a large piece. The idea is, when its cooked with the bread topping, you just dive in and then the bread is used to mop up the ham juices.

Place the ham into a large saucepan, add the onions, carrot, bay leaves and peppercorns then cover with cold water. Bring to the boil rapidly, skim off any scum that rises to the top, reduce the heat, cover and simmer for about 20 minutes per 500g; it will take 2–2¾ hours, depending on size.

To check the ham is cooked, insert a skewer into its centre, then run it against the inside of your wrist: if it's piping hot, it's cooked. Remove from the heat and cool totally in the liquid.

Meanwhile, put the flour, sugar and salt into a large bowl or a food mixer fitted with a dough hook. Put the yeast into a jug with 200ml of water and mix to combine, then turn on the mixer and slowly add the yeast water. Measure 500ml more water into the jug and add gradually it to the dough, making sure you've pulled all the flour into the dough.

Tip out on to a very lightly floured work surface then knead well for 5–10 minutes until elastic. Place into a large bowl, cover and set aside to double in size, about 2 hours.

Preheat the oven to 180°C/350°F/gas mark 4. Remove the ham from the stock and discard the vegetables, reserving the stock. Carefully peel off the ham skin and discard.

Place the potatoes, spring onions, beans, peas and mint and parsley sprigs into a large ovenproof casserole big enough to fit the ham in. Pour over 1.25 litres of the reserved ham stock (use the rest for a soup), then place the ham on top. Brush the outside edge of the casserole with the beaten egg.

Lift the dough out of the bowl, tip out on to a lightly floured work surface and stretch it into a shape big enough to fit over the casserole and ham. Carefully lift it over the ham and stretch to the edges of the casserole. Pinch the dough all the way round to secure it to the casserole, except where the ham bone is (leave it loose around here, allowing the steam to escape).

Place in the oven to bake for 1 hour until golden brown. To check the bread is cooked through, tap it lightly; it should sound hollow. Remove and allow to cool for 15 minutes before serving directly on to the table. Break the bread crust, lift the ham out and carve, then spoon out all the vegetables.

Serves 8–10

For the ham and vegetables

1 raw ham, about 3–4kg, bone in, soaked overnight if necessary (check with your butcher)

2 onions, cut into thick slices

1 carrot, cut into big chunks

2 bay leaves

10 black peppercorns

600g potatoes, peeled and cut into large chunks

8 spring onions, trimmed

350g runner beans, trimmed and cut in half

300g fresh peas

small handful of sprigs of mint, torn in half

small handful of sprigs of flat-leaf parsley, torn in half

1 egg, lightly beaten

For the spelt bread

1kg spelt flour, plus more to dust

2 tsp caster sugar

2 tsp salt

2 x 7g sachets of fast-action yeast

Côte de boeuf with béarnaise sauce

A dish for a legend. When Sir Stirling Moss wanted to learn how to make béarnaise sauce, who was I to say otherwise? And with a côte de boeuf – which is one of the best cuts of meat out there – it creates the best-tasting plate of food there is. Purists will say that the shallots should be strained out, but I like to keep them in. While working for some of the greatest chefs in the world, I saw that they kept the shallots in, and I agree.

Serves 4

1.8kg côte de boeuf

4 large chipping potatoes, peeled and cut into 1cm thick batons

vegetable oil or dripping, for deep-frying

300g unsalted butter

1 small banana shallot, finely chopped

½ tsp white peppercorns

3 tbsp tarragon vinegar

2 egg yolks

1 small bunch of tarragon, leaves picked and finely chopped

sea salt and freshly ground black pepper

1 bunch of watercress, picked

Preheat the oven to 180°C/350°F/gas mark 4. Place the beef on an oven tray and roast for 30–40 minutes until cooked to your liking.

While the beef is cooking, prepare the chips. Heat a deep-fat fryer to 140°C/285°F, or heat the oil for deep-frying in a deep heavy-based frying pan until a breadcrumb sizzles and turns just a very pale gold when dropped into it. (CAUTION: hot oil can be dangerous. Do not leave unattended.) Carefully place the chips in the oil in batches and fry for 4–5 minutes until pale but tender. Remove and drain on kitchen paper. When the beef is nearly ready, turn the oil up to 190°C/375°F.

Remove the beef from the oven and let it rest for 5–10 minutes.

Heat a large frying pan until hot and add 50g of the butter. When it's foaming, add the beef and sear on each side for 1 minute until browned, spooning the butter over the top. Remove from the pan and let it rest on a plate while you make the béarnaise.

Place the rest of the butter in a pan and heat until melted, then skim off any foam.

Place the shallot, peppercorns and vinegar in a small saucepan and bring to the boil. Simmer over a low heat for a few minutes until the liquid has evaporated and there is only 1 tbsp left.

Put the egg yolks into a bowl and whisk together. Whisk in the melted butter, a little at a time initially, then in a thin constant stream, whisking all the time – you want the mixture to emulsify and thicken slightly. Don't add the solids at the bottom of the melted butter – discard them. When all the butter has been added, spoon in the shallot and any liquid, add the chopped tarragon, and season to taste with salt and pepper.

When ready to serve, return the chips to the hot oil and cook for 3–4 minutes until golden and crispy. Drain on kitchen paper, sprinkle with salt and serve immediately.

Carve the côte de boeuf and lay the slices on a plate. Pile the chips alongside, and finish with a dollop of the béarnaise and the watercress.

Classic coq au vin – à la Floyd

This classic French dish – made here in honour of the legend Keith Floyd – traditionally uses wine from Burgundy. However, many regions of France have a version made with their own local wine – from coq au Riesling in Alsace to coq au violet, using beaujolais nouveau wine. There is even a coq au Champagne. Serve the rich chicken and lardons with just some simple, creamy, buttery mashed potatoes.

Serves 4–6

2kg good-quality chicken, cut into 10 pieces
1 tsp plain flour
175g unsalted butter
1 onion, roughly chopped
225g smoked streaky bacon, cut into lardons
500ml red wine
50ml brandy
2 garlic cloves, lightly crushed
3 bay leaves
4 sprigs of thyme
1kg King Edward potatoes, peeled and cut into chunks
sea salt and freshly ground black pepper
200ml double cream
100g silverskin onions
200g baby button mushrooms

Sprinkle the chicken pieces with the flour and toss to coat thoroughly. Heat a large casserole dish until hot and add 50g of the butter. When it's foaming, add the chicken in batches, skin-side down, and cook until brown on each side. Remove from the pan, then add the onion and fry for 1–2 minutes.

Return the chicken to the casserole, then add the bacon and fry for 1 minute. Add the red wine, brandy, garlic, bay leaves and thyme, and bring to the boil. Reduce the heat and simmer for 1 hour until the chicken is cooked through.

While the chicken cooks, make the mash. Place the potatoes in a pan of cold, salted water and bring to the boil, then reduce the heat and simmer for 12–15 minutes, or until the potatoes are tender. Drain and return to the pan, then place over a low heat for a couple of minutes to dry the potatoes slightly.

Pass the potatoes through a ricer, then beat in 100g of the butter and the double cream to form a very smooth mash. Season to taste with salt and pepper.

When the chicken is cooked, heat a frying pan until hot and add the remaining butter. When it's foaming, add the silverskin onions and button mushrooms, and cook until golden. Add them to the chicken, stir through and season to taste.

Serve the coq au vin with a dollop of mash.

Chicken cordon bleu

It's ham, cheese and chicken: that's all. It's a simple dish, but like many things in life, the simplest are the best. Cook the escalope in plenty of butter, not oil. By the time the butter is nut-brown, the chicken should be ready to turn over and cook on the other side. You need to allow the middle to become hot, to melt the cheese inside.

Serves 4

4 boneless skinless chicken breasts
175g Emmental cheese, cut into 8 chunks
4 good-quality thick ham slices
75g plain flour
3 eggs, lightly beaten
150g panko breadcrumbs
sea salt and freshly ground black pepper
150g unsalted butter
300g French beans, trimmed
25g flaked almonds

Cut the chicken breasts in half widthways nearly all the way through then open out to a heart shape. Lay a large piece of clingfilm on a work surface, and place the chicken on top. Cover with another sheet of clingfilm and gently bat out with a rolling pin until about double the size and 1cm thick.

Remove the clingfilm and lay two pieces of cheese over one half of each chicken breast, then fold the ham on top. Fold the other half of the chicken over to enclose the cheese and ham, and press down lightly.

Place the flour, eggs and breadcrumbs in separate bowls, each big enough to take a chicken breast. Season the flour and eggs with salt and pepper, then pass the chicken first through the flour, then the eggs, then the breadcrumbs, coating fully.

Put 125g of the butter into a large frying pan and set over a medium heat. When the butter is just melted, add the chicken and cook for 4–5 minutes on one side until the butter is golden brown, then turn and cook for another 4–5 minutes. Baste the chicken with the melted butter as it cooks, keeping it over a medium heat. You don't want the butter or breadcrumbs to burn, and you want the chicken to be cooked all the way through and the cheese melted.

Bring a pan of salted water to the boil. Add the beans and cook for 3–4 minutes until just tender, then drain. Put the pan back on the heat and add the last of the butter and the flaked almonds. Heat until the butter is melted, then toss the beans into the butter and warm through. Season well.

Serve the chicken with the beans alongside.

Pork and hazelnut terrine with apricot and tomato chutney

People are so often put off making terrines and pâtés until they realise how easy they are, and this one is even simpler than most, as it uses good-quality sausage meat as its base. You can make it with venison sausages and add whatever flavouring you like.

Serves 6

For the pastry

275g plain flour, plus extra for dusting
50g strong white flour
1¼ tsp salt
65g unsalted butter
75g lard
1 egg, lightly beaten

For the filling

1kg pork and apple sausages, skins removed
1 banana shallot, finely chopped
2 tbsp roughly chopped flat-leaf parsley
100g toasted hazelnuts, roughly chopped

For the chutney

150g light muscovado sugar
1 onion, finely chopped
3 tomatoes, roughly chopped
200g soft dried apricots, roughly chopped
½ tsp dried chilli flakes
125ml white wine vinegar
sea salt and freshly ground black pepper

1 bunch of radishes, to serve

Preheat the oven to 200°C/400°F/gas mark 6. Grease a 23 x 10cm terrine mould.

Start by making the pastry. Put both flours and the salt into a bowl.

Pour 175ml of water into a small saucepan, add the butter and lard, and bring to the boil over a low heat until the fats have melted. Pour the mixture onto the flour and stir together until it forms a soft dough. Tip onto a lightly floured board and knead very gently until smooth and cooled slightly. Cut one-third of the dough off and set aside while you make the pie.

Roll the remaining pastry out so that it's as big as the terrine, then gently lay it inside, pressing it into each corner and pulling the pastry so that it comes all the way up the sides of the terrine. Place in the fridge while you make the filling.

Put the sausage meat into a large bowl, then add the shallot, parsley and hazelnuts, and mix well to combine. Spoon a little at a time into the pastry-lined terrine, pressing gently into the corners to make sure there are no gaps.

Take the remaining pastry and roll it out so that it's big enough to fit the top of the terrine. Brush the edges of the pastry in the terrine mould with the beaten egg, then lay the pastry rectangle on top and crimp together at the edges. Decorate with any remaining pastry. Brush with the remaining egg wash and pierce a hole in the centre of the pie, then bake for 1–1¼ hours.

To make the chutney, heat a large frying pan until hot, add the sugar and cook until totally dissolved and starting to caramelise. Stir in the onion, tomatoes, apricots and dried chilli flakes, then deglaze with the vinegar – the mixture will become lumpy, but continue cooking until the lumps dissolve. Boil gently for 5–10 minutes, until the fruit and veg are tender and the mixture has thickened slightly. Season with salt and pepper. You can use it straight away, or decant it into a sterilised jar and keep it in the fridge for 2 weeks.

When the terrine is cooked, remove it from the mould and either serve immediately, or chill and serve cold. Slice and serve with a dollop of chutney and a few radishes.

Rump steak with creamy brioche leeks

Rump steak is a chef's favourite, as it's full of flavour. My advice is to buy the best quality you can, as there are cheap rump steaks that even your dog would find hard to chew.

Serves 4

1 medium potato, peeled and cut into 1cm dice
sea salt and freshly ground black pepper
125g unsalted butter
1 shallot, finely diced
2 garlic cloves, finely chopped
500g leeks, washed and sliced
100ml white wine
250ml double cream
3 sprigs of thyme, leaves picked
3 slices of brioche loaf, cut into 1cm cubes
50g Gruyère cheese, finely grated
4 x 250g rump steaks
1 tbsp rapeseed oil

Preheat the oven to 200°C/400°F/gas mark 6.

Bring a pan of water to the boil. Add the potatoes and a pinch of salt, reduce the heat and simmer for 3–4 minutes, then drain.

Meanwhile, heat a frying pan until just warm. Add 50g of the butter and when it's melted, add the shallot, garlic and leeks and cook for 2–3 minutes, or until softened.

Add the potatoes to the pan and mix to combine, then add the white wine and bring to a simmer. Add the cream and thyme leaves, and simmer for 2–3 minutes. Season to taste with salt and pepper and pour into an ovenproof dish.

Heat a separate frying pan until hot. Add 50g of the butter and the brioche cubes and fry until golden-brown on all sides. Scatter over the top of the leeks, then scatter the cheese over the top to cover. Bake in the oven for 5–10 minutes until golden and bubbling.

Meanwhile, heat a griddle pan until searing hot and rub the steaks with the rapeseed oil. Brush the griddle with a little rapeseed, then add the steaks and cook for 2 minutes without moving them. Turn them 90° and cook for another minute. Season with salt and pepper. Turn the steaks over and cook for 1–2 more minutes, then remove from the pan and place on a plate to rest.

Melt the remaining butter in the brioche pan and brush it over the steaks, spooning any resting liquid back over the meat, then season once more.

Serve the steaks with the leeks alongside and any juices poured over them.

Roast grouse with pear tatin and kale

The king of all game birds, the grouse is available from 12th of August – the glorious 12th, as it's called. The key to cooking all game is not to overcook it and to allow it to rest before serving and carving.

Serves 6

150g caster sugar

1 lemon

3 pears, peeled but left whole

100g unsalted butter

100g ready-made all-butter puff pastry

6 grouse, cleaned

sea salt and freshly ground black pepper

500g celeriac, peeled and cut into small chunks

4 sprigs of thyme, leaves picked

75ml port

200ml reduced chicken stock (start with 400ml and simmer until reduced to 200ml)

300g kale, stalks removed

Preheat the oven to 200°C/400°F/gas mark 6. Butter a six-hole muffin tin or silicone muffin mould.

Half-fill a medium saucepan with water and add 75g of the sugar. Squeeze in the lemon juice, then add the squeezed halves to the pan. Add the pears and bring to a simmer. Poach for 15 minutes until tender, then leave until cool enough to handle.

While the pears cool, make the caramel for the tatin. Put the remaining 75g of caster sugar into a frying pan and heat gently, without stirring, until the sugar turns golden-brown and liquid. Add a knob of butter and swirl around the pan, then remove from the heat and divide between the holes in the muffin tin. Roll the caramel around the bases of the holes and set aside to cool slightly.

Slice two thick discs off of the bottom of each of the pears and set them on top of the caramel. Cut six discs of pastry, each 1cm bigger than the holes of the muffin tin. Prick the pastry with a fork, then place over the pears, tucking the excess pastry in around the edges. Bake for 10–15 minutes until the pastry is golden-brown and cooked through. Remove the tatins from the oven and leave to rest for 1 minute before turning out. Place a large serving plate or baking tray over the top of the muffin tin and turn it over, so that the tarts slip out.

Season the grouse inside and out with salt and pepper. Heat a large frying pan until hot, then add a knob of butter and fry the grouse, breast-side down, until golden-brown on the crown and legs. Set them on their backs in a roasting tray, then scatter the celeriac and thyme around the grouse and roast for 15–20 minutes. The grouse should still be pink.

Place the grouse and celeriac on a plate to rest and put the roasting tray on the heat. Add the port and bring to the boil, then simmer until reduced by half. Add the chicken stock and return to the boil, then cook gently for 10 minutes until reduced just by one-third. Pour through a sieve into a clean pan, whisk in a knob of butter and season to taste.

Heat a frying pan until hot. Add the last of the butter, a splash of water and the kale, and sauté for a couple of minutes until just wilted. Season with salt and pepper.

Spoon the celeriac down the centre of each serving plate and top with the kale. Carve the legs and breasts from the grouse and cut the breasts in half. Place the tatin next to the grouse and drizzle with the port sauce.

Layered sole with langoustines and cauliflower

A bit fancy, but this is a dish to show off with. Amazing langoustines and fresh sole are some of the best foods from around the UK. The strange thing is that we export almost all of them to the French and Spanish!

Serves 4

4 sole, filleted and skinned
275ml double cream
sea salt and freshly ground black pepper
1 cauliflower
1 hard-boiled egg, peeled
1 tbsp finely chopped chives
1 tbsp white balsamic vinegar
3 tbsp extra virgin olive oil
16 cooked langoustines, peeled
fennel fronds, to garnish

Trim the sole fillets so that they are all the same size, then set aside (you will have 16 fillets in all, four per fish). Place four of the fillets and the trimmings into a small food processor with 75ml of the double cream, blitz to a fine paste, then season with salt and pepper, and pulse once more. Place in a piping bag and snip the end off the bag.

Lay four of the trimmed fillets on individual sheets of clingfilm twice their size, season with salt and pepper, then pipe a thin layer of the purée on top of each one. Top each one with another fillet and repeat with another layer of purée, then add a final fillet. You will have three layers of fillet with two layers of purée in between. Wrap the clingfilm around the sole so that you have four clingfilm-wrapped parcels, and place in the fridge until ready to cook.

Cut the cauliflower in half. Set one half aside and chop the other half into small florets. Put half the florets into a saucepan with the remaining 200ml of cream and bring to the boil. Turn the heat down and simmer for 4–5 minutes until soft, then tip straight into a blender and blitz to a fine purée. Season with salt and pepper and set aside.

Bring a pan of salted water to the boil and add the rest of the cauliflower florets. Simmer for 2–3 minutes until just tender, then drain.

Finely grate the other half of the cauliflower into a bowl, then grate the hard-boiled egg in too. Add the chives and mix together.

Whisk the white balsamic vinegar and olive oil together in a separate bowl, then spoon two-thirds of this over the salad and toss to coat. Season with salt and pepper.

Set a steamer on top of a pan of simmering water and add the sole parcels. Cover and steam for 6–8 minutes until just cooked through. Lift out and remove the clingfilm.

Add the cauliflower florets and langoustines to the rest of the dressing and toss gently to coat.

Spoon the cauliflower salad in a line across each plate, then place four langoustines along the top. Spoon the purée to one side and set one of the sole parcels on top of it. Place a few cauliflower florets around the langoustines and finish with a drizzle of dressing and some fennel fronds.

Oyster and seafood pie with samphire

I don't know that 'posh' is the right word for this really, as although it uses oysters and lobster, you can get hold of both of these easily nowadays. It does use a fair bit of Champagne, but you can always use prosecco instead. The grated potatoes make a great topping — just give them a thorough squeeze to remove any excess water.

Serves 4–6

140g unsalted butter

2 heaped tbsp plain flour

600ml double cream

350ml Champagne

sea salt and freshly ground black pepper

500g salmon, boneless and skinless, cut into chunks

400g smoked haddock, boneless and skinless, cut into chunks

1kg cooked lobster, shelled and cut into chunks

8 oysters, shucked

350g raw king prawns, shelled and deveined

100g samphire

1kg white potatoes, peeled and coarsely grated

3 egg yolks

200g frozen peas

Preheat the oven to 220°C/425°F/gas mark 7.

Put 75g of the butter into a saucepan and heat until melted, then add the flour and cook for 2 minutes until thickened and light golden-brown.

Add the cream gradually, whisking all the time, and cook until thickened and smooth. Pour the Champagne in a steady stream into the sauce, still whisking all the time, until thick enough to coat the back of a spoon, then season to taste with salt and pepper.

Place the salmon, smoked haddock, lobster, oysters, prawns and samphire in a large ovenproof dish. Pour the sauce over the top to coat everything.

Put the grated potato into a clean tea towel and squeeze all the liquid from it. Place in a bowl. Melt 50g of the remaining butter in a saucepan, then mix with the potato and egg yolks and plenty of salt and black pepper. Sprinkle over the top of the fish, then place on a baking sheet in the oven and bake for 30 minutes until golden and hot through.

Bring a pan of salted water to the boil, add the peas and cook for 2–3 minutes until tender. Drain and return to the pan, add the remaining butter and season to taste. Serve with the fish pie.

Apple and sage porchetta with apple sauce

I love searching for porchetta in the markets in Italy, and to be fair you don't have to search too hard, as it's a staple over there. It can be eaten hot, but for me it's best served cold cut into thin slices. It is a big piece of pork, though, so it needs a fair amount of time in the oven.

Serves 8–10

4kg pork loin with belly attached, all bones removed

sea salt and freshly ground black pepper

4 medium onions, 2 finely sliced and 2 cut into quarters

4 Bramley apples, 1 sliced and 3 peeled and roughly chopped

1 large bunch of sage, leaves picked and roughly chopped

2 lemons

150g unsalted butter

3 carrots, cut into large chunks

2 garlic bulbs, cut in half horizontally

1 bottle of white wine

2–4 tbsp caster sugar

500g tenderstem broccoli, trimmed

Preheat the oven to 220°C/450°F/gas mark 7.

Season the pork flesh and skin with plenty of salt and pepper and rub it into the pork. Place the pork skin-side down and scatter the sliced onions, sliced apple, sage, lemon zest, 50g of the butter, salt and pepper over the top, pressing down gently.

Starting with the shortest side in front of you, roll the pork up into a long sausage as tightly as possible and secure with string at intervals along the length of it. Make a little noose in the end of the string, then loop it around the pork, pull the string through the noose and pull it tight. Continue down the pork, wrapping the string around, then looping it back through the string, keeping it taut all the time. Tie it at the end to secure it.

Place the quartered onions, carrots and garlic bulbs in a large deep-sided oven tray, then place the pork on top and rub in another 50g of the butter. Pour the white wine into the tray. Roast for 30 minutes, then turn the oven down to 150°C/300°F/gas mark 2 and cook for 3 or even 4 hours.

While the pork roasts, make the apple sauce. Place 20–25ml water, the chopped apples, a squeeze of lemon, 25g of the butter and a little of the sugar in a saucepan, then cover, place over the heat and cook for 4–5 minutes until the apple has broken down. Beat with a spoon until nearly smooth, leaving a few chunks, then season to taste with the rest of the sugar and a little salt.

Remove the pork from the oven and lift it out onto a serving plate to rest for at least 30 minutes before removing the string. Place the tray on the hob over a medium heat, stirring all the time to release the juices stuck to the bottom of the tray. Check the seasoning, then strain through a fine sieve.

Bring a pan of salted water to the boil. Add the tenderstem broccoli and simmer for 3–4 minutes until just tender. Drain and toss with the last 25g of the butter. Serve alongside the pork, with a dollop of apple sauce.

Comforting Summer Nights

Summer veg soup with mussels and salsa verde

This comes straight from my garden and into the bowl (except for the mussels!) and when the summer's in full swing in the veg garden there are few better soups. Add the salsa at the end to keep all the flavour and colour or, better still, let your guests add as much as they need.

Serves 4

For the soup

50g unsalted butter

1 banana shallot, finely chopped

150g courgettes, cut into 1cm cubes

1 fennel bulb, cut into 1cm cubes, fronds reserved

150g carrots, peeled and cut into 1cm cubes

100g celery sticks, cut into 1cm cubes

8 radishes, halved lengthways

500g mussels, scrubbed, beards removed

150ml white wine

750ml vegetable stock

sea salt and freshly ground black pepper

For the salsa verde

2 tbsp roughly chopped mint leaves

2 tbsp roughly chopped dill fronds

2 tbsp roughly chopped tarragon leaves

2 tbsp roughly chopped flat-leaf parsley leaves

2 tbsp roughly chopped watercress leaves

2 tbsp torn basil leaves

1 large shallot, roughly chopped

6 anchovies, roughly chopped

2 tbsp capers, drained and rinsed

juice of ½ lemon

1 tsp Dijon mustard

4 tbsp extra virgin olive oil, plus more to store, if needed

Heat a sauté pan until medium hot, add the butter and all the vegetables and sweat over a low heat until just softened, about 5 minutes.

Add the mussels, wine and stock and bring to the boil, then cover and simmer for 2–3 minutes until all the mussels have opened. Discard any that fail to open.

Meanwhile, make the salsa verde. Place all the chopped herbs into a food processor and blitz to roughly chop, then add the shallot, anchovies, capers, lemon juice, mustard and oil and blitz to a slightly chunky purée. Season with salt and pepper.

Remove the soup from the heat, then stir 2–3 tbsp of salsa verde in, check the seasoning and serve immediately, with the rest of the salsa on the side.

Any leftover salsa verde should be decanted into a sealable container, covered with a thin layer of oil and kept in the fridge for up to 4 days.

British seaside chowder with saffron

Whenever I visit the seaside I'm a sucker for cockles and whelks, but the idea of turning them into a chowder is from farther afield. This is such a quick and simple soup when you have the seafood to hand. Use whatever local shellfish you can get your hands on as long as you stick to the same amounts, but this is a good traditional version.

Serves 4

2 tomatoes

300ml white wine

1kg mixed shellfish: cockles, clams, mussels, winkles, soaked in cold water

50g unsalted butter

1 shallot, finely chopped

1 garlic clove, finely chopped

1 fennel bulb, finely chopped

½ leek, white part only, finely chopped

250g potatoes, peeled and cut into 5mm pieces

2 pinches of saffron strands

1 star anise

500ml chicken stock

175ml double cream

75g samphire, trimmed

12 shelled cooked whelks

2 tbsp finely chopped chives

a handful of celery leaves

sea salt and freshly ground black pepper

First, skin and deseed the tomatoes: bring a saucepan of water to the boil, take out the stalk of the tomatoes and make crosses on the bases.

Drop the tomatoes into the water and simmer for 10–15 seconds until the skin starts to peel away. Lift straight out into a bowl of iced water and peel off the skin. Cut the tomatoes into quarters and remove the seeds, then finely chop the flesh.

Heat a sauté pan until hot, add the wine and the shellfish, cover and cook for 3–4 minutes until just cooked through. Strain into a colander over a bowl, reserving the cooking liquor, and allow to cool slightly before picking the meat out of the shells.

Wipe out the sauté pan, then add the butter, shallot and garlic and sweat for a couple of minutes, then add the fennel, leek, potatoes, saffron and star anise and cook for another 1 minute.

Add the reserved cooking liquor and chicken stock and bring to the boil. Reduce the heat to a simmer and cook for 3–4 minutes until the potatoes are just tender.

Add the cream and samphire then simmer for another couple of minutes until just thickened. Reduce the heat then add the tomatoes and all the shellfish, including the whelks, and gently warm through. Add the chives and celery leaves and season to taste (you probably won't need much salt).

Serve straight away.

Confit duck salad with blue cheese dressing

The great chef Eric Chavot gave me this dressing and I use it all the time; the buttermilk gives it the acidity you need. Duck confit can be found in most supermarkets now in cans, so you can make this dish nice and quickly. I hope you like it; I think it's one of the best salads out there. Whenever I'm doing dinners at mine, this recipe is a must.

Serves 2–4

2 confit duck legs
75g soft light brown sugar
pinch of cayenne pepper
100g pecan nuts
sea salt and freshly ground black pepper
1 head Romaine lettuce, cut into 2.5cm-thick slices

For the blue cheese dressing

75g gorgonzola, roughly chopped
50g St Agur blue cheese, roughly chopped
1 garlic clove, finely chopped
2 tbsp runny honey
50ml buttermilk
60g crème fraîche
juice of 1 lemon
2 dashes of Worcestershire sauce
dash of Tabasco
1 tbsp red wine vinegar
75g mayonnaise

Preheat the oven to 200°C/400°F/gas mark 6. Put the duck legs on to a tray and place in the oven for 10 minutes to heat through.

Meanwhile, heat a frying pan until hot, add the sugar and cayenne pepper then, when the sugar stars to melt, add 50ml of water and swirl to combine.

Cook over a high heat until a deep caramel, then add the pecan nuts and stir to coat. Add a pinch of salt. Tip out on to a baking tray and place in the oven for 5 minutes while you make the dressing.

Put both cheeses into a bowl and whisk to break down the cheese slightly, then add the garlic, honey, buttermilk and crème fraîche and whisk together well.

Add the lemon juice, Worcestershire sauce, Tabasco, vinegar and mayonnaise and whisk well, then season with salt and pepper.

Remove the duck and pecans from the oven and wait until they're cool enough to handle, then shred the duck from the bone.

Toss the lettuce with some of the cheese dressing – just enough to coat the leaves – then add the shredded duck and pecans and toss together.

Pile into a large bowl, drizzle with more of the dressing and serve straight away, with the remaining dressing in a bowl alongside.

What a treat; fresh seafood is one of the joys of being alive. I have this whenever I can. Home-made rye bread is what I love to eat it with it and whipping the butter makes it light. Mayonnaise is all you need alongside. This is all about the best-quality shellfish and, around the UK, we have some of the best in the world.

Fruits de mer with home-made rye bread and whipped butter

Serves 4

For the rye bread and butter

500g whole grain rye flour, plus more to dust

25g dark brown muscovado sugar

10g salt

10g fast-action dried yeast

200g unsalted butter, softened

For the fruits de mer

12 langoustines

12 razor clams, scrubbed

400g clams in the shell, scrubbed

1 x 1kg cooked lobster

1 cooked medium brown crab

8 oysters, shucked

16 cooked shrimps in the shell

200g cooked brown shrimps

For the mayonnaise

3 egg yolks

1 tbsp Dijon mustard

2 tbsp cider vinegar

finely grated zest and juice of 1 unwaxed lemon

300ml rapeseed oil

sea salt and freshly ground black pepper

Start the rye bread the day before. Place the flour, sugar and salt into a large bowl or a food mixer fitted with a dough hook. Put the yeast into a jug with 200ml of water and mix to combine, then turn on the mixer and slowly add the yeasted water. Measure 150ml more water into the jug and gradually add it to the dough, making sure you've pulled all the flour from the bottom into the dough.

Tip out on to a lightly floured work surface, then knead well for at least 5–10 minutes until elastic.

Form into a long log shape, then set on to a baking parchment-lined baking sheet, cover loosely with cling film to allow for the dough to double in size, but make a good seal around the edges to keep it as airtight as possible. Set aside to prove for at least 6 hours, but preferably overnight.

Preheat the oven to 220°C/425°F/gas mark 7. Uncover the dough and dust with a little rye flour, then slash the top diagonally a few times with a sharp knife. Place the loaf into the oven and bake for 30 minutes. When the bread is risen and golden brown, tap the base of the loaf: it should sound hollow when it is ready. Allow to cool.

Place the softened butter into a food processor and blitz until light and fluffy, then scrape into a serving dish.

Place the langoustines into a steamer insert set on a saucepan half filled with water, then place the razor clams and clams into a second level of steamer on top. Cover with a lid and steam for 5–8 minutes until they are all cooked through. Set aside.

Prepare the lobster by cutting it in half lengthways, remove any gubbins in the head and remove the claws. Break down into knuckles and claws, then tap firmly with the back of a heavy knife to crack them. Pick the meat out of both and pile back into the shell.

Prepare the crab by opening the shell, remove the dead man's fingers and discard. Remove the claws and repeat as for the lobster, then pile back into the crab shell.

For the mayonnaise, whisk the egg yolks, mustard, vinegar and lemon juice in a bowl or small processor. Still whisking, start adding the rapeseed oil in a very thin trickle; the mixture should be thick and light once the oil is incorporated. Stir in the lemon zest and season to taste, then decant into a serving bowl.

Pile the seafood, including the brown shrimps, on to a big platter and serve with the lemon mayonnaise, sliced rye bread and whipped butter.

Cauliflower 'couscous' with barbecued chicken and honeyed tomatoes

I love this salad. Henry Dimbleby showed me the idea, but I've done it slightly differently. It's like couscous… but tastier. I love the dressing with the maple syrup and vinegar mixed together. You could just roast the chicken in the oven if you wish rather than barbecue; either way this is all about the great salad that goes with it. Remember to season the cauliflower well.

Serves 4

3 tbsp olive oil

4 chicken breasts on the bone, cut in half

sea salt and freshly ground black pepper

8 sprigs of thyme

4 ripe tomatoes, halved widthways

3 tbsp runny honey

1 large cauliflower, cored and broken into florets

100g toasted flaked almonds

75g shelled pistachio nuts, roughly chopped

1 heaped tsp curry powder

6 tbsp white wine vinegar

100ml maple syrup

6 spring onions, sliced diagonally

3 tbsp chopped mint leaves

3 tbsp chopped coriander leaves

Prepare a barbecue until the flames have died down and the coals are just glowing. Drizzle 1 tbsp of the oil over the chicken breasts and season with salt and pepper, then add half the thyme and toss to coat. Place the chicken skin side down on the barbecue and cook for 8–10 minutes on each side until golden brown and cooked through.

Place the tomatoes on a sheet of foil cut sides down, fold the foil up around the sides to make a little 'tray', then drizzle 1 tbsp of the oil, add the honey, scatter the remaining thyme on top and season with salt and pepper. Place on the barbecue alongside the chicken and roast for 12–15 minutes.

Meanwhile, blitz the cauliflower in a food processor to tiny pieces, then tip into a large bowl. Heat a frying pan until hot, add the remaining 1 tbsp of oil, the flaked almonds and pistachio nuts and toast for 1 minute until golden. Then add the curry powder and fry for 1 minute. Reduce the heat to medium, add the vinegar and maple syrup and cook for another 2–3 minutes until just reduced.

Tip into the bowl with the cauliflower, add the spring onions and herbs and stir well, then season to taste with salt and pepper.

Pile the cauliflower 'couscous' into a serving bowl, top with the chicken and tomatoes and drizzle the juices from the tomatoes over the top.

Salmon and watercress pan bagnat

This really is a treat and – to be honest – it's massive! But the idea is you make it and it lasts four to five days in the fridge, or you take it on a picnic and feed the masses. Making the pesto-style sauce with watercress gives a peppery result and uses the masses of watercress for which Hampshire – where I live – is so famous. If you ask me, we should use a lot more of it instead of rocket. It has a great taste and we can grow it naturally all year round.

Serves 8–10

1.5kg salmon fillet
1 lemon, sliced
sea salt and freshly ground black pepper
a few black peppercorns
leaves from a large bunch of basil
2 garlic cloves
60g toasted pine nuts
400g watercress, coarse stalks removed
400ml extra virgin olive oil
6 courgettes, thinly sliced lengthways
2 tbsp olive oil
1 large good-quality pain de campagne loaf
2 red onions, finely sliced
3 x 200g jars roasted piquillo red peppers, opened out

Preheat the oven to 200°C/400°F/gas mark 6. Place the salmon into a deep-sided tray with the lemon slices, adding salt and black peppercorns. Cover with water, then place in the oven for 15–20 minutes until just cooked through. Remove and allow to cool slightly before flaking the fish into large pieces.

Make the pesto by putting a little salt, the basil, garlic, pine nuts and two-thirds of the watercress into a processor and blitz until slightly chunky, then add the virgin oil gradually until it forms a thick paste.

Heat a griddle pan until very hot. Toss the courgettes with the regular oil, salt and pepper then place on the griddle in batches and cook for 1–2 minutes until just cooked through. Remove and set aside to cool.

Meanwhile, take the loaf and cut off the top one-quarter. Spread with pesto and set aside. Scoop out all the crumb from inside the loaf and keep for making breadcrumbs. Spread some of the pesto into the bottom of the loaf.

Arrange one-quarter of the onion slices and piquillo peppers over the pesto.

Place one-quarter of the courgettes on top and press down lightly. Place one-quarter of the remaining watercress on top and press down. Top with one-quarter of the salmon. Repeat the layers, including the pesto, until the loaf is full to the brim, then replace the 'lid' on top.

Wrap very tightly in cling film and place in the fridge for at least 1 hour, but preferably overnight or even up to 3 days, then unwrap and cut into wedges to serve.

This was an idea we had in my restaurant in Malton. These are simple flavours and it is simple to make, too. Even better, these can be assembled in advance for the perfect dinner party dish, sort of a fishy sausage roll! Mackerel, even more than most fish, needs to be spanking fresh.

Mackerel en croûte with gooseberry chutney

Serves 4

For the chutney

125g caster sugar

50g sultanas

leaves from 2 sprigs of thyme

40g piece of ginger, peeled and finely chopped

½ shallot, finely chopped

100ml cider vinegar

300g gooseberries, cleaned, topped and tailed

sea salt and freshly ground black pepper

For the mackerel

250g salmon fillet, skinned, pin-boned and roughly chopped

juice of 1 lemon

110ml double cream

4 mackerel, heads removed, gutted and deboned, tails left on (ask your fishmonger to do this)

leaves from 4 sprigs of tarragon

600g all-butter puff pastry, rolled to 5mm thick

2 eggs, lightly beaten

unsalted butter, for the foil

For the chutney, put the sugar into a heavy-based pan and heat, without stirring, until it has melted and turned to a golden-brown caramel, swirling the pan from time to time. Stir in the sultanas, thyme, ginger and shallot.

Add the cider vinegar and gooseberries, return to the heat and bring to the boil, then simmer gently for 8–10 minutes until the gooseberries are soft, stirring occasionally. Season with salt and pepper and set aside to cool slightly.

To prepare the mackerel, preheat the oven to 220°C/425°F/gas mark 7.

Place the salmon fillet into a food processor with the lemon juice and blitz to a fine paste, then gradually add the cream with the processor still running until thickened. Season with salt and pepper.

Place the mackerel on their sides and open up the cavities, then stuff with the tarragon leaves and the salmon mousse, being careful, so that the fish doesn't tear.

Cut the pastry into 4 rectangles, each about 18cm x 15cm; the width should be about half the length of the fish, and the length long enough to wrap around the stuffed fish. Brush the pastry with egg, then wrap around the centre of the fish, overlapping the ends underneath.

Place on to a baking tray in a row, then mark the pastry with the end of an apple corer or similar to replicate fish scales and brush with egg. Wrap the tails in buttered foil to stop them from burning.

Sprinkle with some sea salt, then bake in the hot oven for 20 minutes until golden and cooked through. Remove from the oven and rest for 5 minutes.

Remove the foil from the tails, cut the fish in half and place the tail end upright on to serving plates, with the other half lying alongside. Finish with a dollop of gooseberry chutney.

Tip

Get the fishmonger to remove the bones from the mackerel, but try to keep the fillets together or it may fall apart (that's why I leave the tail on).

*Looks weird, I know, and while you're making it you might feel the same…
but good things will come of it in the end. Salt crust cooking is nothing new;
from fish to veg, most things can be cooked this way and you will be amazed
at the flavour it creates, seasoning as it cooks. Vegetarians will love the simple
flavours and it's good hot or cold. You have to serve it simply as you want
the flavour to come through. I use it for dinner parties at mine; it's a good
talking point.*

Salt crust dough-baked celeriac with crème fraîche and chive dressing

Serves 4

500g strong white bread flour

200g fine sea salt

4 egg whites

2 medium or 1 large celeriac, washed thoroughly

100g crème fraîche

2 tbsp extra virgin olive oil

freshly ground black pepper

3 tbsp finely chopped chives

50g watercress, coarse stalks removed

a handful of chive flowers (optional)

Place the flour and salt into a large bowl or food mixer and mix until combined, then add the egg whites and 100–125ml of water and mix for about 5 minutes, until it forms a soft, smooth dough.

Remove and flatten into a 2cm-thick disc, wrap in cling film and chill in the fridge for 30 minutes.

Preheat the oven to 180°C/350°F/gas mark 4. Roll out the dough to about 1cm thick. Set aside a small piece. Place a celeriac in the centre of each half of dough, or just use the whole piece for a big one, and wrap to cover totally.

Place on a baking tray and roast in the oven for 1–1½ hours or until the pastry is hard and the celeriac tender; to check if it's tender, insert a skewer into the centre, there should be very little resistance.

Meanwhile, make the dressing: whisk the crème fraîche and olive oil together in a bowl then season well with pepper and stir in the chives (or scatter the chives separately). Set aside in the fridge until ready to use.

When the celeriac is tender, remove and cool slightly before cracking the pastry off.

Finely slice the celeriac and lay across a serving plate, then drizzle the dressing over the top, add the chives if you didn't stir them into the crème fraîche and arrange the watercress and chive flowers (if using) on top.

Hazelnut and Parmesan-crusted chicken

The key to this dish is to cook the chicken in plenty of butter. It will colour the meat while keeping it moist. Using just oil can cause it to burn before it's cooked through. You can use almonds as well as, or instead of, the hazelnuts if you wish.

Serves 4

4 boneless skinless chicken breasts

40g hazelnuts

25g Parmesan cheese, freshly grated, plus more to serve

2 lemons, zested, then cut in half

2 sprigs of thyme, leaves picked

40g panko breadcrumbs

75g plain flour

sea salt and freshly ground black pepper

2 eggs, beaten

250g unsalted butter

2 heads of little gem lettuce, leaves separated

Put the chicken between two pieces of greaseproof paper and bat out with a rolling pin to about 1cm thick.

Place the hazelnuts, Parmesan, lemon zest and thyme in a food processor, and blitz to fine crumbs. Add the breadcrumbs and pulse quickly to just break them up, then tip out onto a plate.

Season the flour with salt and pepper, then dust the chicken with the flour. Dip into the beaten egg, then into the hazelnut breadcrumbs, making sure to coat each side of the chicken thoroughly.

Heat the butter in a large frying pan, then add the chicken breasts and fry until golden – about 5 minutes on each side – basting with the butter as you go. Drain on some kitchen paper, then finish with a little more Parmesan.

Lay the chicken on serving plates, drizzle over all the remaining butter in the frying pan and finish with a squeeze of lemon juice. Pile the lettuce leaves alongside, with a wedge of lemon.

Veal escalopes with salsa verde

When everyone gets bored with sausages and burgers, try this and you might never go back. Veal is the perfect meat for the barbecue. It can be cooked just like steak, but the key to cooking this particular cut of meat well is not to overcook it, as it's very lean and can easily dry out.

Serves 6–8

5 lemons
1 small bunch of mint
1 small bunch of flat-leaf parsley
½ small bunch of dill
½ small bunch of chervil
1 small bunch of tarragon
1 bulb of garlic, cut in half, plus 2 garlic cloves
250ml extra virgin olive oil
1kg veal cushion, cut into 2cm thick slices
1 shallot, finely chopped
2 sprigs of basil
3 anchovies, finely chopped
1 tbsp Dijon mustard
1 tbsp capers, drained
sea salt and freshly ground black pepper
300g spinach leaves

Heat a barbecue until the coals are glowing, or heat a griddle pan until very hot.

Zest 2 of the lemons into a large bowl and squeeze in the juice. Add a few sprigs of mint, parsley, dill, chervil and tarragon, and the halved garlic bulb. Add 150ml of the extra virgin olive oil, mix to combine and set aside.

Place a long sheet of clingfilm on a board, then lay all the slices of veal on it and cover with a second sheet of clingfilm. Bash with a rolling pin until about 1cm thick, then place the pieces of veal in the herby oil. Toss to coat, then set aside while you make the salsa verde.

Chop the shallot, garlic cloves and the remaining herbs, including the basil, together finely on a board. Add the zest of 2 more lemons, then chop again. Add the anchovies and chop all together, then finally add the Dijon mustard and capers, and chop until you have a fine mixture. Season with salt and pepper, then make a hollow in the centre.

Lift the veal out of the marinade and onto the barbecue or griddle and cook for 2–3 minutes, then turn over and cook for another 2 minutes. Remove and put straight onto a serving platter.

While the veal cooks, heat a sauté pan until hot. Add 50ml of the extra virgin olive oil and the spinach leaves, and sauté until just wilted, then spoon over the veal.

Pour the last of the extra virgin olive oil into the centre of the herb pile and mix together until it forms a thick paste. Spoon over the top of the veal and spinach, and serve with the last lemon, cut into wedges.

Flageolet bean and bacon salad

When you want a meal that's ready in just 10 minutes, tinned beans and other pulses are great to have in your cupboard. Either hot or cold, they can form the main part of a simple and very quick dish like this. Buy good-quality ones, though, as some are in a strong brine that doesn't taste very nice. A nice dressing is the key.

Serves 4

1 tbsp rapeseed oil
8 slices of smoked streaky bacon
2 tbsp cider vinegar
1 shallot, finely sliced
400g tin flageolet beans, drained and rinsed
1 tsp truffle oil
3 tbsp vegetable oil
sea salt and freshly ground black pepper
50g rocket leaves
1 head of romaine lettuce, roughly chopped
40g Parmesan cheese, broken into small nuggets

Heat a frying pan until hot. Add the rapeseed oil and bacon, and fry on each side for a couple of minutes until golden-brown and crispy. Drain on kitchen paper, then roughly chop.

Return the frying pan to the heat, then add the cider vinegar and deglaze the pan, scraping up all the meaty bits from the bottom of the pan. Add the shallot and flageolet beans, and warm through.

Mix the truffle and vegetable oils together in a bowl, then add the flageolet bean mixture and toss to coat in the dressing. Season with pepper and a touch of salt to taste.

Divide the rocket and romaine lettuce between your serving plates and spoon the beans over the top, finishing with a scattering of Parmesan nuggets.

Fresh crab and chilli linguine

People often ask me what my own personal food heaven or food hell would be. One of my top three for food heaven would definitely be fresh crab. There's nothing better than fresh white crabmeat served with just a touch of lemon. This linguine dish takes it one step further, with a spicy hit from the chilli: simple yet full of flavour. You could use dark crabmeat or a combination of the two; just make sure it's very good quality.

Serves 4

300g dried linguine
50ml olive oil
2 shallots, finely chopped
2 garlic cloves, finely chopped
1 red chilli, finely chopped
½ tsp crushed red chilli flakes
100g fresh brown crabmeat, picked
300g fresh white crabmeat, picked
100ml white wine
2 tbsp roughly chopped flat-leaf parsley
1 lemon, zested and juiced
sea salt and freshly ground black pepper
1–2 tbsp extra virgin olive oil

Cook the linguine according to the packet instructions, then drain, reserving 100ml of the pasta water.

Heat a large sauté pan until hot. Add the olive oil, shallots, garlic, chilli and chilli flakes, and sweat for 3–4 minutes until softened. Add the crabmeat and toss to combine, then add the white wine and cook until the wine has reduced by half and the crab is hot through. Add the parsley and lemon zest, and toss together, then add lemon juice, salt and black pepper to taste.

Add the drained pasta and the reserved pasta water, and toss together, checking the seasoning once more.

Divide between serving plates and serve with a drizzle of extra virgin olive oil.

Artichoke and broad bean risotto

My artichoke plants have been in the garden some eight years now, and still produce a great crop year on year. If you can, try to get the smaller artichokes for this recipe, as they're easier to prepare and cook. The little bit of lemon at the end makes all the difference to this dish.

Serves 4

1 lemon
6 baby purple artichokes
200ml extra virgin olive oil
25g unsalted butter
2 shallots, finely chopped
1 garlic clove, finely chopped
3 sprigs of fresh thyme, leaves only
100g risotto rice
200ml white wine
750ml hot chicken or vegetable stock
150g podded broad beans, inner skins removed
4 heaped tbsp grated Parmesan cheese, plus extra to serve
2 tbsp finely chopped chives
50ml double cream
salt and freshly ground black pepper
1 chive flower, to garnish

Remove the zest from half the lemon and set aside. Cut the lemon in half. Peel the stalk of one artichoke, then trim to about 2.5cm below the base and remove the tough outer leaves. Cut the top third off and discard, then rub immediately with the halved lemon. Repeat with the rest of the artichokes.

Put 200ml of water into a sauté pan, then add the olive oil and bring to a simmer. Cut the artichokes in half lengthways, then add to the pan, cover with a lid and simmer for 10–15 minutes until tender. Check with the tip of a knife to see if they are cooked through – there should be no resistance. Remove from the heat and cool slightly, then cut in half lengthways.

Heat a sauté pan until medium hot. Add a knob of the butter, the shallots, garlic and thyme, and cook for a couple of minutes without colouring. Tip in the rice and stir well, then add the wine and cook until reduced to nothing.

Add a ladleful of hot stock and bring to a simmer, stirring occasionally, until the rice has absorbed it all. Keep adding stock a ladleful at a time, waiting until it has been absorbed before adding more. After you've been adding the stock for 5–6 minutes, add the broad beans and continue adding the stock until it has been used and the rice is tender – it should take 12–15 minutes.

When the rice is cooked through, add the artichokes, Parmesan, chives, lemon zest and cream, and season with salt and pepper to taste. Add a little more stock if needed to keep the risotto loose.

Serve with extra Parmesan grated over the top and the chive flower.

A great chef mate of mine – Stephen Terry – runs a fab place called the Hardwick at Abergavenny in Wales. If it's a nice day, I often take one of the old cars for a spin and go there for lunch. This was a dish I saw Stephen make and it's so good that I've nicked it both for this book and for me at home. It's very clever cooking from a top-class chef, using just a hint of spice, but the lemon calms it down. Trust me, you will like it.

Sausage, radicchio and lemon gnocchi

For the gnocchi, preheat the oven to 170°C/340°F/gas mark 3½.

Rub the potatoes with a little oil then place on a small pile of rock salt on a baking tray. Bake in the oven for 1½ hours, or until tender. When cooked, remove from the oven and set aside until cool enough to handle.

Cut the potatoes in half and scoop out the flesh, then pass through a potato ricer or sieve into a large bowl. Add the flour and egg yolk, season, then mix lightly until it forms a soft dough.

Tip on to a floured work surface, divide into quarters and roll each into a long sausage. Cut into 2cm pieces and lightly pinch each in the middle.

Once all the gnocchi are cut, drop them into a large pan of boiling salted water. When the gnocchi bob to the surface, they are ready. Remove with a slotted spoon and place in a bowl of ice-cold water to cool.

To make the sauce, heat a frying pan until medium hot, add the sausagemeat and half the butter and fry until golden-brown all over. Add the shallots, garlic and chilli flakes and cook for 2 minutes.

Pour in the chicken stock and simmer until it is reduced by half and the sausagemeat is cooked through. Add the cream, drained gnocchi, capers, parsley and lemon zest and simmer for 2 minutes.

Heat a griddle pan until hot, toss the radicchio with the olive oil, then char on the griddle pan for 1 minute on each side.

Heat a small frying pan until medium hot, add the remaining butter and, when it's foaming, add the breadcrumbs and fry until golden. Season with salt and pepper. Tip the crumbs on to kitchen paper to cool.

Place the radicchio on to a serving plate, then spoon the sauce over the top. Finish with some Parmesan and a sprinkling of crunchy breadcrumbs.

Tip

If you make these ahead, blanch the gnocchi in boiling water as in the recipe, then drain and place on an oiled tray. They will keep better in the fridge and won't turn soft.

Serves 4

For the gnocchi

4 large floury potatoes
olive oil, for the potatoes
4 tbsp rock salt
75g '00' flour, plus more to dust
1 egg yolk
sea salt and freshly ground black pepper
25g Parmesan, finely grated

For the sauce

4 good-quality pork sausages, skins removed, roughly chopped
50g unsalted butter
2 shallots, finely chopped
2 garlic cloves, finely chopped
1 tsp chilli flakes, or to taste
300ml chicken stock
100ml double cream
25g capers, rinsed, roughly chopped
2 tbsp roughly chopped flat-leaf parsley leaves, plus more to serve
finely grated zest of 2 unwaxed lemons
1 large head of radicchio, cut into wedges through the root
1 tbsp olive oil
50g fresh white breadcrumbs

One of the first things I did when I moved into the house was dig the foundations for the greenhouse. Both my granddad and uncle had greenhouses at the bottom of the garden and taught me so much about growing amazing produce. Over the years we've just about mastered the art of growing tomatoes, often ending up with SO many of them! This is a great dish for using up a glut of seasonal tomatoes. Just purée them, then hang the purée in muslin or a tea towel and let it drip down into a bowl below. The flavour is incredible. You can also freeze it and use it for bloody Marys.

Tomato consommé

Serves 4–6

2kg ripe tomatoes, chopped

2 shallots, roughly chopped

½ tsp Tabasco sauce

1 tbsp Worcestershire sauce

a small handful of basil leaves

sea salt

12 mixed heritage tomatoes, halved or quartered

1 tbsp tiny basil leaves

Place the chopped tomatoes, shallots, Tabasco, Worcestershire sauce and basil leaves in a food processor and blitz for 8–10 seconds, until just broken up but not puréed – a bit like gazpacho. Season with salt, then pulse again and check the seasoning once more.

Line a colander with a large piece of muslin, then set it over a large bowl. Tip the tomato mixture into the muslin and seal with pegs or string, then place in the fridge and leave to drip through for at least 4 hours or overnight, without pressing or squeezing at all.

Lift out the muslin bag (don't discard the contents, you can make a great tomato sauce with it – just add a little olive oil and cook for 15 minutes). Check the tomato consommé for flavour balance, adding extra Tabasco and Worcestershire sauce as desired. Cover and chill in the fridge until ready to serve.

Ladle into bowls, and garnish with the pieces of heritage tomato and a scattering of tiny basil leaves.

Tip

You can serve this cold or warm, and if you have any left over, freeze it in ice cube trays to use in a Bloody Mary.

Cheddar, smoked bacon and courgette quiches

There are a couple of quiches in this book: when they're made with good-quality ingredients, including courgettes freshly picked from the garden, there's little better for a lunchtime snack. The key is in the cooking: nice, thin pastry (you don't need to bake it blind, just reduce the temperature and bake it for longer).

Serves 6

For the pastry

250g plain flour, plus extra for dusting
150g cold unsalted butter, cubed
a pinch of sea salt
1 egg, beaten

For the filling

6 slices of dry-cured smoked streaky bacon
5 egg yolks
300ml double cream
sea salt and freshly ground black pepper
75g mature Cheddar cheese, finely grated
1 small courgette, finely diced
4 sprigs of thyme, leaves picked

For the salad

1 tsp grainy mustard
1 tsp red wine vinegar
1 tbsp rapeseed oil
1 bag of salad leaves
1 head of little gem lettuce, leaves picked

To make the pastry, put the flour into a bowl, add the butter and rub together with your fingertips until breadcrumbs form. Add the salt and egg, and bring together, then knead very lightly to form a soft dough. Cover and place in the fridge for 10–15 minutes to firm up.

Preheat the oven to 180°C/350°F/gas mark 4 and grease six loose-bottomed tart tins 9cm in diameter and 4cm deep.

Roll the pastry out on a lightly floured surface to a thickness of 3mm and cut it into six discs larger than the tart tins, re-rolling the last of the pastry for the last two tins. Lay the pastry over the tins and press gently into the base and sides. Trim the sides so the pastry is flush to the edge.

For the filling, heat a frying pan until medium–hot, then add the bacon and fry for 3–4 minutes, until golden-brown and just crispy. Drain on kitchen paper, then roughly chop and set aside.

Whisk the egg yolks and cream together, whisk once more, then season with salt and pepper. Sprinkle half the cheese into the bottom of the tart cases, and follow with half the bacon, the courgette, then the last of the cheese and bacon. Finish with a little thyme, then pull the oven rack out slightly and set the tins near the edge. Pour in the egg mixture, then slide the quiches fully into the oven and bake for 15–20 minutes until just set and golden-brown. Remove and cool slightly before serving.

For the salad, put the mustard, vinegar and rapeseed oil into a small jar with a lid, and shake vigorously to emulsify together. Put the salad into a resealable bag, then, when ready to serve, tip the dressing into the bag and shake to coat all the leaves.

Serve the quiches at room temperature, with the salad.

Ricotta and herb cappellacci with pesto, peas and beans

I love Gennaro Contaldo – he's a great friend and a true gent, and was one of the first to sign up for the show. He said it was about the food, though I reckon it was all about the cars … but when I did manage to prise him out of the garage he gave me a helping hand with this dish.

Serves 4

For the cappellacci

400g '00' pasta flour
4 eggs, plus 1–2 tbsp water if needed
200g ricotta cheese, drained
1 tbsp freshly grated Parmesan cheese, plus to serve
4 tsp finely chopped chives
1 tbsp finely chopped basil leaves
1 tsp finely chopped marjoram leaves
1 tsp finely chopped oregano leaves
sea salt and freshly ground black pepper

For the pesto, peas and beans

60g basil leaves
1 garlic clove, finely chopped
50g Parmesan cheese, grated
75ml extra virgin olive oil
100g fresh peas
100g runner beans, cut into 2cm pieces
a few sprigs of mint

To make the cappellacci, place the flour and eggs in a bowl or food processor and rub together or pulse until the mixture forms small crumbs. Remove from the processor, if using, pull together to form a dough, then knead lightly for 2–3 minutes, until the dough is smooth and elastic. Cover and place in the fridge for 20 minutes – you can cut the pasta you don't wish to use into portions and freeze any extra for another dish.

Meanwhile, place the ricotta, Parmesan and herbs in a bowl, and mix to combine then season to taste with salt and pepper.

Roll out the pasta to 2mm thick, using a pasta machine or by hand with a rolling pin. Lay a sheet of pasta on the work surface and cut into 7.5cm squares. Brush one of the squares lightly with a little water around the edges, then place a spoonful of the ricotta mixture in the centre. Fold the pasta over the filling to form a triangle and press lightly around the edges to seal. Pressing gently on the edges, carefully roll the back long edge of the triangle up and over the filled area. Twist the two long ends of the triangle around, away from the tip, then press the long ends together, using a little more water to seal if necessary. Repeat with the remaining pasta and filling.

To make the pesto, place the basil, garlic and Parmesan in a food processor or a pestle and mortar and blitz to a fine purée. Add the olive oil and blitz again until well combined. Check the seasoning, then tip into a sauté pan. Bring a pan of salted water to the boil, add the peas and beans, and simmer for 3–4 minutes until tender. Drain and tip into the sauté pan with the pesto.

Bring a large pan of salted water to the boil, add the cappellacci and cook for 1–2 minutes until they float to the top of the pan. Lift out with a slotted spoon and add them to the pesto, peas and beans, then add a couple of spoonfuls of pasta water and toss well to combine and warm the whole dish through.

Serve with extra Parmesan grated over the top and a few sprigs of mint.

Carpaccio of tuna with caramelised watermelon

This is one of my favourite fish dishes – it's so simple. The idea comes from a dish I had in a restaurant in New York when I was there on a bit of a food tour. It's a simpler dish made this way, but the taste is great and it can be made at home. The keys to it are fresh tuna and really good extra virgin olive oil.

Serves 4

¼ watermelon, peeled and cut into 1cm thick slices
sea salt and freshly ground black pepper
2 thin slices of sourdough bread
4 x 50–75g fresh tuna loin steaks
1 lemon, juiced
2 tbsp very finely chopped chives
1 shallot, very finely chopped
50g unsalted butter
2 tbsp extra virgin olive oil

Place the watermelon in a resealable bag with a pinch of salt and place in the fridge for 2–3 days.

Preheat the oven to 150°C/300°F/gas mark 2.

Toast the bread in a toaster, then slice in half horizontally so you have one toasted side and one untoasted side. Place between two thin baking trays and bake in the oven for 5 minutes until crisp. Remove and cool between the trays.

Spread a sheet of clingfilm on a work surface and lay a piece of tuna on it, then cover with a second sheet of clingfilm. Bat the tuna very gently with a rolling pin so that you have an evenly thin piece, finishing by rolling it flat – about 2mm thick. Repeat with each piece of tuna.

Take a bowl the same size as the centre of the plate you are going to serve on, then turn it upside down and place it on one of the pieces of clingfilmed tuna. Cut around the bowl so you are left with a disc of tuna, then set the disc aside. Repeat with the rest of the tuna. Remove the clingfilm from the trimmings, then chop them very finely and place in a bowl.

Add a squeeze of lemon juice, two-thirds of the chives and shallot, season with salt and pepper, and mix together to form a tuna tartare.

Slice the watermelon into pieces. Heat a frying pan until hot, add the butter, and only when it's nut-brown add the watermelon and fry on each side for 1 minute, or until browned and hot through. Add a pinch of salt and tip onto a plate.

Place a spoonful of tuna tartare on each piece of toast and place a piece of the fried watermelon on top. Place on a serving plate. Lift the clingfilm off one side of the tuna discs and flip over. Lay them on top of the tartare and lift off the second sheet of clingfilm. Drizzle with the extra virgin olive oil and brush it all over the tuna.

Garnish with the rest of the shallot and chives, and add a squeeze of lemon juice and some pepper.

Deep-fried aubergine with halibut and miso

The idea for this came from a trip to the Indian Ocean – weird, I guess, considering none of the ingredients comes from there. I've added the fish to make it a main course, but this is also a great vegetarian dish made with just the aubergines as a base. You do need to keep an eye on the sauce as it simmers – because of the sugar it can burn easily.

Serves 4

150ml white miso

150g caster sugar

vegetable oil, for deep-frying

2 aubergines, cut into 1–2cm cubes

2 tbsp roughly chopped coriander

50g unsalted butter

500g halibut fillets, skinned, pin-boned and cut into 8 chunks

100g edamame beans

1 tbsp white sesame seeds

1 tbsp black sesame seeds

2 tbsp mixed micro cress – red amaranth and bronze fennel fronds

Put the miso and sugar into a saucepan with 50ml of water and bring to the boil. Reduce the heat and simmer gently for 10 minutes until thickened and just darkened in colour. Decant into a squeezy bottle fitted with a small nozzle lid – it can be kept like this in the fridge for one week.

Heat a deep-fat fryer to 180°C/350°F, or heat the oil for deep-frying in a deep heavy-based frying pan until a breadcrumb sizzles and turns brown when dropped into it. (CAUTION: hot oil can be dangerous. Do not leave unattended.)

Deep-fry the diced aubergine for 2–3 minutes, or until golden brown and crisp. Set aside to drain on kitchen paper, then add the chopped coriander and toss together.

Heat a large frying pan until hot. Add the butter and when it's foaming, add the halibut and fry on each side for 2 minutes, until golden-brown and just cooked through. Add the edamame beans and warm through.

Mix the two types of sesame seeds together.

To serve, place the aubergine on the serving plates, scatter with the edamame beans, then sprinkle the sesame seeds on top. Finish with two pieces of fish and a drizzle of the miso sauce. Garnish with the cress.

Comforting Sunday Night Bites

A lovely simple soup that can be made with either white or brown crab meat. The brown crab meat version will be richer and the white crab meat a little lighter. Or you can, of course, use a mixture of both. You can also use canned or frozen sweetcorn, so you can make this soup all year round.

Sweetcorn soup with crab and home-soured cream

Serves 4

25g unsalted butter

1 banana shallot, finely sliced

½ tsp curry powder

340g can of sweetcorn, or frozen sweetcorn

75ml white wine

200ml double cream

sea salt and freshly ground black pepper

juice of 1 lemon

100g picked white or brown crab meat, or a mixture

a little rapeseed oil, to serve

Heat a saucepan until medium hot, add the butter, shallot and curry powder and cook without colour for 2–3 minutes until the shallot has just softened.

Add the sweetcorn (and all the liquid from the can, if you're using canned), then add the wine and enough water to just cover.

Bring to a simmer, add half the cream, then season with salt and pepper.

Pour into a blender, making sure to fill it only one-third full, cover with the lid and blitz to a purée. (You will probably have to blend the soup in batches.) You'll know your blender better than I do, but you need to make sure the centre part of the lid is slightly ajar, or it can create a vacuum which can pop the lid off and spray hot soup around the kitchen. Be careful.

Return the soup to the pan and heat through gently, adding a squeeze of lemon juice, salt and pepper to taste.

Pour the remaining cream into a bowl with the remaining lemon juice then whisk until thickened (this is home-made soured cream!). Season with salt.

Ladle the soup into serving bowls, then top with a little of the crab, a spoonful of the soured cream and a drizzle of rapeseed oil.

A 'French-trimmed' chicken breast is a skin-on breast with the wing bone attached, but the end of the bone is trimmed down like a French-trimmed rack of lamb. You're best off asking your butcher to cut them for you. And most people wouldn't think you can cook squash in super-quick time… but you can and it's so easy.

Quick spiced squash with chicken

Serves 2

1 butternut or tromboncino squash

2 French-trimmed skin-on chicken breasts (wing bones attached)

sea salt and freshly ground black pepper

50g unsalted butter

1 tbsp olive oil

1 shallot, finely chopped

2 garlic cloves, finely sliced

1 tbsp caster sugar

5cm piece of ginger, peeled and finely grated

½ tsp turmeric

¼ tsp fenugreek seeds

1½ tsp black onion seeds

1 red chilli, deseeded and finely chopped

2 tbsp roughly chopped coriander leaves

2 tbsp mango chutney

Preheat the oven to 200°C/400°F/gas mark 6. Cut a 6cm piece of squash and peel it, then cut into four 1.5cm-thick slices and set aside.

Cut another piece of squash about 300g in weight, peel it and chop into 1cm pieces.

Season the chicken breasts with salt and pepper.

Heat an ovenproof frying pan until hot, making sure it is large enough to hold the chicken and squash slices in a single layer. Add half the butter, the olive oil and the chicken, skin-side down. Cook on each side for 1–2 minutes until golden brown. Now add the squash slices, turn to coat and place in the oven for 15 minutes, until both are cooked through. The squash should be tender to the point of a knife, and the chicken, when cut at its thickest point, should show no trace of pink. (If it does, return to the oven for a few minutes, then test again.)

Meanwhile, heat a sauté pan until hot, add the remaining butter and the shallot, garlic and chopped squash and cook for a couple of minutes.

Add the sugar and cook until just caramelising, then add a splash of water with the ginger, turmeric, fenugreek and black onion seeds and cook for another couple of minutes.

Pour in 50–75ml of water and stir to combine, then add the chilli, coriander and a good pinch of salt and cook for a further 2 minutes. Remove from the heat and stir in the mango chutney.

Place two slices of squash on to each plate, top with a chicken breast, then spoon some spiced squash alongside.

Grilled vegetable pan bagnat

When you're making this it all looks a bit weird, but it will come together when you actually serve it. The chargrilled veg are layered with cheese, and you can add salmon, tuna, ham – whatever you want. You can even buy the roasted veg if you don't want to make your own. It's best left to sit in the fridge for a couple of hours so that all the flavours are absorbed into the bread.

Serves 4

1 aubergine, cut into 5mm dice

1 red onion, thickly sliced

6 asparagus stems, trimmed and cut into 1cm pieces

3 tbsp olive oil

sea salt and freshly ground black pepper

130g sunblushed tomatoes, drained, and 100ml of the oil reserved

50g toasted pine nuts

50g pecorino cheese, freshly grated

4 ciabatta rolls

a large handful of basil leaves

1 ball of mozzarella cheese, drained and thinly sliced

Preheat the oven to 180°C/350°F/gas mark 4.

Heat a griddle pan until very hot. Toss the aubergine, red onion and asparagus with 1 tbsp of the olive oil, season with salt and pepper, then place on the griddle in batches and grill for 2–3 minutes, until just cooked through. Remove and set aside to cool.

Put the sunblushed tomatoes into a food processor or a pestle and mortar with the 100ml of olive oil from the jar, and blitz to a chunky purée. Add the pine nuts and pecorino, and pulse until combined but still slightly chunky. Season the pesto with pepper and a pinch of salt.

Cut off the top quarter from the rolls. Set these aside – they will be the lids. Scoop out all the bread from inside the rolls and keep for making breadcrumbs. Brush the inside of the rolls with the remaining olive oil and place on a tray in the oven for 8–10 minutes, to crisp up.

Spread some of the tomato pesto in the bottom of the rolls, then layer in some mozzarella and basil leaves.

Divide the griddled vegetables between the rolls, then top with more pesto, mozzarella and basil leaves. Place the lids on top and press down lightly.

This can be eaten immediately, or wrapped in clingfilm and kept in the fridge for up to 3 days, then either eaten cold or heated through in the oven preheated to 200°C/400°F/gas mark 6 for 15 minutes until hot through.

Tartiflette and bacon fat salad

I'm not into skiing, although I did try it once and – apart from nearly breaking my leg – I also took out seven school kids and a fence. I haven't and wouldn't do it again. You should stop wearing things on your feet other than shoes and slippers after the age of five. The French Alps are good for some things though, including tartiflette.

Serves 6–8

1.5kg red-skinned potatoes, such as Desiree, well scrubbed
75g unsalted butter, plus more to brush
1 large onion, finely sliced
2 sprigs of thyme
1 garlic clove
10 thick rashers of smoked dry-cured streaky bacon
250g whole petit Reblochon cheese, rind removed
sea salt and freshly ground black pepper
1 tsp Dijon mustard
1½ tbsp white wine vinegar
1 egg yolk
2 tbsp vegetable oil
100g mixed salad leaves

Preheat the oven to 200°C/400°F/gas mark 6.

Place the potatoes into a large pan and bring to the boil in their skins. Cook for 10 minutes.

Meanwhile, heat a frying pan until medium hot, add a knob of the butter, the onion and thyme and cook for 5–8 minutes until softened, but not coloured at all.

Drain the potatoes and, when they are cool enough, scrape off the skins with a table knife. Cut into slices around 5mm thick.

Take an ovenproof dish, cut the garlic in half and rub the cut side all over the dish, then smear on some butter.

Lay the onion into the dish and spread out over the base, then lay six rashers of bacon across that. Lay the potatoes in concentric circles over the top, then place the cheese in the centre.

Dot with half the remaining butter, pepper and a touch of salt and place in the oven for 45 minutes, until the potatoes are lovely and crisp at the edges and the cheese is totally melted.

Meanwhile, melt most of the remaining butter in a frying pan and chop the remaining four rashers of bacon into lardons. Add to the pan and cook over a medium heat until the fat starts to render, then increase the heat and cook until crisp and browned. Remove with a slotted spoon and place on kitchen paper.

Whisk the Dijon mustard, vinegar and egg yolk together until paler, then whisk in the vegetable oil to emulsify. Pour into the hot fat in the bacon pan and whisk until thickened and cooled slightly. Check the seasoning. Toss the crispy bacon with the salad leaves, then dress with a little of the dressing.

Remove the tartiflette from the oven, melt the remaining butter in a small saucepan and brush the tartiflette with the melted butter. Serve with the salad.

The simplest ingredients often taste the best, and this is a great example of that. I'm not much of a fan of goat's cheese but I do like the milder types that aren't chalky. If you're not sure, give it a try!

Parma ham and goat's cheese en croûte with chilli apple chutney

Serves 2

For the goat's cheese en croute

2 tbsp unsalted butter

100g baby spinach leaves

grated nutmeg

sea salt and freshly ground black pepper

4 slices of Parma ham

200g unrinded soft goat's cheese, cut into 4 discs

325g puff pastry, rolled out to 3mm thick

1 egg, beaten

green salad, to serve

For the chilli apple chutney

100g dark muscovado sugar

1 shallot, finely chopped

2cm piece of ginger, peeled and finely chopped

1 tsp mixed spice

½ tsp dried chilli flakes

2 apples, grated

150g sultanas

150ml white wine vinegar

Preheat the oven to 200°C/400°F/gas mark 6.

Heat a frying pan until hot, then add the butter and spinach, and cook until just wilted. Season with nutmeg, salt and pepper, then tip out onto a paper-lined plate and leave to cool.

Wrap the Parma ham around the cheese to cover it on all sides.

Divide the pastry into eight equal rectangles and place the spinach on top of four of them. Place the cheese on top and season well. Brush the edge of the pastry with the some of the egg and top with the remaining pieces of pastry. Press down lightly around the edges, then crimp the edges. Brush with the remaining eggwash and place on a baking tray. Bake for 20 minutes until cooked through and golden brown.

To make the chutney, heat a saucepan until medium hot, then add the sugar and cook until just melted, stirring occasionally. Add all the remaining ingredients and cook for 15–20 minutes until the apples are tender and the chutney has thickened slightly.

Remove from the heat and allow to cool slightly, then serve with the goat's cheese en croute and a green salad.

Whenever I go to France I make a beeline for Le Fouquet's on the Champs-Elysées, in the shadow of the Arc de Triomphe. The keys to a good onion soup like this are the stock and the cooking time, plus a little sherry. Get those three things right and it's the best-tasting soup out there, plus of course the melted cheese croutons on the top.

French onion soup with cheesy croutons

Serves 4

3 tbsp olive oil
3 large onions, finely sliced
2 sprigs of thyme, leaves picked
1 tbsp soft brown sugar
2 garlic cloves, finely sliced
200ml white wine
1 heaped tbsp plain flour
50ml brandy
50ml dry sherry
1 litre fresh dark beef stock
½ baguette, sliced thickly into chunks
sea salt and freshly ground black pepper
110g Gruyère cheese, grated

Heat a large sauté pan until hot, then add 2 tbsp of the olive oil, the onions, thyme and soft brown sugar, and fry for 10–15 minutes over a medium–low heat, or until the onions are softened and golden-brown, stirring occasionally so they don't catch on the bottom of the pan.

Add the garlic and cook for 1 minute, then add the white wine and cook until reduced by half. Stir in the flour and cook for 2 minutes. Add the brandy and sherry, then pour in the stock and bring to the boil. Reduce the heat slightly and cook gently for about 10–15 minutes.

While the soup simmers, heat a griddle until hot. Drizzle the remaining oil over the bread and toast on one side, then set aside.

Check the seasoning of the soup, adding plenty of salt and a little pepper, and adding more sugar or alcohol if necessary to suit your own taste.

Preheat the grill to high. Ladle the soup into bowls and top with the toasted bread, then add the cheese and return to the grill until bubbling and golden-brown.

Any leftover soup can be frozen for up to 4 weeks.

'Nduja and sheep's cheese pizza

'Nduja is one of the ingredients I came across while working with another chef, Francesco Mazzi. It comes from, Calabria, his region of Italy. It's a wonderful spicy – and I mean spicy – soft sausage that contains so much flavour. I love it with gnocchi, but on this pizza, made in my oven in the garden, it tastes amazing.

Serves 6

For the pizza dough

200g semolina flour

800g '00' white flour, plus extra for dusting

1 tbsp caster sugar

1 tsp salt

7g fresh yeast

650ml warm water

For the topping

400g tin San Marzano tomatoes (see page 10)

400g sheep's cheese, sliced and crumbled

300g 'nduja (soft spicy salami from Calabria, Italy)

a large handful of basil leaves

1 tbsp peanut oil

Place the flours, sugar and salt in a large bowl, and stir. Mix the yeast to a paste with a little of the warm water, then pour onto the flour. Add the rest of the water, gradually mixing in the flour to form a soft dough.

Tip the dough out onto a lightly floured work surface and knead until smooth and elastic. Place in a bowl and leave to rise for 1½ hours, then knock back and divide into six equal portions. Roll each piece into a ball, then place on a tray, cover and leave to rise for 4 hours or overnight in the fridge.

Preheat the oven to as high as it will go. Place a heavy baking tray or pizza stone in the oven to heat up.

Roll each piece of dough out on a lightly floured surface, until about 5mm thick, then place on an upturned floured tray.

Place the tomatoes in a food processor and blitz to a purée. Spoon the tomato purée thinly over the bases, just to the edges. Scatter over the sheep's cheese, 'nduja and basil leaves, and drizzle over the peanut oil.

Scoot into the oven, pushing the pizza onto the heated baking tray or pizza stone, and cook for 5–8 minutes until cooked through and bubbling. You will need to cook the pizzas in batches. Serve immediately.

Mrs Baxter's chicken livers

This was the dish that got me into so much trouble at school. Little did my twelve-year-old self know that bringing in a bottle of alcohol was going to be such a problem! It tasted nice though – the dish I mean.

Serves 2–3

1 slice of white bread
1 tbsp olive oil
7 slices of dry-cured streaky bacon
400g chicken livers, trimmed
50ml brandy
1 tbsp sherry vinegar
50ml double cream
50g mangetout, sliced
sea salt and freshly ground black pepper
2 handfuls of rocket leaves

Heat a griddle pan until hot. Drizzle both sides of the bread with the olive oil, then place on the griddle, toast on both sides and set aside.

Heat a frying pan until warm, then add the bacon and cook until golden brown and crisp. Lift out onto a plate and set aside. Dip the bread in the hot bacon fat in the pan, then set aside again.

Return the frying pan to the heat, then add the chicken livers and cook for 2–3 minutes until browned on the outside but still pink on the inside. Deglaze the pan with the brandy, then add the sherry vinegar, cream and mangetout, and cook for a couple of minutes. Season with salt and pepper.

Pile the rocket into a serving bowl, then roughly chop the toasted bread and the crispy bacon, and scatter over the top. Spoon the chicken livers and juices over and serve straight away.

Morel mushrooms en cocotte with duck egg

Wild mushrooms are one of the joys of autumn, and cooked this way their taste stays fresh and clean. I love the simple nature of this dish and it's a perfect home comforts recipe. You can use smoked salmon on the base instead of the mushrooms, if you wish.

Serves 4

25g unsalted butter, plus extra for greasing

2 shallots, finely chopped

150g morel, wild or field mushrooms, cleaned and roughly chopped

sea salt and freshly ground black pepper

1 tbsp finely chopped chives

1 tsp truffle oil

200ml double cream

4 duck eggs

crusty bread and a dressed green salad, to serve

Preheat the oven to 180°C/350°F/gas mark 4 and butter four ovenproof ramekins.

Heat a frying pan until hot. Add the butter and when it's foaming, add the shallots, mushrooms and a pinch of salt, and fry for 2–3 minutes until wilted and nearly all the moisture has evaporated. Remove from the heat and stir in the chives and half the truffle oil, then season well with salt and pepper. Set aside while you prepare the cream.

Pour the cream into a jug, add the remaining truffle oil, and season well with salt and pepper.

Place the ramekins in a deep-sided roasting tray and divide the mushrooms equally between them. Crack an egg into each ramekin and pour the cream over the top to cover. Fill the tray with warm water until it comes halfway up the ramekins, then place in the oven for 15–20 minutes until the eggs are just cooked through.

Remove from the tray and place on serving plates. Serve with crusty bread and a dressed green salad.

Artichoke with smoked bacon fat mayonnaise

Sounds weird, but the dressing does work – lots of chefs are doing this sort of thing now, and some are even using the fat to distill and make drinks such as lamb fat vodka. Odd, I know.

Serves 4

4 globe artichokes

2 lemons, cut in half

sea salt and freshly ground black pepper

100g plain flour

8 rashers of streaky smoked bacon, roughly chopped

2 egg yolks

1 tsp Dijon mustard

400ml rapeseed oil

Pull off the tough leaves from each artichoke and cut off the stalks and top of the leaves and discard. Rub each artichoke with the cut side of a lemon to stop them discolouring, then put straight into a bowl of water while you repeat with all the other artichokes.

Squeeze the juice from the lemons into a large saucepan, add a pinch of salt and the flour, then fill the pan with cold water. Add the artichokes, set on the heat and bring to the boil. Reduce the heat to a simmer and cook for 15 minutes until tender when pierced with a knife. The flour will rise to the top of the pan and create a crust, keeping the artichokes from discolouring.

While the artichokes cook, make the mayonnaise. Heat a frying pan until hot, then add the bacon and cook over a medium heat until the fat is rendered out and the bacon crispy. Tip into a bowl and allow to cool.

Place the egg yolks and mustard in a food processor, and blend until pale and creamy. With the motor running, pour in the oil in a steady stream, until the mayonnaise is thick, then add the fat from the cooked bacon. Add the crispy bacon pieces, then pulse to combine and break down the bacon a little. Season with a tiny amount of salt and plenty of pepper.

Remove the artichokes and drain upside down on kitchen paper. Allow to cool slightly, then serve with the bacon mayonnaise alongside.

Spanish beans on toast

I've never been a fan of baked beans. In my childhood I used to live on banana and chocolate flake sandwiches (don't ask!), or dripping sandwiches, while my friends tucked into baked beans when they got home from school. These days I find myself making my own beans. It's a simple recipe and one that will bring out the kid in everybody!

Serves 4–6

3 tbsp olive oil

300g cooking chorizo sausages, roughly chopped

2 shallots, finely chopped

2 garlic cloves, finely chopped

1 red chilli, finely chopped

1 tsp smoked sweet paprika

1 tsp smoked hot paprika

400g tin chopped tomatoes

200ml chicken stock

400g tin or jar of haricot beans, drained and rinsed

400g tin or jar of large butter beans, drained and rinsed

2 tbsp roughly chopped flat-leaf parsley

sea salt and freshly ground black pepper

4–6 thick slices of sourdough bread

2 tbsp extra virgin olive oil

Heat a frying pan until hot, then add 2 tbsp of the olive oil and the chopped chorizo sausages, and cook over a medium heat until just browning and the oil is turning red.

Add the shallots and cook for 2 minutes, then add the garlic, chilli and smoked paprikas, and cook for another minute before adding the tinned tomatoes. Bring to a simmer, then add the stock and beans and cook for 5–6 minutes until the sauce has thickened slightly. Add the parsley and season with salt and pepper.

Heat a griddle pan until hot, then drizzle the last tablespoon of the olive oil over the sourdough bread and toast on each side until golden.

Serve the beans and sausages spooned over the bread, with a drizzle of extra virgin olive oil.

I love rarebit and, when you make a batch of the cheese sauce at home, it can sit in the fridge, covered, for about a week, ready to use on toast or just as it is here. It is even great spooned over cooked smoked fish such as haddock. Use a good Cheddar though and don't boil it, or the fat will spill out of the cheese and the mixture will split.

Bacon rarebit with apple chutney

Serves 4

For the apple chutney

150g soft light brown sugar
100g sultanas
125ml malt vinegar
2 eating apples, roughly chopped
3 tomatoes, roughly chopped
1 onion, finely chopped
sea salt and freshly ground black pepper

For the rarebit

8 rashers of dry-cured back bacon
350g grated mature Cheddar cheese
50ml beer (I mean ale, not lager)
1 tsp English mustard
3–4 dashes Tabasco sauce
1 tsp Worcestershire sauce
2 tbsp plain flour
4 thick slices of white bread

To sterilise jars for keeping preserves, you have two choices. Either place the jars in a dishwasher on a normal cycle, then fill (taking care not to touch any of the inside of the jar or lid). Or wash the jars in hot soapy water, dry carefully, then place in an oven preheated to 150°C/300°F/gas mark 2 for 15 minutes. Remove carefully and fill immediately.

To make the chutney, heat a sauté pan until hot, add the brown sugar and sultanas and heat until just melting. Don't stir, but swirl the pan from time to time. Add the vinegar and cook until totally dissolved and starting to caramelise, then add the apples, tomatoes and onion and cook for 10 minutes until the apple is tender and the mixture thickened. Season with salt, remove from the heat and decant into a sterilised jar or jars while both chutney and jar are still hot.

For the rarebit, preheat the grill to high. Place the bacon on a tray and grill for 4–6 minutes, turning once, until the rashers are golden at the edges and just cooked through.

Place the cheese and beer into a frying pan and heat over a low heat until the cheese starts to melt. Heat until bubbling and smooth, then stir in the mustard, Tabasco and Worcestershire sauces, then stir in the flour and cook until just thickened. Season with salt and pepper.

Meanwhile, toast the bread on each side then lay into an ovenproof dish. Top each piece with two rashers of the bacon and spoon the cheese mixture over the top.

Grill for 2–3 minutes until golden and bubbling. Serve with a dollop of the apple chutney.

The only dish my grandad was allowed to make and – given my gran was such a great cook – that means a lot. It's simple but it tastes great. You must use proper natural smoked haddock to make it, none of 'that sprayed stuff', as grandad used to call it.

Poached haddock and egg with mustard sauce

Serves 2

500ml whole milk, plus more if needed
½ onion, thickly sliced
1 bay leaf
2 x 175g natural smoked haddock fillets, pin-boned, skin on
sea salt and freshly ground black pepper
2 tbsp white wine vinegar
2 large eggs
40g unsalted butter
1 tbsp plain flour
1 tbsp English mustard
juice of ½ lemon
200g baby spinach leaves

Preheat the oven to 140°C/275°F/gas mark 1. Pour the milk into a large sauté pan, add the sliced onion and bay leaf and bring to a simmer.

Carefully place the haddock, skin-side down, into the liquid and simmer for 2 minutes, then turn and simmer for another 2 minutes.

Meanwhile, bring a small saucepan of water to the boil, add salt and the white wine vinegar, whisk to create a vortex, then crack one egg into the water and cook for 3 minutes. Remove with a slotted spoon and place straight into iced water, then repeat with the second egg. Keep the pan of water simmering.

Lift the haddock out of the milk with a slotted spoon and place on a plate, then cover and keep the fish warm in the low oven.

Strain the fish poaching milk into a jug, then wipe out the pan and return it to the heat. Add 25g of the butter and, when it has melted, add the flour and cook over a low heat for 2–3 minutes, stirring with a wooden spoon. Gradually whisk in the reserved milk, a little at a time, whisking constantly to avoid any lumps. Continue until all the milk has been added, then reduce the heat to very low and cook for a further 2–3 minutes until you have a smooth, shiny sauce.

Add the mustard and check the seasoning and consistency, adding a little more milk if necessary to make it thick enough to coat the back of a spoon. Add lemon juice to taste.

Heat a frying pan until hot, add the remaining butter and the spinach and cook until wilted and hot through. Drain on kitchen paper, then place on serving plates.

Drop the poached eggs back into the pan of simmering water for 20–30 seconds to reheat.

Place a smoked haddock fillet on each pile of spinach, followed by a poached egg, then finish with the mustard sauce over the top.

Lebanese spiced lamb flatbread

This is a recipe I've tweaked: it was for chunks of lamb, but I changed it to mince to speed it up. Instead of bread I've used a pizza base, as I love my pizza oven in the garden. You can buy a pizza stone for your regular oven and heat it with the oven on full whack and you get a similar effect.

Serves 8

1 quantity pizza dough (see page 226)
1 tbsp vegetable oil
1 shallot, finely chopped
1 garlic clove, finely chopped
1 tsp ground coriander
1 tsp ground cumin
1 tbsp ground baharat spice mix
500g minced lamb
75g sultanas
300ml chicken stock
sea salt and freshly ground black pepper
250ml natural yogurt
2 green chillies, finely chopped
leaves from 4 sprigs of mint
leaves from 16 sprigs of coriander

Start the day before by making the dough, following the instructions on page 226.

Divide into four and roll each into a ball, then place on a tray, cover and leave to rise for 24 hours.

For the filling, heat a sauté pan until hot, add the oil, shallot, garlic and spices and cook for 2 minutes. Add the lamb and cook over a high heat, turning frequently and breaking up with the spoon, until browned.

Add the sultanas and chicken stock and bring to the boil, then reduce the heat and simmer for 20 minutes until the lamb is tender and the liquid virtually gone. Season to taste, then allow to cool totally.

Preheat the oven to as high as it will go. Place a heavy baking tray or pizza stone in the oven and allow to heat.

Roll each piece of dough out on a lightly floured surface into an oval roughly 20 x 15cm, and about 5mm thick, then place on to an upturned, floured baking tray.

Cover the dough bases with the lamb mixture, then evenly scatter over the yogurt and chillies and season with salt and pepper.

Place on the heated tray or stone (you may have to cook them in batches) and cook for 5–10 minutes until golden and crispy. Scatter with the herbs and serve immediately.

This started off with me just wanting to make fish and chips, and it turned into something else. Let's face it, you can't have fish and chips without bread and butter, and homemade lemon mayo brings the whole thing together in one sandwich. A bit extravagant, I know, but my goodness, it tastes delicious.

Battered pollock, mushy pea and lemon mayo baguette

Serves 4–6

For the mushy peas

225g dried marrowfat peas
1 tsp bicarbonate of soda
25g unsalted butter
sea salt and freshly ground black pepper

For the pollock

200g plain flour
15g fresh yeast or 8g fast-action dried yeast
a pinch of caster sugar
a pinch of sea salt
1 tbsp cider vinegar
300ml beer
vegetable oil and dripping, for deep-frying
1kg pollock fillets, skin on, pin-boned and cut into 5cm pieces

For the lemon mayonnaise

2 egg yolks
1 tsp English mustard
300ml rapeseed oil
2 lemons, zested and juiced

To serve

50g softened unsalted butter
1 long baguette, split horizontally

Soak the peas in a large bowl in three times their volume of water with the bicarbonate of soda, for at least 12 hours, preferably overnight.

Drain the peas, rinse under cold running water, then place on the stove in a large pan and cover with water. Cover and bring to the boil, then reduce the heat and simmer the peas for 20–30 minutes, stirring from time to time. They should be soft and mushy in texture, but not too dry. If they are wet, continue cooking them with the lid off to dry them out a little. Beat in the butter and season with salt and pepper.

To make the lemon mayo, place the egg yolks and mustard in a food processor, and blend until pale and creamy. With the motor running, pour in the oil in a slow, steady stream, until the mayonnaise is thick (you may not need all the oil). Mix in the lemon zest and juice, and season to taste.

To cook the pollock, mix the flour, yeast, sugar, salt and vinegar together in a bowl. Add the beer and whisk until the mixture forms a thick batter. Set aside to ferment for about 30 minutes – it is ready to use when the mixture starts to bubble.

Heat a deep-fat fryer to 190°C/375°F, or heat the oil for deep-frying in a deep heavy-based frying pan until a breadcrumb sizzles and turns brown when dropped into it. (CAUTION: Hot oil can be dangerous. Do not leave unattended.)

Dip each piece of fish into the batter to coat thoroughly. Lower carefully into the fryer and cook one at a time. Fry for 4–6 minutes, until the fish is cooked through and the batter is golden-brown. Scatter the remaining batter into the fat fryer and fry until golden-brown. Drain the fish on kitchen paper and season with salt.

To serve, spread the softened butter along the length of the baguette and top with the mushy peas. Place pieces of pollock all along the mushy peas and drizzle over the lemon mayonnaise. Add the batter scraps, then cover with the top of the baguette and gently press down. Serve in one long piece and carve at the table.

Chilli beef with a sticky rice omelette

Make sure you reduce the sauce for the beef down until sticky, as you want the meat to be coated in the sauce. The usual warnings about using cold cooked rice apply (see page 4).

Heat a deep-fat fryer to 190°C/375°F or heat the oil for deep-frying in a deep heavy-based frying pan until a breadcrumb sizzles and turns brown when dropped into it. (CAUTION: hot oil can be dangerous. Do not leave unattended.)

Toss the beef strips with the 2 tbsp of vegetable oil.

Place the Szechuan peppercorns into a mortar and pestle and crush to a fine powder. Place them in large bowl with the lime and orange zests and rice flour, then toss well to combine. Add the beef and toss to coat each piece.

Drop a small batch of the beef into the fat fryer and cook for 2 minutes. Don't overcrowd the pan. Drain on kitchen paper to blot off the excess fat. Keep warm while you cook the rest.

Now make the sauce. Heat a frying pan or wok until hot, add the sugar, rice wine, vinegar and soy sauce and bring to the boil. Add the chillies, chilli flakes, ginger, lemon grass and lime leaves, then cook for 5–8 minutes until thickened, sticky and glossy looking.

Add the cooked beef to the sauce, remove from the heat and toss well so that all the beef is coated in sticky chilli sauce.

Now for the omelette. Heat a wok until hot, add the oil and swirl to coat before very carefully wiping the wok out with kitchen towel, removing any excess oil.

Whisk the eggs together with the soy sauce then pour into the hot wok, lifting the wok up and rolling the egg around the sides of it so you have one very large omelette.

Add the cooked rice to the centre of the omelette then carefully peel the omelette away from the sides of the wok to cover the rice.

When the rice is hot through and the omelette set, roll out on to a board and cut into four.

Pile the beef on to a plate or into bowls and serve the rice omelette on a board alongside it.

Serves 3–4

For the chilli beef

flavourless vegetable oil, to deep-fry, plus 2 tbsp

400g beef fillet, cut into thin strips

1 tbsp Szechuan peppercorns

finely grated zest of 2 limes

finely grated zest of 1 orange

3 heaped tbsp rice flour, potato flour or cornflour

For the sauce

150g caster sugar

150ml Shaoxing rice wine

25ml rice wine vinegar

2 tbsp soy sauce

1½ red chillies, deseeded and finely chopped

2 tsp chilli flakes

10cm piece of ginger, peeled and finely chopped

2 lemon grass stalks, outer leaves removed, finely chopped

4 lime leaves, finely chopped

For the sticky rice omelette

1 tbsp vegetable oil

4 eggs

2 tbsp soy sauce

400g sticky rice, cooked and drained, at room temperature

Comforting Sweet Treats

Jelly and ice cream for grown ups! Of course you can leave out the vodka if you prefer, or if you are serving this to children.

Raspberry jelly with lime syrup and home-made vanilla ice cream

Serves 8–10

For the jelly

450g caster sugar

8 gelatine leaves

50ml raspberry cordial, or raspberry and rose cordial

75–100ml vodka

flavourless vegetable oil, for the moulds

350g raspberries

For the ice cream

500ml whole milk

500ml double cream

1 vanilla pod, split, seeds scraped out

8 egg yolks

200g caster sugar

For the sauce

50ml lime cordial

1½ tsp arrowroot

finely grated zest of 3 limes

To make the jelly, put the sugar into a pan with 1 litre of water and bring to the boil. Meanwhile, soak the gelatine in a little cold water until softened. When the syrup has boiled, measure 1 litre of it into a jug (reserve the 200ml left over for the sauce), then squeeze the gelatine to remove any excess water. Add the gelatine to the measured syrup and mix gently to dissolve. Add the raspberry cordial and vodka and mix to combine.

Brush the inside of two 500g terrine moulds with the oil, then lay in cling film to cover it totally, with at least 2cm hanging over the edge. Place the moulds on a tray filled with ice.

Spoon enough jelly into the moulds to make a 1cm layer. Arrange a layer of the raspberries over the jelly, then cover with another layer of jelly. Allow this layer to partially set in the fridge for 30–45 minutes before adding more raspberries and jelly, reserving a few raspberries to serve (if the remaining jelly has set too much to pour, gently heat it to liquefy first). Place in the fridge for at least 4 hours to set.

For the ice cream, place the milk, cream and vanilla seeds into a saucepan and bring to the boil. Whisk the egg yolks and sugar in a bowl.

Pour the boiling cream mixture over the eggs, whisking all the time, then tip back into the saucepan, place over a high heat and cook, still whisking all the time, until the mixture thickens. Remove from the heat and pass through a fine sieve into a bowl to cool down. Once cool, transfer to an ice cream maker and churn until frozen.

Scoop into a lidded freezerproof container and freeze until needed.

To make the sauce, place the remaining 200ml sugar syrup into a pan with the lime cordial and bring to a simmer. Dissolve the arrowroot in a little cold water, then whisk it into the syrup and cook until it is thick enough to coat the back of a spoon. Remove from the heat, stir in the lime zest and allow to cool.

Turn the jelly out of the moulds and remove the cling film, then cut into slices. Serve with the reserved raspberries, some ice cream and a drizzle of the lime syrup.

I learned to make real doughnuts at one of the oldest bake shops in the USA. They made all fancy shapes, but the biggest seller was the regular kind. Better still if you make small doughnuts like these, as you don't have to prove them for a second time, you can just fry them straight away.

Peach melba with sugar-roasted doughnuts

Serves 4

For the doughnuts

250g strong white bread flour
pinch of salt
25g caster sugar, plus 75g to dust
25g unsalted butter, softened and chopped
2 x 7g sachets of fast-action yeast
flavourless vegetable oil, to deep-fry

For the rest

75g caster sugar
2 tbsp brandy
juice of 1 orange
200g canned sliced peaches
25g flaked almonds
25g pistachio nuts
100g raspberries
500g vanilla ice cream

To make the doughnuts, place the flour, salt, sugar and butter into a bowl. Put the yeast into a jug and mix with 150ml of water until smooth, then pour into the flour mixture.

Mix well, then knead to a smooth dough. Put in a bowl, cover and rest for 1 hour, until doubled in size.

When the dough has proved, heat the oil for deep-frying in a deep-fat fryer to 150°C/300°F. Alternatively, heat the oil in a deep, heavy-based saucepan until a breadcrumb sizzles and turns brown when dropped into it. (CAUTION: hot oil can be dangerous. Do not leave unattended.)

Take small golf ball-sized pieces of the dough and roll into balls.

Carefully lower the dough balls into the hot oil in batches and deep-fry for 3–4 minutes, or until golden-brown. Remove from the pan using a slotted spoon and set aside to drain on kitchen paper. Roll in the 75g of sugar.

For the sauce, heat a frying pan until hot, add the caster sugar and heat until it forms a caramel, swirling the pan occasionally (don't stir it).

Add the brandy, stand well back and set light to the pan then, when the flames subside, pour in the orange juice and swirl to combine.

Add the peaches, almonds, pistachio nuts and raspberries and heat through for 2 minutes only; you don't want to let the raspberries break down.

Place two spoonfuls of ice cream into each bowl, add a few doughnuts, then pour the sauce on top.

The good thing with this meringue is that you can make it with lots of other fruits such as cherries, raspberries, blueberries or blackberries. All the versions are just as good. I have some greengages growing in the garden at home, so that's why they are in this. The meringue turns lovely and sticky when cooked.

Greengage meringues with ice cream

Serves 4

750g greengages, pitted and quartered
270g caster sugar
5 egg whites
150g icing sugar
300ml double cream
1 vanilla pod, split, seeds scraped out

Preheat the oven to 100°C/200°F/gas mark ¼.

Put 2 tbsp of water, the greengages and 120g of the caster sugar into a pan and cook for 15–20 minutes until they are soft with a sticky syrup. Remove from the heat and allow to cool totally.

Beat the egg whites in a clean bowl, using electric beaters, until the mixture forms soft peaks, then add the remaining 150g of caster sugar and beat until stiff peaks form. Sift the icing sugar over, then continue to beat until the mixture forms stiff peaks again and is really smooth and shiny.

Line a baking sheet with baking parchment, or a silicone sheet, and secure the paper with a few dabs of meringue mixture.

Fold half the cooled greengages into the meringue mixture, taking care not to knock out too much air, then place eight spoonfuls on to the baking tray.

Place into the oven and bake for 2 hours, then turn the oven off and open the door a bit (propping it open with a wooden spoon is a good trick). Leave the meringues to cool in the oven.

Whisk the double cream with the vanilla seeds until soft peaks form.

Spoon some of the reserved greengages into the centre of each plate. Sandwich the meringues together with the vanilla cream, set on top of the greengages and serve immediately.

You will need a waffle maker for this recipe. I never knew how simple waffles were to make, or how quick, before I used one. I've only used strawberries because I have bucket-loads of them in my garden; other fruits such as raspberries and apricots would be just as good.

Home-made waffles with strawberry compote

Serves 4

For the waffles

250g plain flour

1½ tsp baking powder

1 tsp salt

1 tbsp caster sugar

3 eggs, lightly beaten

425ml whole milk

110g unsalted butter, melted, plus more
 for the waffle maker

For the strawberry compote

75g caster sugar

25g unsalted butter

250g strawberries, hulled

finely grated zest of 1 unwaxed lemon

500ml vanilla ice cream, to serve

4–8 tbsp maple syrup, to serve

For the waffles, preheat a waffle maker to a medium setting and preheat the oven to 140°C/275°F/gas mark 1.

Mix the flour, baking powder, salt and sugar in a large mixing bowl. Whisk in the eggs, milk and butter.

Butter the waffle maker lightly, then ladle some of the batter into each well of the waffle maker, close the lid and cook for 5 minutes, or until golden-brown and crispy. Remove and place on a tray in the oven to keep warm while you cook the rest.

To make the compote, place the sugar and 75ml of water with the butter into a small sauté pan, then add the strawberries and lemon zest and simmer for 5 minutes.

Stack the waffles on to a plate, top with some strawberry compote and a dollop of vanilla ice cream. Finish with a drizzle of maple syrup.

I love this. Part of the process is a bit cheffy for sure — with the Pacojet to make the ice cream — but I do it in the restaurant and at demos around the UK. The crux of this are the galettes, which are ace, simple to make and taste so good. If you don't want to spend on a fancy machine, just serve this with good bought vanilla ice cream.

Fast chocolate bar ice cream with blueberry galettes

Serves 8

For the chocolate bar ice cream

300ml whole milk

200ml double cream

75g caster sugar

6 egg yolks

3 chocolate and peanut bars, one end cut off

For the galettes

200g plain flour, plus more to dust

75g caster sugar

150g unsalted butter, chopped

2 egg yolks

400g blueberries

1 vanilla pod, split, seeds scraped out

2 tbsp cornflour

juice of 1 lemon

2 tbsp demerara sugar

Start with the ice cream. Heat the milk and cream in a saucepan until just simmering. Meanwhile, place the caster sugar and egg yolks into a bowl and whisk, then pour the warm milk and cream on to them, whisking all the time. Return the mixture to the saucepan and whisk until it thickens enough to coat the back of a spoon. Put in the fridge to chill.

If you're using a Pacojet, when the mixture is cold, place the chocolate bars into the container, then pour over the cold custard (it must not come up further than the 'fill here' mark on the inside of the container). Freeze for at least 4 hours, until frozen solid.

Or, if you do not have a Pacojet, roughly chop the chocolate bars, make the custard as above until it has thickened, then add the chocolate bars and melt into the custard. Transfer to an ice cream machine and churn until frozen, then transfer to a lidded container and freeze until needed.

Make the galettes. Put the flour, 25g of the caster sugar and the butter into a bowl and rub with your fingertips until the mixture looks like crumbs. Add one of the egg yolks and mix to form a dough. It will be quite tight, so knead until it becomes smooth. Flatten to a disc about 2cm thick, wrap in cling film and chill for 30 minutes.

Meanwhile, put the blueberries, remaining 50g of caster sugar, vanilla seeds, cornflour and lemon juice into a bowl and toss together to mix.

Roll the pastry out on a lightly floured surface to 5mm thick, then stamp out eight 12cm discs and pull the sides up to form little pastry cases. Transfer to a large baking sheet lined with baking parchment, then fill with the blueberries. Brush the pastry with the remaining egg yolk, then sprinkle over the demerara. Place in the fridge for 30 minutes to firm up. Preheat the oven to 200°C/400°F/gas mark 6.

Bake the galettes in the oven for 25 minutes until deep golden and crispy.

Place the container into the Pacojet and blitz to form ice cream, or remove the churned ice cream from the freezer to soften slightly. Spoon the ice cream on to the warm galettes and serve straight away.

Home-made marshmallows with chocolate sauce

I remember when I was a kid that Flumps were the sweet of choice for me. But, these days, they're hard to find. So now for parties at mine I make this. It really is easy, a marshmallow is basically just a meringue with gelatine and that's about it.

Serves 6–8

For the marshmallows

450g granulated sugar

1 tbsp liquid glucose

9 sheets of gelatine

2 large egg whites

1 tsp vanilla extract

2 tbsp flavourless vegetable oil, for the baking tray

5–6 tbsp icing sugar, to dust

5–6 tbsp cornflour, to dust

For the chocolate sauce

75g caster sugar

200g dark chocolate, roughly chopped

To make the meringues, place the granulated sugar, glucose and 200ml of water into a heavy-based saucepan and bring to the boil. Cook over a medium-high heat until a sugar thermometer shows 127°C/260°F. Meanwhile, soak the gelatine in 140ml of water. Add the soaked gelatine sheets and their soaking water to the hot sugar syrup very carefully. Stir to dissolve, then pour into a jug.

Place the egg whites into a clean grease-free bowl and whisk to firm peaks. Continuing to whisk, pour the sugar syrup on to the egg whites, until the mixture is shiny.

Add the vanilla extract and continue to whisk for 5–10 minutes until the mixture is thick enough to hold its shape on a whisk.

Lightly oil a 30 x 20cm baking tray.

Dust the tray with icing sugar and cornflour then spoon in the marshmallow, smoothing the top with a wet palette knife. Place in the fridge for at least 1 hour to set.

Dust some more icing sugar and cornflour over a work surface. Loosen the edge of the marshmallow, then turn out on to the work surface. Cut into squares and roll in the icing sugar and cornflour to coat totally.

For the chocolate sauce, place the sugar and 110ml of water into a saucepan and bring to a simmer. Cook for 1–2 minutes until all the sugar has dissolved, then add the chocolate. Whisk until smooth, then remove from the heat.

Carefully thread the marshmallows on to skewers. Place on a hot griddle, under a grill, over an open fire or into a tandoor and grill for 1–2 minutes until a bit charred and gooey.

Serve the skewers of marshmallows with a bowl of chocolate sauce.

Ginger parkin with rhubarb and spiced syrup

This is best when made in advance and kept in an airtight tin for two or three days, as it will become really sticky all the way through. Serve with vanilla ice cream, if you like — for a home-made recipe, see page 242.

Serves 8

For the parkin

150g softened unsalted butter, plus more for the tin

150g soft light brown sugar

250g golden syrup

75g black treacle

125g rolled oats

175g self-raising flour

3 tbsp ground ginger

1 tsp ground nutmeg

1 tsp mixed spice

pinch of salt

2 eggs, lightly beaten

25ml milk

For the rhubarb

50g unsalted butter

75g caster sugar

finely grated zest of 1 orange

4 rhubarb sticks, cut into 5cm lengths

For the sauce

200g golden syrup

100ml dry cider

½ tsp mixed spice

½ tsp ground ginger

¼ tsp ground nutmeg

For the parkin, preheat the oven to 140°C/275°F/gas mark 1 and butter a 30 x 20cm cake tin.

Put the 150g of butter, soft brown sugar, syrup and treacle into a small saucepan and melt over a gentle heat. Tip the oats, flour, spices and salt into a bowl, mix together, then add the eggs and milk. Pour the contents of the saucepan on to the flour mixture and stir together with a whisk until combined.

Pour into the prepared tin and bake for 1¼ hours, or until firm to the touch in the centre.

Remove from the oven and leave in the tin to cool before turning out. When cold, store in an airtight tin, ideally for a couple of days.

To cook the rhubarb, put the butter, sugar and 75ml of water into a sauté pan with the orange zest and rhubarb and set over a gentle heat to poach for 4–5 minutes until just tender, then remove from the heat.

For the sauce, place the syrup, cider and spices into a saucepan and bring to the boil, then cook for 3–4 minutes until just thickened.

Cut the parkin into squares and place them on plates. Spoon the rhubarb to one side and pour a little syrup over the top.

God knows how many calories this has in it; I certainly don't but – believe me – someone out there will and I'll get letters! To those people who don't care, you can serve this with toffee sauce and vanilla ice cream. Just enjoy these for what they are, as the flavours are off the scale. You need good-quality flour to bake great cinnamon rolls and NR Stoate & Sons, the Dorset mill we visited on the TV show, is a great example of the artisan millers which are popping up all over the country.

The best cinnamon rolls

Serves 6–8

For the dough, place the flour, sugar, salt and yeast into a mixer fitted with a dough hook and slowly mix in about 450ml of water, adding more or less as needed to make a dough. Process until it starts sticking to the edge of the bowl and feels elastic.

Turn off the machine, lift out the hook and cover the bowl with a tea towel. Leave it in a warm place for the dough to rise for about 20 minutes, or until doubled in size. Now knock the air out of it and roll out on a floured surface into a rectangle measuring 60 x 30cm.

Slice the butter 1cm thick and arrange over half the dough, lengthways, leaving a border. Fold the other half of the dough over and press down lightly at the edges to seal in the butter.

On a well-floured surface, beat the dough with the rolling pin, then roll into a 60 x 30cm rectangle again. Fold one short side over by one-third, then the other short side on top of it, as though you were folding a business letter. Repeat the rolling, beating and folding process three times. Wrap the dough in cling film and leave to rest in the fridge for 1 hour.

Roll the dough out into a rectangle about 1cm thick.

For the filling, mix the cream cheese, vanilla seeds and cinnamon. Cover the dough with the mixture, then roll up from a longer side. Cut into slices about 5cm thick.

Butter and line a 23cm springform tin. Place the slices, cut-sides up, around the edge and one in the middle, making sure they are not too tightly packed. Leave in a warm place to prove until doubled in size; it should take about 40 minutes.

When ready to bake, preheat the oven to 200°C/400°F/gas mark 6. Brush the dough with the beaten egg and bake for 45 minutes until golden brown.

While the rolls are cooling slightly, make the glaze by mixing the icing sugar, maple syrup and bourbon together until smooth.

Lift the 'cake' of rolls out of the tin and set on a serving plate, then drizzle the glaze over the top, back and forth. Leave to set. Tear off the rolls to serve.

For the dough

625g strong white bread flour, plus more to dust

75g caster sugar

pinch of sea salt

20g fast-action dried yeast

500g cold unsalted butter, plus more for the tin

For the filling

300g full-fat cream cheese

1 vanilla pod, split, seeds scraped out

1 tsp ground cinnamon

2 egg yolks, lightly beaten

For the glaze

200g icing sugar, sifted

100ml maple syrup

25ml bourbon whiskey

If you ever wondered what goes into making a croissant… well, now you know: a fair bit of elbow grease. But the rewards are great. Good-quality butter is a must for this and that's why the French croissants taste so good. The butter needs to be cold and firm. (You can't make these with margarine, before you dare to ask!) You need to start these the day before you want them.

Home-made buttery croissants

Makes 16

625g strong white bread flour, plus more to dust

75g caster sugar

12g fine sea salt

40g fresh yeast

500g unsalted butter, chilled

1 egg and 1 egg yolk, lightly beaten

The day before you want to bake the croissants, place the flour, sugar, salt and yeast in a food mixer fitted with a dough hook, or a large mixing bowl, add 350–400ml of water and mix to a soft dough. Tip on to a floured work surface and knead really well until it feels elastic, then set aside.

Place the chilled butter between two sheets of greaseproof paper and bash flat with a rolling pin to a 30 x 20cm rectangle about 1cm thick. Place in the fridge while you roll out the dough.

Lift the dough back out on to a floured surface and roll out to a large rectangle, about 60 x 30cm.

Put the butter in the centre of the dough and fold one side of the dough over the butter, then fold the other side over to meet it, covering the butter. Fold it all in half lengthways.

Turn 90°, then roll out again to a 60 x 30cm rectangle. Fold one-quarter of the dough across to the centre, then fold the other side over to meet it. Fold it in half lengthways, then repeat the whole process twice more. Fold over, then cover and place in the fridge to rest overnight.

Roll the dough out to 3mm thick, then cut into two 16cm-wide strips. Cut each strip into triangles about 12cm wide at the base.

Place a dough triangle with the narrow point facing away from you, then stretch the bottom points out sideways. Roll it over itself and curl it into a traditional crescent shape. Repeat to shape all the croissants.

Place on baking trays lined with silicone paper, brush with egg and leave to rise for 30–45 minutes. They can be frozen at this point, or left in the fridge overnight to prove.

When ready to bake, preheat the oven to 190°C/375°F/gas mark 5. Bake for 20 minutes until golden brown.

Tip

Once you've shaped the crossiants, you can place them in the fridge, cover and bake them when you need. They keep for about 12 hours just fine.

Bramley marzipan slice

This is so simple to make. You can even use ready-made Bramley apple sauce, would you believe. But whether bought or home-made, the apple sauce must be made with Bramleys as it's their sharpness combined with the sweet marzipan that makes this work so well.

Serves 4–6

750g Bramley apples, peeled, cored and roughly chopped

50–75g caster sugar

25g unsalted butter, plus more for the tray

2 x 320g all-butter puff pastry sheets (about 35 x 23cm)

250g natural marzipan, thinly sliced

1 egg, lightly beaten

2 tbsp demerara sugar

200g clotted cream, to serve

Preheat the oven to 200°C/400°F/gas mark 6.

Place the apples and 50g of the caster sugar into a saucepan with the butter and 3 tbsp of water. Bring to the boil, cover and cook for 3–5 minutes until the apple has softened. Remove the lid and stir to combine, then cook for another 2–3 minutes until totally softened and purée-like. Taste to see if it needs the rest of the caster sugar. If it does, stir it in while the purée is hot, so it dissolves. Remove from the heat and allow to cool. Roll the marzipan out into a rectangle about 30 x 20cm and 5mm thick.

Put one of the sheets of pastry on a buttered baking tray and lay the sheet of marzipan over, leaving a border of 2cm all the way around, then spread the cooled apple purée over the marzipan. Brush some of the beaten egg around the pastry border.

Fold the second sheet of puff pastry in half lengthways and carefully slice through from the fold towards the edges at 1cm intervals down the length of the pastry, making sure to leave 2cm intact at the edges.

Unfold and you will have a piece of puff pastry that has a 2cm border and the centre sliced. Lay this on top of the apple-covered pastry, making sure that it sits directly over, crimp the edges, then trim them so they are straight.

Brush with the remaining egg and scatter the demerara over the top. Bake in the oven for 30 minutes until golden brown and crispy.

Serve warm with the clotted cream.

Banana and maple syrup cake

Chefs are always on the look-out for new and different ingredients, and once they've found something new they generally stick with it for a while. Well, that ingredient for me at the moment is maple syrup. I can't get enough of the stuff. I love it. There are many grades, but get the best you can afford, as you really can taste the difference.

Serves 6–8

4 ripe bananas, peeled and roughly chopped

200ml maple syrup

50ml milk (only if needed and if the bananas are firm)

200g softened unsalted butter, plus extra for greasing

150g caster sugar

4 eggs

2 tsp baking powder

100g pecan nuts, roughly chopped

400g plain flour, plus extra for the tin

200ml double cream

Preheat the oven to 170°C/325°F/gas mark 3. Butter, line and flour a 23cm springform cake tin.

Place the bananas in a food processor and blitz until chunky, then add 75ml of the maple syrup (and the milk if needed) and blitz until smooth.

In a large bowl, whisk the butter and sugar together until pale and very soft, then add the eggs one at a time, whisking well in between. Add the baking powder, then fold in the banana mixture, three-quarters of the pecans and finally the flour.

Spoon into the cake tin, then carefully drop the tin from a height of about 15cm onto the work surface twice, to settle the mixture. Sprinkle the remaining chopped pecans over the top of the cake and bake for 45–60 minutes, until golden, risen and firm to the touch.

Cool in the tin for 10 minutes, then turn out and leave to cool on a wire rack.

While the cake cooks, put the cream and remaining maple syrup into a saucepan and bring to the boil. Boil for 3–5 minutes until reduced and thickened, then set aside to cool completely.

When the cake is cold, spoon the maple glaze over the top of the cake, allowing it to drizzle down the sides slightly. Set aside for 10 minutes, then cut into slices and serve.

Still one of my favourite recipes to cook at home and, in fact, one of my favourite recipes in this book. You can make one big or eight small tarts but, in either case, don't overfill the tins as the mixture rises and expands and, importantly, never refrigerate the cooked tarts as the frangipane will set hard and they will end up tasting like shop-bought versions. Not that they will even make it to the fridge; they taste too good.

Frangipane tarts with home-made custard

Serves 8

For the pastry

125g cold unsalted butter, chopped
250g plain flour, plus more to dust
1 egg, lightly beaten

For the filling

225g raspberry jam
225g unsalted butter, softened
1 vanilla pod, split, seeds scraped out
225g caster sugar
5 eggs
225g ground almonds
75g whole blanched almonds

1 quantity of custard (see page 70), to serve

For the pastry, put the butter and flour into a food mixer and pulse-blend until it looks like crumbs, then add the egg and mix until it forms a firm dough. Wrap in cling film and put in the fridge to rest for 30 minutes.

To make the tart, roll the pastry out to about 3mm thick on to a work surface lightly dusted with flour.

Carefully line eight 10cm loose-bottomed tart tins, or a 23cm deep-sided loose-bottomed tart tin, with the pastry, pressing it into the edges. Spread the jam over the base or bases, then leave to rest in the fridge for 10 minutes. Preheat the oven to 180°C/350°F/gas mark 4.

For the filling, beat the butter, vanilla seeds and sugar together in a bowl until pale and fluffy (save the empty vanilla pod). Crack in the eggs, one at a time, beating well after each addition, until they have all been fully incorporated. Carefully fold in the ground almonds.

Spread the filling over the jam, smoothing it to the edges, then decorate with the almonds, in concentric circles.

Place the tart or tarts in the oven and cook for 25 minutes for the tartlets or 35–40 minutes for the large tart, or until the filling has risen and is cooked through and the surface is an even pale golden-brown.

Make the custard as on page 270, but without the vanilla seeds (just use the empty pod).

To serve, cut the tart into wedges or place a tartlet on a plate and pour the custard alongside.

Having this recipe in a book will have my chef mates laughing… but trust me, if this was on a dessert buffet it would be the first one they would go for. I grow my own soft fruit in my garden – the raspberry plants come from Scotland, the home of the best raspberries in the world – and this is the perfect way to use up what I have left. It's not a jam recipe as you know it; this is quicker to make and will do nicely. Let the sponge cool fully before rolling and, if the tea towel you use to roll it up is damp, it shouldn't crack.

Swiss roll with fresh raspberry jam

Serves 6

For the jam

450g raspberries
400g jam sugar

For the sponge

5 eggs
125g caster sugar, plus more to dust
2 vanilla pods, split, seeds scraped out
95g self-raising flour

To assemble

500ml double cream
75g raspberries
8 tiny sprigs of mint or lemon verbena
1 tbsp chopped pistachio nuts (optional)

Make the raspberry jam first. Place a large saucepan on the heat with the raspberries, sugar and 3 tbsp of water and cook gently for 2–3 minutes until the sugar has dissolved. Increase the heat and cook for a further 6–7 minutes until just thick enough to coat the back of a spoon. Remove from the heat, pour into hot, sterilised jars (see page 232) and cool.

For the sponge, preheat the oven to 190°C/375°F/gas mark 5 and line a 38 x 25cm Swiss roll tin with a sheet of baking parchment.

Place the eggs, sugar and the seeds from one of the vanilla pods into a bowl and whisk until very light, fluffy and thickened. Sift the flour over the mixture and fold it in with your hand; carefully lifting and mixing until it is all incorporated.

Pour into the lined tin and smooth with a spatula until evenly spread out. Bake for 10–12 minutes, or until just firm to the touch.

Place a damp, wrung-out tea towel that is slightly bigger than the Swiss roll tin on a work surface and dust it with caster sugar. Turn the sponge out on to the tea towel, then peel off the parchment on the bottom of the sponge. Starting at the longest edge nearest you, roll the sponge up in the tea towel, pressing gently as you go, then unroll and allow to cool.

When you're ready to assemble the dish, whip the double cream and remaining vanilla seeds to firm peaks.

Spread the raspberry jam over the cooled sponge, leaving a 2cm border at the furthest long edge.

Spread most of the whipped cream over the top, then, taking the longest edge and using the tea towel to help, roll up the sponge quite tightly, making sure the filling stays inside.

Roll the sponge off the tea towel on to a serving plate and dust with more sugar.

Serve with the raspberries and sprigs of mint or lemn verbena. If you like – and are feeling flash – you can make 'quenelles' of leftover cream with two hot spoons, to decorate the Swiss roll, or sprinkle it with chopped pistachios.

A classic from France, madeleines need the correct moulds. Mine are old tins I ended up buying on an auction site, but you can get new tins that work better. The batter can be made, covered and stored in the fridge before cooking for up to one day, as the key to these is to bake and serve them on the same day. I've done a nice twist on a caramel sauce here, but they are just as good with chocolate sauce (for a recipe, see page 250).

Cinnamon madeleines with winter-spiced caramel sauce

Serves 4–6

For the madeleines

225g unsalted butter, plus more for the tin(s)

250g caster sugar, plus 75g to dust

250g plain flour

1 vanilla pod, split, seeds scraped out

2 tbsp runny honey

3 eggs, lightly beaten

½ tsp ground cinnamon

For the caramel sauce

100g caster sugar

350ml double cream

1 star anise

½ cinnamon stick

25g unsalted butter

To make the madeleines, preheat the oven to 160°C/325°F/gas mark 3 and butter the madeleine tins. If you've only got one madeleine tin (more likely!), just bake them in batches.

Gently heat the butter in a saucepan until just melted.

Mix the sugar and flour in a bowl, then add the vanilla seeds (reserve the pod), honey and eggs. Whisk in the melted butter until you have a nice smooth batter. Spoon into the tins, only half filling each indent.

Bake for 12–15 minutes for larger madeleines, or 8–10 minutes for smaller, depending on your tin.

While the madeleines are still warm, place the sugar for dusting in a broad, shallow dish with the ground cinnamon. Roll them around to coat. They can be kept in an airtight container for up to 1 week.

For the sauce, put the sugar into a pan and heat until a light golden brown. Don't stir the pan, but swirl it occasionally. Pour in half the cream and bring to the boil, stirring well.

Add the star anise, cinnamon, reserved vanilla pod and butter, then pour in the remaining cream and cook for 2–3 minutes until thickened and smooth. Strain through a fine sieve into a serving bowl.

Serve the madeleines with the sauce.

Tip

Don't overfill the madeleine tins or they will come out shapeless; you want the pretty shell-like shape here.

Bread pudding

Milk puddings have fallen out of favour in recent years, which is a real shame as, made well, they can be really great. Don't keep this bread pudding in the fridge though, as it won't taste as good.

Serves 6–8

100g unsalted butter, plus extra for greasing
500g sultanas
100g whisky
600ml milk
150g soft light brown sugar
1 orange, zested
2 tsp mixed spice
2 tsp ground ginger
500g wholemeal bread
2 eggs, beaten
50g demerara sugar

Preheat the oven to 180°C/350°F/gas mark 4. Grease and line the base of a 20cm square cake tin.

Put the sultanas and whisky into a bowl, swirl around, then set aside to soak for 30 minutes.

Put the milk into a saucepan along with the soft light brown sugar and butter, and set over a medium heat. Heat until the butter has melted, then remove from the heat, stir in the orange zest and spices, and leave for another 15 minutes for the sultanas to soften.

Blitz the bread in a food processor until it forms breadcrumbs, then add to the liquid and mix well. Add the eggs and whisk to combine. Pour into the prepared tin and press down lightly into the corners, then sprinkle with the demerara sugar. Bake for 1 hour until golden brown and just set.

Remove from the oven and leave to cool on a wire rack, then turn out and cut into squares to serve.

Apple milk pancakes with roasted apples, pears and walnuts, and a vanilla syrup

Pancakes should always be in any book of home comfort recipes. They are so simple to make and they also freeze really well – these ones included. Once you've made them, layer them between sheets of greaseproof paper and pop them into the freezer. To use them, allow them to defrost and then reheat.

Serves 4

For the pancakes

100g plain flour
40g caster sugar
1 tsp baking powder
3 eggs
100ml almond milk
2 tbsp vegetable oil

For the apples and pears

2 apples, cut into chunks
2 pears, cut into chunks
4 tbsp honey
75g walnuts

For the vanilla syrup

1 tsp vanilla bean paste
100g caster sugar
100ml almond milk

To make the pancakes, place the flour, sugar and baking powder in a bowl and whisk until combined. Make a hollow in the centre, then crack in the eggs and pour in the almond milk. Whisk gently from the centre outwards until all the flour is taken in and you have a smooth batter.

Heat a frying pan until hot, then add the vegetable oil and a large spoonful of batter. Fry over a medium heat until golden-brown and little bubbles have appeared over the surface, then flip and cook for a further minute until cooked through. Set aside and repeat with the remaining batter.

Heat a frying pan until hot and add the apples and pears. Fry for 2–3 minutes, then add the honey and 4 tbsp of water and bring to the boil. Toss the apples and pears to coat, then add the walnuts.

For the vanilla syrup, put the vanilla bean paste, sugar and almond milk into a saucepan, and bring to the boil, then reduce the heat slightly and simmer until thickened.

Divide the pancakes between the plates, then surround with the apple mixture and drizzle with the syrup.

Dark and white chocolate cherry brownies

When I was in the States, I learnt many things: never drive the wrong way down a one-way street as the police don't like it very much, and never say 'kind regards', as they don't know what it means. The recipe for these brownies is another example of some of the very useful knowledge I brought back with me.

Makes 12 pieces

350g dark chocolate (55–60% cocoa solids)

250g unsalted butter

3 large eggs

250g dark soft brown sugar

110g plain flour

1 tsp baking powder

150g fresh cherries, stoned and halved

150g white chocolate, roughly chopped

1–2 tbsp cocoa powder, for dusting

Preheat the oven to 170°C/325°F/gas mark 3. Grease and line a 30 x 23cm traybake or roasting tin.

Put the dark chocolate and butter into a saucepan and heat until melted, stirring so that it doesn't get too hot, then remove from the heat and cool.

Crack the eggs into a kitchen mixer or a large bowl, then add the sugar and whisk until thickened and paler in colour. Whisk in the cooled chocolate mixture, then gently fold in the flour, baking powder and half the cherries. Spoon into the prepared tin, and scatter the remaining cherries and the white chocolate over the top.

Bake for 30–35 minutes, or until the surface is set. The brownie will be cooked when a skewer inserted into the middle comes out with just a little mixture sticking to it.

Place on a wire rack to cool completely in the tin before removing, dusting with cocoa powder and cutting into squares.

Billionaire's shortbread (or peanut butter caramel shortbread)

It was one of my chefs' ideas to call this billionaire's shortbread – because millionaire's shortbread is simply not a good enough name for this one. It certainly packs a high calorific value. It will definitely keep anyone at home happy for a few hours, as they won't be wanting anything else.

Serves 6–8

For the shortbread

250g softened unsalted butter, plus extra for greasing

150g caster sugar

1 egg

150g cornflour

300g plain flour

For the topping

300g caster sugar

175ml double cream

275g crunchy peanut butter

400g dark chocolate, roughly chopped

Preheat the oven to 180°C/350°F/gas mark 4. Grease and line the base and sides of a 30 x 23cm traybake tin.

To make the shortbread, mix the butter and sugar together in a bowl with an electric whisk until softened and lightened in colour. Add the egg and whisk together, then fold in the cornflour and plain flour to form a soft dough.

Tip the dough out onto a lightly floured work surface and knead very gently until smooth. Press into the base of the prepared tin, spreading it evenly into the corners. Prick all over with a fork, then place in the fridge to rest for 15 minutes.

Bake for about 25 minutes until just lightly coloured and firm to the touch.

Meanwhile, make the topping. Put the caster sugar into a frying pan and heat gently, without stirring, until the sugar turns golden-brown and liquid. Whisk in the cream and cook until thickened and smooth, then whisk in the peanut butter – you want a thick, light golden-brown mixture. Remove from the heat and leave to cool until the shortbread is out of the oven.

Pour the caramel over the shortbread, spreading it to the edges so there's an even layer, then set aside to cool for at least 1 hour.

Put the chocolate into a bowl set over a pan of simmering water until it has melted. Pour three-quarters of the chocolate over the cooled caramel topping, tipping the tray so that it coats all the caramel. Set aside at room temperature to cool for 30 minutes, then drizzle the remaining chocolate over the top. Set the tray aside until the chocolate has set – at least 1 hour.

Lift the shortbread out of the tin by the edge of the silicone paper, and cut into triangles to serve.

Blueberry cobbler with custard

This is an American version of our simple crumble, the difference being that the topping is more like a scone. But as it cooks, the scones separate out to reveal an almost crumble-like topping underneath.

Serves 6

For the filling

500g blueberries
30g vanilla sugar
1 tbsp plain flour
1 lemon, zested and juiced

For the topping

200g plain flour, plus extra for dusting
1 tbsp baking powder
50g caster sugar
50g unsalted butter, softened
1 large egg
200ml natural yoghurt
1 tbsp granulated sugar

For the custard

250ml whole milk
250ml double cream
1 vanilla pod, split, seeds scraped out
100g caster sugar
6 egg yolks

Preheat the oven to 180°C/350°F/gas mark 4. Butter a 15cm x 25cm ovenproof baking dish.

For the filling, tip the blueberries into the baking dish. Add the vanilla sugar, flour, lemon zest and juice, and toss to combine, then set aside.

To make the topping, mix the plain flour, baking powder and sugar together in a bowl, then rub in the butter until it forms a breadcrumb-like texture. Mix the egg and yoghurt together, and stir into mixture until you have a soft, sticky dough.

Tip the dough out onto a lightly floured work surface and knead gently until smooth. Push out into a rough rectangle about 4cm thick, then fold each side into the centre and fold in half, as if shutting a book. Cut the dough into 10 even-sized pieces and place on top of the blueberries – you don't want to handle it too much.

Scatter the granulated sugar over the top and bake for 35–40 minutes until golden and bubbling around the edges.

Meanwhile, make the custard. Put the milk and cream into a shallow saucepan with the vanilla pod, set over a medium heat and bring to the boil. Whisk the sugar and egg yolks in a bowl. When the milk is boiling, pour it onto the eggs, whisking all the time, then return the whole mixture to the pan and cook over a gentle heat, whisking occasionally, until thick enough to coat the back of a wooden spoon.

Strain into a clean pan and warm through when the cobbler is ready.

English apricot and almond bake

When you make the frangipane, make sure to mix the butter and sugar together until they are white, and then fold in the flour by hand to help keep it as light as possible. It's best not to keep the bake in the fridge, as the butter will harden up – if you have to, warm it through in a low oven before serving.

Makes 15 pieces

375g shop-bought sweet pastry

200g unsalted butter, softened, plus extra for greasing

200g caster sugar

3 large eggs

200g plain flour

125g ground almonds

½ tsp baking powder

150g apricot jam

8 fresh apricots, stoned and quartered

Preheat the oven to 170°C/325°F/gas mark 3. Grease and line a 30 x 23cm traybake tin.

Roll out the pastry to 5mm thick and about 2cm larger than your tin. Roll it onto the rolling pin, then roll it over the tin. Press gently into the corners, then trim the excess from the edges. Place in the fridge while you make the filling.

Place the butter and sugar in a food mixer or a large bowl, and beat for 5 minutes until light and fluffy, then beat in the eggs one at a time. Remove from the mixer, if using, and fold in the flour, ground almonds and baking powder.

Cover the pastry with the apricot jam, then spoon over the filling and smooth out to the edges. Lay the apricot halves gently on top, in rows, and bake for 35–40 minutes until golden-brown and risen. A skewer inserted into the centre of the cake should come out clean; if it doesn't, return it to the oven for a further 5 minutes and repeat.

Leave the cake to cool in the tin, then cut into rectangles to serve.

Chocolate truffles

Saves buying them and means you can flavour the truffles with whatever you wish. The key is not to use chocolate that is too rich or that has too high a cocoa solid content as, to me, it doesn't taste as good. Still, buy the best-quality chocolate you can afford for these.

Serves 6–8

350ml double cream

400g dark chocolate (60% cocoa solids), broken into pieces

3–4 tbsp sifted cocoa powder

Pour the cream into a saucepan and bring to the boil. Put the chocolate into a bowl, then pour over the boiling cream and mix well until the mixture is smooth.

Set aside to cool, then cover and place into the fridge to chill and become firm for about 2 hours.

Sift the cocoa powder on to a plate and, using a teaspoon, curl balls of chocolate and drop straight into the cocoa, then roll to coat.

Place on a clean plate to firm up, then serve, or keep in a sealed container in the fridge for up to 4 weeks.

Honeycomb

This is so easy to make. The trick is to cook the sugar and cool it for a minute before whisking in the bicarb. That way the mix will rise and stay up. If the bicarb is added too soon, the bubbles burst and the mix collapses as it cools.

Serves 6–8

200g caster sugar

50ml runny honey

1 tbsp liquid glucose

¾ tsp bicarbonate of soda

Place the sugar, honey, glucose and 50ml of water into a saucepan and bring to the boil. Continue to cook until the temperature reaches 160°C/320°F on a sugar thermometer.

Remove from the heat, allow to cool for 30 seconds so the bubbles disperse, then quickly beat in the bicarbonate of soda, stirring constantly.

Pour on to a silicone-lined baking sheet and leave to cool for 30 minutes.

Break into shards and store in a sealed container until you want to serve it. It will keep well for up to 1 week.

Comforting
Posh Puds

As a keen gardener, there are few things I look forward to more in my garden than fresh strawberries: the one ingredient that, to me, signals that summer is here. When you have fruit this good, cooking it would be a waste. Sure the glaze is cooked, but it's only a small part of the dish and it's delicious. The cheesecake is so simple and quick and, in this recipe, using a sponge base tastes better than biscuit.

Strawberry and white chocolate cheesecake

Serves 6–8

200g white chocolate, roughly chopped

750g strawberries, hulled and halved

100g caster sugar

2 leaves of gelatine, soaked in cold water

1 large sponge flan case

2–3 tbsp fruit liqueur, brandy or whisky (optional)

200g full-fat cream cheese

200ml crème fraîche

325ml double cream

1 vanilla pod, split, seeds scraped out

Melt the white chocolate in a bowl set over a pan of simmering water (the bowl should not touch the water). When totally melted, pour on to a large baking sheet lined with greaseproof paper and tip from side to side until it covers the tray in a layer about 5mm thick. Place in the freezer for about 10–20 minutes until frozen.

Place 300g of the strawberries into a saucepan with 25g of the caster sugar and 40ml of water and bring to the boil. Reduce the heat and simmer for 8–10 minutes.

Pass through a fine sieve into a bowl, then add the soaked gelatine – squeezing out any excess liquid – and stir until totally dissolved. Allow to cool to room temperature.

Use a 20–25cm stainless steel ring to cut out the centre of the flan case. We used a triangle mould for the photo because we were feeling poncey. With a sharp knife, cut the sponge in half horizontally so you end up with two thin pieces. Set one half on a serving plate and save the other half for another time, or blitz for cake crumbs. Place the ring back over the sponge disc, then drizzle over the fruit liqueur (if using).

Put the cream cheese, crème fraîche, double cream, remaining sugar and vanilla seeds into a bowl and whisk until well combined.

Spoon the cheese mixture into the ring, making sure that it is pressed into the edges. Smooth the top with a palette knife.

Cover the top of the cheesecake with the rest of the strawberries, then lift the ring off (warming quickly with a blowtorch is the best way to remove the ring cleanly; if you haven't got one, dip a cloth into hot water and run around the ring).

Drizzle over the strawberry glaze.

Break the frozen white chocolate into shards and press around the edge of the cheesecake until totally covered.

Serve straight away.

Passion fruit crème with coconut and cherry biscotti

I love this. For me, the flavour of passion fruit gives so much bang for its buck. Baking your own biscotti is something you will do again and again once you taste them. And they are so simple with this recipe.

Serves 4

For the passion fruit crème

600ml double cream

250g caster sugar

juice of 1 lime

150ml passion fruit pulp (passed through a fine sieve)

2 leaves of gelatine

For the biscotti

250g plain flour, plus more to dust

250g caster sugar

60g grated fresh coconut

200g natural glacé cherries, roughly chopped

finely grated zest of 1 unwaxed lemon

1¼ tsp baking powder

pinch of salt

3 eggs, lightly beaten

Begin with the passion fruit crème. Put the double cream and 150g of the sugar into a large saucepan. Gently bring to the boil, then remove from the heat. Add the lime juice and 75ml of the passion fruit pulp and whisk to combine.

Pour into four large martini glasses and place in the fridge to set for at least 2 hours.

Meanwhile, soak the gelatine leaves in cold water. Put the remaining 100g of caster sugar into a saucepan with 100ml of water, bring to the boil, then reduce the heat and simmer for 3–4 minutes until just thickened. Add the remaining 75ml sieved passion fruit pulp. Squeeze any excess water out of the gelatine, then add to the hot passion fruit syrup, remove from the heat and stir until totally dissolved. Set aside to cool.

When the mixture in the martini glasses has chilled, pour over the cold passion fruit crème to cover (this layer only needs to be about 5mm thick). Return to the fridge to set for another hour. Remove from the fridge for 30 minutes before serving.

Meanwhile, make the biscotti, Preheat the oven to 180°C/350°F/gas mark 4 and line a baking tray with a layer of baking parchment.

Mix all the ingredients in a bowl and mix together to a soft, sticky dough. Form it into two long sausages on a lightly floured work surface, place on the baking tray, then bake in the oven for 20–30 minutes until golden brown.

Remove from the oven and leave for 10 minutes to cool and firm up.

Using a serrated knife, cut the biscotti on an angle into slices 1cm thick, then lay them back on to the baking tray (you may well need two trays now).

Return to the oven and cook for 8 minutes, then turn the slices over and cook for a further 10–15 minutes or until a pale golden colour on both sides. Remove from the oven and cool on wire racks.

Serve the passion fruit crème with the biscotti alongside.

Steamed chocolate and clementine sponge with orange sauce

You can make this with oranges if you wish, but it is definitely a winter pudding. At Christmas, we all seem to have a glut of clementines left over after the frantic stocking up for the festive period. This is an excellent way to use them up and a great rib-sticking pud to indulge yourself with in the cold weather.

Serves 4–6

For the sponge

175g unsalted butter, softened, plus more for the bowl
8 clementines
175g golden caster sugar
3 eggs, lightly beaten
125g self-raising flour
50g cocoa powder
1 tsp baking powder
pinch of salt

For the orange sauce

75g caster sugar
½ vanilla pod, split, seeds scraped out
50ml orange liqueur
100ml orange juice
juice of 1 clementine
40g unsalted butter
200g crème fraîche, to serve

Start with the sponge. Butter a 1.2-litre heatproof bowl. Carefully cut the skin from the clementines and cut into thick slices. Pat dry, then lay the clementine slices into the buttered bowl, one in the centre then five around it, repeating all the way up the side of the bowl.

Place the butter, sugar, eggs, flour, cocoa, baking powder and salt into a bowl and whisk until light and fluffy. Spoon carefully into the clementine-lined bowl.

Lay a sheet of greaseproof paper on to a sheet of foil, pleat both layers in the centre to create an overlap, then tie – greaseproof side down – around the bowl with string. Take a long piece of foil and fold lengthways in half to make a handle.

Place a cloth in the base of a large saucepan, then put an upside-down saucer or small plate on it. Fill halfway up with water. Place the foil-covered bowl on to the long folded over piece of foil, then into the saucepan (this acts as a handle later to lift the pudding bowl out of the saucepan). Cover and bring to a boil, then reduce the heat and simmer for 1½–2 hours.

For the sauce, heat a sauté pan until hot, add the caster sugar and vanilla seeds and heat, without stirring, until it turns to a light golden caramel, shaking the pan from time to time. Add the orange liqueur and, standing well back, set alight. When the flames die down, add the orange and clementine juices and cook for 2–3 minutes until it comes together into a thin sauce. Add the butter and swirl to combine and thicken.

Use the foil strip to lift the pudding bowl out of the saucepan, then discard the foil and baking parchment. Place a plate on top and turn over, tipping the pudding on to the plate. Pour the sauce over the top, offer some crème fraîche on the side, then dig in!

Tip

You can use oranges for this, too. Make sure you pat the sliced fruit dry slightly before using it to line the dish.

Raspberry, white chocolate and caramel pavlova

Look at the picture. Just look at it. If that doesn't tempt you to make this, I don't know what will.

Serves 6–8

6 egg whites

500g caster sugar

1 tbsp cornflour

1 tbsp white wine vinegar

200g white chocolate, roughly chopped

500ml double cream

200ml ready-made vanilla custard

2–3 punnets of raspberries, depending how generous you are feeling

lemon verbena leaves, or mint leaves, to serve

Preheat the oven to 150°C/300°F/gas mark 2. Line a large baking tray with baking parchment.

Whisk the egg whites with an electric whisk on high speed and add 300g of the sugar a spoonful at a time, whisking until smooth and glossy. Reduce the speed of the whisk and add the cornflour and vinegar. Return the whisk to high speed and whisk until the mixture is stiff.

Spread with a spatula – or pipe it, if you prefer – into a round on the prepared tray and place in the oven for 2–3 hours. Now turn off the oven and leave the pavlova in there for 6–8 hours or overnight to dry out, then place on a serving plate.

Melt the white chocolate in a heatproof bowl over a pan of simmering (not boiling) water. The bowl should not touch the water. Brush the white chocolate over the meringue and allow to cool.

Whisk the cream until soft peaks form, then whisk in the custard until at the soft peaks stage once more. Spread the cream over the cooled chocolate.

Heat the remaining 200g caster sugar in a saucepan over a medium heat until liquid and golden. Don't stir it, but swirl the pan from time to time.

Arrange the raspberries on the cream, then drizzle the caramel over the top. Sprinkle with lemon verbena or mint leaves, to serve.

White chocolate and whisky croissant pudding with honeycomb foam and whisky ice cream

My trademark dish, or so people tell me: bucket loads of butter, cream and calories. Just forget all that and enjoy it as it hasn't been off my restaurant menu in 22 years and is still one of the biggest sellers. Obviously, this is not for kids! You can buy lecithin in some supermarkets now, but also from health food shops and online.

Serves 6

For the whisky ice cream

100ml double cream

400ml whole milk

empty vanilla pod

6 egg yolks

100g caster sugar

100ml whisky

For the pudding

3 large all-butter croissants, thickly sliced

25g sultanas

40g unsalted butter, softened

500ml double cream

500ml whole milk

1 vanilla pod, split, seeds scraped out

300g white chocolate, roughly chopped

3 whole eggs, plus 6 egg yolks

200g caster sugar

75ml whisky

2 tbsp icing sugar, to dust

For the honeycomb foam

400ml whole milk

75g honeycomb, roughly chopped (for home-made, see page 275)

1 tsp lecithin powder

For the ice cream, put the cream and milk into a saucepan with the vanilla pod and bring to a simmer. Whisk the egg yolks and sugar together.

Add the whisky to the hot cream and return to a simmer, then pour over the eggs, whisking constantly to combine. Return to the pan and, whisking constantly, heat gently until thick enough to coat the back of a spoon.

Churn in an ice cream machine, then decant into a lidded freezerproof container and freeze until needed.

To make the pudding, lay the croissants into an ovenproof dish with the sultanas layered in between, then dot with the softened butter. Try to make sure no sultanas show on top, or they could burn.

Place the cream, milk and vanilla seeds into a saucepan and bring to the boil, then add the chocolate and whisk until totally melted and smooth.

Place the eggs, egg yolks and sugar into a bowl and whisk to combine.

Pour the hot chocolate custard through a sieve over the eggs (reserve the vanilla pod) and whisk to combine, pour in the whisky, then ladle it through a fine sieve over the croissant pudding and set aside for 20 minutes to soak. Preheat the oven to 180°C/350°F/gas mark 4.

Cover the pudding with foil and place in the oven for 25–30 minutes until golden and just set.

Remove from the oven and dust with the icing sugar. Place under a hot grill to caramelise, or use a blowtorch.

To create the foam, place the milk, honeycomb and lecithin into a small saucepan and heat until simmering, then froth with a stick blender until it is foaming.

Place a serving of the pudding into the centre of a plate, with some of the sauce from the dish, top with ice cream and add a spoonful of foam.

Gâteau St Honoré

Named after the patron saint of pastry chefs, this should be on every menu around. I wish it was, anyway, but it's a bit of a fiddle to make and that's the reason it isn't.

Preheat the oven to 200°C/400°F/gas mark 6. Line two baking sheets with silicone mats or paper.

Put the milk, 125ml of water, the butter and sugar into a saucepan and set over a high heat until the butter has melted (do not boil). Add the flour, beating well with a spatula and cook for 1 minute. Tip into a food mixer and beat for a couple of minutes to cool the mixture. Add the eggs, one at a time, beating well after each addition until the mixture is smooth.

Place into a piping bag and pipe a large Catherine wheel shape, about 24cm in diameter, keeping it only about 1cm deep. Pipe the remaining mixture into small balls, lifting off to a peak on each. Using a wet finger, gently pat down the peaks to flatten.

Place in the oven for 25 minutes until golden brown, then remove and set aside to cool. Pierce the sides of the small buns once with a small knife, and of the larger circle several times, to let the steam out.

Whisk the double cream and custard to soft peaks, then add the orange liqueur and whisk until the cream is holding its shape. Spoon one-third of the cream into a piping bag and snip the top off, creating a small nozzle.

Pierce the flat base of 16 of the small choux buns with the tips of a pair of scissors then fill with cream, piping until you feel pressure pushing back and the bun is full. (Any leftover unfilled buns freeze very well.)

Heat the sugar in a frying pan over a high heat until it forms a light golden caramel; swirl the pan, but don't stir. Quickly dip the rounded sides of the filled choux buns in the caramel to coat, then return to the tray to harden.

Place the big choux circle on a serving plate. Set two large tablespoons into hot water, then drag one at a time through the remaining cream to form small oval balls, placing on top of the choux base to cover, leaving a small border around the outside (keeping the spoons in hot water makes it easier to form quenelles).

Place the caramel-topped choux buns around the outside of the quenelles on the choux base, then decorate with the soft fruit and a few little twisted willow sprigs (if using) and serve.

Serves 8-10

For the choux pastry

125ml whole milk

100g unsalted butter, cut into small cubes

1 tsp caster sugar

175g plain flour

4 eggs

For the filling

300ml double cream

200ml vanilla custard (for home-made, see page 270)

50ml orange liqueur

100g caster sugar

200g mixed soft fruit, such as strawberries, raspberries, blackberries and currants

2 small twisted willow sprigs, to decorate (optional)

Raspberry and pistachio trifle

Who doesn't like a trifle? This one uses pistachio paste which you can now buy online and in some speciality cake shops as the popularity of cake baking continues to increase. It won't turn green; the reason commercial pistachio cakes are green is down to food colouring. The paste will give the cake a great pistachio taste, though.

Serves 6–8

For the pistachio sponge

25g unsalted butter, melted, plus more for the tin

175g plain flour, plus more for the tin

6 eggs

175g caster sugar

25g pistachio paste

For the trifle

1kg raspberries

25g flaked almonds

500ml double cream, whipped

3 tbsp icing sugar, sifted

125ml kirsch

500ml home-made vanilla custard, cooled (see page 270)

40g shelled pistachio nuts, roughly chopped

To make the sponge, preheat the oven to 200°C/400°F/gas mark 6.

Butter and flour a 23cm springform cake tin and line the base with greaseproof paper.

Place the eggs and sugar into a large bowl and whisk for about 5 minutes until really pale and thick, then add the pistachio paste and mix for another minute until totally incorporated.

Fold the flour and melted butter into the mixture quickly without knocking out too much air, then pour into the tin and bake for 25 minutes until golden, risen and firm.

Cool in the tin for 10 minutes, then turn out and cool on a wire rack.

To assemble the trifle, set 100g of raspberries aside, Place one-third (300g) of the remaining berries into a food processor with 2 tbsp of water. Blitz to a purée, then set aside.

Cut the cooled pistachio cake into 2cm-thick slices.

Place the flaked almonds in a small, dry frying pan and set over a medium heat. Stir until they turn a shade darker and smell toasty, then immediately tip on to a plate to stop the cooking.

Whip the cream with the icing sugar until soft peaks form.

Take a large glass serving bowl and layer in the sponge, drizzle over the kirsch, then top with some raspberry sauce, raspberries and custard, then repeat, until all the sponge, kirsch, raspberry sauce, raspberries and custard have been used up.

Top with the whipped sweetened cream, then sprinkle with the reserved 100g of raspberries, flaked almonds and chopped pistachios. Serve straight away, or chill until ready to serve.

Instant coffee meringue gâteau

You might not think, looking at it, that you could do this or that it's easy… but I proved the camera crew on the photoshoot wrong. It's not for the diet conscious, but my desserts never are. Using bought meringues and marshmallows saves masses of time. I hope you like it as much as the crew did. They're all on the treadmill now, mind…

Serves 6–8

For the gâteau

5 egg whites
150g caster sugar
150g icing sugar, sifted
2 tbsp coffee essence
500g mascarpone cheese
175ml double cream
1 vanilla pod, split, seeds scraped out
2 x 250g large sponge flan cases
175ml cold espresso

To serve

10 small meringue shells
10 small marshmallows
2 tbsp cocoa powder
2 tbsp icing sugar
50g dark chocolate, finely grated

Place the egg whites in a large clean bowl and whisk until the mixture forms stiff peaks. Add the caster and icing sugars and continue to beat for about 5 minutes, until the mixture is smooth and shiny. Beat in the coffee essence, then set aside.

Beat the mascarpone, cream and vanilla seeds together until smooth. Cut each disc of sponge in half horizontally.

Place one piece of cake on to a serving plate, drizzle over a third of the cold coffee, then spread over half the mascarpone cream mixture. Repeat with two more layers of cake and sponge, retaining a little of the mascarpone mixture: you will end up with three layers of cake and two of cream (freeze the fourth layer of cake for another day).

Dollop the coffee meringue on top, spread it roughly around the sides of the cake, then sear with a kitchen blowtorch until light golden brown.

Stick a meringue to a marshmallow with a little of the mascarpone then place on top of the cake in a little cluster. Dust with cocoa powder, icing sugar and grated chocolate, then serve.

There are lemon tarts and lemon tarts. Good versions, like the one you should be able to produce with this recipe, are good enough to grace Michelin three-star restaurant menus. It is a true test of any cook. Get it right and it's the best dessert in the world. Get it wrong and not only will it taste rubbish, it will leak all over the oven and take two days to clean up. The pastry must be thin and cooked through; if it's too thick it will not taste nice. But the real trick is in the oven temperature and knowing when your tart is just done: overcook it and the filling will crack and split; have the oven too hot and the mixture will soufflé up and separate; have the oven too cool and the pastry will go soft and leak. Good luck!

Lemon tart

Serves 6–8

For the pastry

250g plain flour, plus more to dust

100g cold unsalted butter, chopped, plus more for the tart ring

25g icing sugar

pinch of salt

1 egg, lightly beaten, plus extra for brushing

For the filling

14 eggs

550g caster sugar

700ml double cream

finely grated zest and juice of 10 large unwaxed lemons

icing sugar, to glaze

crème fraîche, to serve

To make the pastry, put the flour, butter, icing sugar and salt into a bowl and rub with your fingertips until it has the texture of fine crumbs. Add the egg and mix together until it forms a dough, then knead lightly on a board until smooth. Roll into a ball, wrap in cling film and put in the fridge to rest for 30 minutes.

Meanwhile, preheat the oven to 160°C/ 325°F/gas mark 3. Make the filling: break the eggs into a bowl, add the sugar, cream, lemon zest and juice and whisk. Strain through a fine sieve, then cover and refrigerate.

Roll the pastry out on a work surface lightly dusted with flour to about 3mm thick. Keep turning the pastry a quarter turn every time you roll it, so you end up with a perfect circle.

Butter the inside of a 25cm, 4.5cm-deep tart ring and a baking sheet. Place the ring on the sheet, then line it with the pastry, carefully lifting the pastry then pressing it into the base, so it hangs over the edge. Line with several sheets of ovenproof cling film or one sheet of baking parchment to hang over by 10cm, then fill with flour, baking beans or raw rice. Fold the cling film

or baking parchment back over that and bake for 15 minutes.

Remove the cling film or parchment and its contents, brush the inside of the tart with the beaten egg and return to the oven for another 3–4 minutes until just golden.

Reduce the oven temperature to 150°C/ 300°F/gas mark 2.

Skim any bubbles from the top of the filling and discard. Remove the tart from the oven, add half the filling, then transfer to the oven shelf. Now pull the oven shelf out and ladle the rest of the filling in, then carefully push the tray back into the oven and bake for one hour. (This lessens the risk of spilling the filling all over the floor!) Remove when it still just wobbles in the centre, then leave to cool to room temperature.

To serve, cut the tart into wedges and dust with icing sugar, then glaze either under the grill or with a blowtorch. Serve with some crème fraîche.

There are few desserts that look as impressive as a millefeuille and it's a favourite of my old mate, the top chef Pierre Koffmann. Making your own puff pastry is ideal as it will taste far better, though I admit it is more time-consuming. And let's face it, if you had one of the world's greatest chefs coming round for dinner, what would you do? Panic. Well you're not alone, as I still do that!

Apple and blackberry millefeuille tart

Serves 8–10

1 quantity rough puff pastry (see page 49)
25g icing sugar
40g unsalted butter
2 large Bramley apples, peeled, cored and roughly chopped
1 vanilla pod, split, seeds scraped out
juice of 1 lemon
125g blackberries
300ml double cream

Make the pastry as on page 49 and leave in the fridge to chill while you preheat the oven to 220°C/425°F/gas mark 7.

Roll the pastry out on a lightly floured surface to a 22.5 x 15cm rectangle about 3mm thick, then cut into three rectangles, each 15 x 7.5cm. Dredge two of them with icing sugar, to cover. Lift on to a baking tray and bake for 15 minutes.

Meanwhile, make the filling. Heat a small sauté pan until hot, add the butter and apples and cook for a minute, then add 2–3 tbsp of water and continue to cook. Add the vanilla pod and seeds, lemon juice and blackberries and cook for 5–6 minutes until softened and pulpy. Allow to cool, then chill in the fridge.

Whisk the double cream to firm peaks, then spoon into a piping bag.

Slice the cooled pastry sheets in half horizontally through the depth of the pastry; you will now have six very thin rectangles. Set aside the two glazed pieces for the tops.

Spoon some of the blackberry mix on a piece of pastry, then pipe the cream over. Place another piece of pastry on top then repeat with another layer of blackberry and cream. Finish with an icing sugar-glazed piece of pastry. Repeat to make another millefeuille. Serve immediately.

Lavender crème caramel with lavender shortbread

I have masses of lavender in my garden and cook it with lamb as well as in this pudding.

Place six 7.5cm diameter, 4cm-deep ramekins into a deep roasting tray. Preheat the oven to 150°C/300°F/gas mark 2.

Put 150g of the caster sugar into a saucepan over a high heat and cook without stirring until a golden brown caramel, swirling the pan from time to time. Remove the pan from the heat and carefully add 2 tbsp of hot water; it will spit and splutter a little but swirl to combine, then divide equally between the ramekins and roll around the sides to coat evenly.

Place the milk, cream and lavender into a saucepan and heat gently until just simmering. Meanwhile, put the eggs and remaining 75g of the sugar into a bowl and whisk until combined, then pour on the simmering milk, whisking constantly, until smooth. Strain the custard through a fine sieve into the ramekins and half-fill the roasting tray with hot water so that the water comes two-thirds of the way up the sides of the ramekins.

Carefully place in the oven and bake for 45 minutes until just set, then remove. Allow to cool to room temperature, then remove the ramekins from the tin and chill in the fridge for at least 1 hour.

Make the shortbread. Preheat the oven to 180°C/350°F/gas mark 4 and butter a 30 x 20cm baking tin.

Put the butter and icing sugar into a bowl and beat until light and fluffy, with an electric whisk if you like, then fold in the lavender, cornflour and plain flour and mix to a firm dough. Press into the tin to lie about 1cm thick, prick all over with a fork and scatter the caster sugar over the top (if using).

Bake in the oven for 12–15 minutes until light golden brown and cooked through. Leave to cool briefly in the tin, then break into shards.

To remove the crème caramels from the ramekins, run a knife around each, then press the knife lightly into one side, before inverting on to plates. Serve with the shortbread.

Tip

The key to using lavender in cooking is not to use too much, or it can overpower food and make it taste like your auntie's soap.

Serves 6

For the crème caramel

225g caster sugar

150ml whole milk

300ml double cream

½–1 tbsp dried lavender tips (check the strength first!)

4 eggs, lightly beaten

For the lavender shortbread

175g unsalted butter, softened, plus more for the tin

100g icing sugar

½–1 tbsp dried lavender tips (check the strength first!)

100g cornflour

200g plain flour

2 tbsp caster sugar (optional)

Orange and rapeseed oil cake with cream cheese frosting

Olive oil cake is nothing new to anyone who is familiar with Italian cooking. It keeps the cake lovely and moist. Rapeseed oil is a great alternative, as it has a slightly milder flavour.

Serves 8–10

unsalted butter, for greasing
5 large oranges
100ml rapeseed oil
4 eggs
450g caster sugar
125g self-raising flour
125g ground almonds
2 tsp baking powder
150g cream cheese
150g crème fraîche
25g icing sugar
25g walnut halves, crumbled
1 tablespoon basil cress or tiny basil leaves

Preheat the oven to 170°C/325°F/gas mark 3. Lightly butter a 23cm springform cake tin.

Remove the zest from three of the oranges and set aside, then remove the pith and discard. Roughly chop the flesh, then either place in a saucepan with the rapeseed oil and blitz until puréed with a stick blender, or blitz with the oil in a food blender.

Whisk the orange zest, eggs and 250g of the caster sugar in a food mixer or a large bowl with an electric whisk, until the mixture is very light and ribbons form when the whisk is lifted out.

Mix the flour, ground almonds and baking powder together in a separate bowl.

Fold half the puréed orange into the eggs, then add all the flour and the rest of the puréed orange.

Pour into the cake tin and bake for 1 hour until golden-brown and risen. Check the cake is cooked by inserting a clean skewer or knife into the centre – if it comes out clean, the cake is ready; if not, cook for a further 5 minutes and check once more.

While the cake cooks, prepare the topping. Whisk the cream cheese, crème fraîche and icing sugar together in a bowl until smooth and thickened, and chill in the fridge until needed.

Peel the last two oranges using a vegetable peeler, then slice the peel very finely into julienne. Put 150ml of water into a saucepan with 150g of caster sugar and the julienned orange peel. Bring to the boil and simmer for 8–10 minutes. Strain into a sieve set over a bowl and press through lightly to remove the sugar syrup. You can use this for a salad dressing or in another cake.

Place the last 50g of caster sugar on a plate and toss the julienned orange peel into it, moving it around with your hands to make sure all the strands are coated.

Remove the cake from the oven and allow it to cool in the tin before turning it out and cooling completely on a wire rack.

Spread the frosting over the top of the cooled cake and decorate with crumbled walnut pieces, the candied julienne strips and basil cress.

Without the cress the cake will keep in an airtight container in the fridge for up to 1 week.

This is one of the simplest desserts you'll ever make, as most of the ingredients are already done for you. All you need is whipped cream, a few strawberries, a ready-made sponge flan and a little bit of imagination. Make sure you use a sharp-sided mould so you get a neat, clean edge. The only bit of real work is cutting the sponge flan in half. Best of luck.

Strawberry gâteau

Serves 8–10

1 large shop-bought flan case
50ml Drambuie
800ml double cream
1 tablespoon vanilla bean paste
75g icing sugar
400g large strawberries, trimmed and cut in half lengthways
125g caster sugar
125g small strawberries
50g each of raspberries, blueberries and blackberries
3–4 sprigs of mint
pouring cream, to serve (optional)

Place a 20–25cm stainless steel ring on the flan case and use it to cut through, discarding the outer sponge. Cut the flan in half widthways so you end up with two thin layers. Place the steel ring on a large flat serving plate, then place one of the sponge layers inside and press down lightly. Sprinkle 2 tbsp of the Drambuie over the sponge and set aside.

Put the double cream into a bowl with the vanilla bean paste, the remaining Drambuie and 60g of the icing sugar, and whip to semi-firm peaks.

Line the ring with the large strawberry halves, cut-side against the ring. Carefully spoon the whipped cream into the centre and spread out gently to fill the whole ring – adding as much cream as necessary to fill to the top of the strawberries. Place the remaining sponge layer on top and press down lightly.

Remove the ring by carefully warming the edges with a hot cloth or blowtorch and lifting it straight off. Dust the top of the sponge with the remaining icing sugar.

Put the caster sugar into a very clean frying pan and place over a medium heat to caramelise. Once it is caramelised, remove from the heat and place the base of the pan in a bowl or pan filled with cold water to stop the caramel overcooking.

While the caramel is cooling, heat a metal skewer over a flame or on a hob until very, very hot (taking care to hold the skewer with a cloth), then score the top of the sponge in lines to create a diamond-style pattern. Decorate the top with the small strawberries and the mixed berries, and garnish with the sprigs of fresh mint.

To finish, dip a small spoon into the caramel and as the caramel falls off the spoon, twist it around a metal rod or handle (I used a knife sharpener but you could use the rounded handle of any kitchen utensil) to create some curls, then balance them on top of the gâteau.

Serve cut into wedges, with pouring cream if needed.

One of the best cheesecakes I've ever tasted was in New York, at Eileen's Special Cheesecake bakery. All she sells is cheesecakes, in all manner of sizes and flavours. The bakery where she makes them is at one end, the shop is at the other end, and the queue outside is immense.

Chocolate and salted caramel banoffee cheesecake

Serves 2

100g full-fat cream cheese
100ml crème fraîche
125ml double cream
1 vanilla pod, split and seeds scraped
50g dulce de leche
½ tsp sea salt
40g caster sugar
25g unsalted butter
2 bananas, peeled
2 chocolate digestive biscuits
25g dark chocolate

Put the cream cheese, crème fraîche, 75ml of the double cream and the vanilla seeds into a bowl and whisk until well combined.

Put the dulce de leche and salt into a bowl, and whisk together, then lightly fold into the cream mixture until just marbled through. Set aside.

Heat the sugar in a frying pan until golden and liquid, then add the bananas and coat in the caramel. Whisk in the butter and the rest of the cream and coat once more.

Crumble each biscuit onto a serving plate, place the caramel-coated bananas on top, drizzle the sauce around, and finish with a quenelle of dulce de leche cream. Finally, grate the chocolate over the top.

Sticky toffee roulade

This is an even more indulgent version of classic sticky toffee pudding, with a hint of bourbon in the sauce. It has a deep flavour and rich colour – exactly what you want from a sticky toffee pudding.

Serves 6–8

For the sponge

150g dates, roughly chopped
4 eggs, separated
75g soft dark brown sugar
1 tsp vanilla extract
½ tsp bicarbonate of soda
100g plain flour
1–2 tbsp caster sugar, for sprinkling

For the sauce

200ml double cream
200g unsalted butter
200g soft dark brown sugar
50ml bourbon

Preheat the oven to 230°C/450°F/gas mark 8. Grease and line a 35 x 25cm Swiss roll tin.

Put the dates and 225ml of water into a saucepan, set over a low heat and bring to the boil.

Meanwhile, whisk the egg yolks and dark brown sugar in a kitchen mixer or a large bowl with an electric whisk, until the sugar has dissolved, then set aside.

Pour the dates and water into a blender and blitz to a fine purée.

Whisk the egg whites in a large bowl with an electric whisk until soft peaks form.

Now you're ready to put it all together you need to work quickly. Add the vanilla extract to the sugar and egg yolk mixture, then add the bicarbonate of soda and puréed dates, and mix together. Fold in the flour and mix to combine, then beat in half the egg whites for 10 seconds. Beat in the remaining egg whites until fully incorporated.

Pour straight into the Swiss roll tin and smooth to the edges, then bake in the oven for 11–12 minutes until risen and golden-brown.

While the cake bakes, make the sauce. Put the cream, butter, brown sugar and bourbon into a saucepan set over a medium heat. Bring to the boil, whisking until smooth, then simmer for a few minutes until thickened.

Set a damp clean tea towel on a work surface and dust with the caster sugar. When the cake comes out of the oven, turn it top-down onto the damp tea towel and peel off the lining paper. Spoon one-third of the sauce over the sponge and gently roll the sponge up from the short side to form a fat roll.

Transfer to a serving platter, then spoon some more of the sauce over the top, and serve with the rest of the sauce alongside in a jug.

Elderflower jelly with peaches and strawberry with quick strawberry ice cream

Jelly and ice cream make such a perfect combination. Even this grown-up version made with elderflower cordial reminds me of when I was young, when my mother would serve me jelly and ice cream when I was poorly. It's easier to get the right amount of gelatine if you use the leaf form, as the powdered type sometimes doesn't dissolve properly and you can end up with too much – resulting in a jelly that has set too firm.

Serves 4

For the jelly

450ml sparkling elderflower pressé
50g caster sugar
5 leaves of gelatine, soaked in cold water
1 peach, stoned and finely diced
50g small strawberries, quartered
a small handful of Greek basil

For the ice cream

500g strawberries, hulled
½ vanilla pod, seeds scraped
300ml thick double cream

To make the jelly, heat 100ml of the sparking elderflower pressé and the caster sugar in a saucepan until hot, then add the soaked gelatine and stir gently until it has dissolved. Add the rest of the elderflower pressé and stir to combine.

Pour the jelly into a soup plate or lipped plate and place in the fridge for 30 minutes to set.

To make the ice cream, place the strawberries in a sealable food bag and freeze for at least 4 hours, but preferably overnight. When they're frozen and you're ready to serve the jelly, tip the strawberries into a food processor with the vanilla seeds and half the cream, and blitz until they start to break down. Continue blitzing for 3–4 minutes until it becomes smoother, then add the remaining cream and blitz until it forms a smooth frozen cream.

With the jelly still in the plate, lay a line of chopped peaches down one side of the jelly, then top them with the strawberries and Greek basil. Place spoonfuls of the ice cream in a line alongside and serve immediately, with the remainder of the ice cream in a separate bowl.

Individual hot chocolate and hazelnut mousse cake with pouring cream

This simple little dish contains no flour at all, so it's the perfect dessert if you are gluten-intolerant or need it to be gluten-free. Make sure to serve it at room temperature or while it is still warm, as it will go very hard in the fridge because of its lack of flour.

Serves 6

60g chopped toasted hazelnuts
200g dark chocolate
100g unsalted butter
4 eggs, separated
50g caster sugar
250ml pouring cream, to serve

Preheat the oven to 180°C/350°F/gas mark 4. Line the bases of a six-hole large muffin tin with discs of silicone paper.

Blitz the toasted hazelnuts to a powder in a food processor or blender and set aside.

Put the dark chocolate and butter in a bowl set over a saucepan of simmering water and heat until melted, stirring so that it doesn't get too hot, then remove from the heat and cool slightly.

Put the egg yolks into a bowl with half the sugar and set over the pan of simmering water. Whisk until thickened and pale in colour, then set aside.

Make sure your bowl and whisk are very clean, free of grease and completely dry, as any water or grease will affect the meringue. Place the egg whites in the bowl and whisk with a food mixer or an electric whisk on high speed, to soft peaks. Add the remaining caster sugar, whisking until the mixture is smooth and glossy. You should hear the machine dropping down a gear as it gets to the correct consistency.

Pour the melted chocolate mixture onto the egg yolks and mix to combine, then fold in the ground hazelnuts and half the whisked egg whites. Whisk well to combine, then carefully fold in the rest of the egg whites and divide equally between the muffin tins.

Bake for 8–10 minutes, or until the surface is set – there should still be a wobble. Remove and cool slightly before turning out.

Serve with pouring cream.

Lemon posset with figs, strawberries and Gran's shortbreads

Traditionally, a posset was a hot drink made from curdled milk with wine or ale added to it, and sometimes spiced with nutmeg and cloves. It was often used as a cold or flu remedy. Nowadays, it's more similar to a syllabub. It's amazing how only a few simple ingredients can produce a dessert as intense as this – sharp to the taste and so easy to make.

Serves 4–6

For the posset

600ml double cream
150g caster sugar
2 large lemons, zested and juiced
8 strawberries
2 figs, cut into wedges
a handful of tiny mint sprigs, to garnish

For the shortbread

175g plain flour
90g icing sugar
60g ground almonds
25g cornflour
250g unsalted butter, cut into cubes
200g strawberry jam

First make the posset. Bring the cream and sugar to the boil in a saucepan, then remove from the heat and whisk in the lemon zest and juice. Whisk well, then pour into serving bowls and place in the fridge to set for 1 hour.

Preheat the oven to 180°C/350°F/gas mark 4.

To make the shortbread, mix the plain flour, icing sugar, ground almonds and cornflour together in a bowl. Rub the butter into the flour until it forms a breadcrumb-like texture, then pull together very lightly to form a soft dough.

Divide the dough into small balls and press into a 24-hole silicone bun tin or fairy cake tin. Bake for 10–12 minutes until they are a light golden colour. If you have dough left over, make a second batch. The shortbread mix makes more than you need for this recipe, but keeps well in an airtight tin.

While the shortbreads are baking, put the jam into a saucepan with 50ml of water and bring to the boil. Simmer for a few minutes until it has a thick syrup texture.

Remove the shortbreads from the oven and carefully make a small dent in the centre of each one with your finger, to create a hollow to put the strawberry jam. Spoon the warm jam into the dent and set aside to cool on a wire rack, still in the tin.

Take the posset out of the fridge and decorate with the strawberries, figs and mint sprigs. Serve with the shortbread.

I was first introduced to making meringue roulade by the great Mary Berry, and ever since then I've always made this dessert at home. The cooking times and temperatures are really vital, so that the meringue stays nice and soft and pliable in the centre. If it's too hot, it cracks; if it's too cold, it firms up and you won't be able to roll it.

Lemon and plum meringue roulade

Serves 8–10

5 egg whites

400g caster sugar

2 sprigs of lemon verbena, leaves picked, plus extra to garnish

8 plums, quartered and stoned

400ml double cream

225g good-quality lemon curd

Preheat the oven to 180°C/350°F/gas mark 4. Grease a 35 x 25cm Swiss roll tin and line with silicone paper.

Make sure your bowl and whisk are very clean, free of grease and completely dry, as any water or grease will affect the meringue. Place the egg whites in the bowl and whisk with a food mixer or an electric whisk on high speed, to soft peaks. Add 275g of the caster sugar, whisking until the mixture is smooth and glossy. You should hear the machine dropping down a gear as it gets to the correct consistency.

Spoon the meringue into the prepared tin and spread evenly to the edges using a palette knife, then scatter the lemon verbena over the top. Bake for 8 minutes until golden-brown, then lower the oven temperature to 170°C/325°F/gas mark 3 and bake for a further 10 minutes until crisp.

Remove from the oven and turn out of the tin onto a clean tea towel. Remove the paper from the base of the meringue and allow to cool.

Put the plums into a saucepan with 100g of the sugar and 100ml of water. Bring to the boil, then cook for 10 minutes until the plums are softened.

Whisk the double cream in a large bowl until very soft peaks form, then whisk in the last 25g of the sugar and the lemon curd, and mix gently until it just holds a peak.

Spread the lemon cream over the cooled meringue all the way to the edges, leaving a 1cm gap along one long edge, then spoon three-quarters of the cooked plums over the top. Starting at the long end with the border, roll up the meringue using the tea towel to help you. Roll it carefully off the tea towel onto a serving platter, and decorate with any remaining plums and lemon verbena.

St Emilion is a famous wine region of Bordeaux, and I was fortunate enough to visit it a lot as a young nipper. Not to taste the wine, but because my family used to work over there. In the main square of St Emilion was a macaron shop, and I'd often pop in on the way home. The macarons were cooked and served on cardboard and you'd end up pulling them off with your teeth. Crunchy on the outside and soft in the middle, good macarons are a real joy.

St Emilion macarons

Serves 2, plus extra macarons

For the macarons

100g icing sugar
100g ground almonds
100g caster sugar
50ml water
2 egg whites

For the chocolate mousse

150g good-quality plain chocolate, broken into pieces
40g unsalted butter, melted
4 eggs, separated
50g caster sugar
150ml good-quality red wine, ideally St Emilion or Merlot

Preheat the oven to 130°C/260°F/gas mark ¾ and line two baking sheets with silicone paper. Make 24 circles, 4.5cm in diameter – this is your template for piping. Flip the paper over so the pencil line is on the underside but the outline can still be seen.

Place the icing sugar and ground almonds in a food processor and blitz to a fine powder, scraping down the sides halfway through, then set aside.

Put the caster sugar and 50ml of water into a saucepan and bring to the boil. Continue to boil until the mixture reaches 110°C/230°F, or soft boil, on a thermometer.

Make sure the bowl and whisk you are using for the next step are very clean, free of grease and dry, as any water or grease will affect the meringue. Place the egg whites in the bowl and whisk with a food mixer or an electric whisk on high speed until soft peaks form. Add the sugar syrup, whisking until the mixture is smooth and glossy and has cooled slightly, at least 2 minutes.

Transfer half the meringue to a clean bowl, then sieve in the ground almond mixture and whisk together to form a thick paste. Fold in the remaining meringue – you will end up with a smooth, pipeable mixture. Transfer it to a piping bag fitted with a 7mm plain nozzle, and secure the silicone paper to the baking sheets with a dab of the mixture.

Pipe the mixture onto the template so that it just fills each circle – hold the bag upright and press down lightly to fill the circle before lifting off quickly. Use a wet finger to lightly press the peak down on the macaron, then set aside for at least 30 minutes until the mixture has spread slightly.

Bake for 25 minutes until crusted and risen. Remove from the oven and leave to cool on the baking sheets.

To make the mousse, melt the chocolate and butter together in a bowl set over a pan of simmering water.

Whisk the egg yolks and sugar together in a bowl set over a second pan of simmering water until light and thick. Remove both pans from the heat, but leave the bowls set over the pans of water to keep warm.

Make sure the bowl and whisk you are using for the next step are clean, free of grease and dry, as any water or grease will affect the meringue. Place the egg whites in the bowl and whisk with a food mixer or an electric whisk on high speed until soft peaks form.

Fill the bottom of two large wine glasses with a few macarons, then divide the red wine between the glasses.

Whisk the warm chocolate mixture into the eggs and sugar, then lift the bowl off of the saucepan and fold in the egg whites, a spoonful at a time, until totally incorporated.

Pour the mousse over the wine-covered macarons, and top each with one more macaron. Put into the fridge to set for a couple of hours before serving.

Churros with peaches and custard

This is a kind of fried dough pastry that is very similar to choux pastry in an eclair, but is deep-fried and rolled in sugar. Churros are very popular in France, Spain, Portugal and South America. It's best to use a star-shaped nozzle to give the churros their distinctive shape – and also so that they can hold in more sauce. Make sure to use fresh oil when you fry the churros so you don't taint their flavour.

Serves 4

For the peaches

4 peaches, stoned and roughly chopped

25g caster sugar

75g unsalted butter

2 large sprigs of basil, leaves picked and roughly torn

For the churros

vegetable oil, for deep-frying

50g caster sugar, plus extra for dusting

75g unsalted butter

200g plain flour

¼ tsp baking powder

1 egg

1 quantity of custard (see page 270), to serve

Start by making the custard, following the instructions on page 270. Strain into a bowl and set aside.

Put the peaches, sugar and butter into a sauté pan with 50ml of water and set over a medium heat. Add the basil leaves, cover and cook for 5–10 minutes until tender and softened. Place in a serving dish.

To make the churros, heat a deep-fat fryer to 150°C/300°F, or heat the oil for deep-frying in a deep heavy-based frying pan until a breadcrumb sizzles and turns brown when dropped into it. (CAUTION: hot oil can be dangerous. Do not leave unattended.)

Bring 250ml of water, the sugar and butter to the boil in a saucepan set over a medium heat. When boiling, add the flour and baking powder, and beat to a smooth batter. Remove from the heat and beat in the egg, continuing to beat until the batter is smooth and shiny.

Place a large star nozzle in a piping bag and fill with half the batter, then pipe directly into the fat fryer or frying pan in lines, cutting by dipping a pair of metal scissors into the hot oil, then snipping through the batter. Cook for 5–6 minutes until golden and crispy, then lift out and drain on kitchen paper. Repeat with the remaining batter. Toss the churros with caster sugar to coat.

Spoon the custard and peaches into separate bowls, then pile the churros on one big plate and tuck in!

Fruit meringue gâteau

This is a very simple dish. The key is to keep it in the fridge for 3–4 hours before serving. The fruit, cream and meringue start to stick together and the meringue softens up – in a similar way to an Eton mess.

Serves 6–8

6 egg whites
400g caster sugar
1 litre double cream
1 tbsp vanilla bean paste
500g strawberries, hulled and cut in half
4 plums, halved, stoned and finely sliced
5 figs, cut into small wedges
2 tbsp toasted flaked almonds

Preheat the oven to 110°C/225°F/gas mark ½. Draw four 20cm circles, using a cake tin as a template, on four sheets of silicone paper. Turn the sheets of paper over, so that the pencil line is on the underside but can still be seen through the paper, and place on four flat baking sheets (or two large, if your oven is big enough.)

Make sure your bowl and whisk are very clean, free of grease and completely dry, as any water or grease will affect the meringue. Place the egg whites in the bowl and whisk with a food mixer or an electric whisk on high speed, to soft peaks. Add 300g of the sugar, continuing to whisk until the mixture is smooth and glossy. You should hear the machine dropping down a gear as it gets to the correct consistency.

Spoon into a piping bag fitted with a 1cm plain nozzle and pipe a little meringue onto the back of each sheet of silicone paper to secure the paper to the tray. Pipe a disc of meringue onto each template, starting in the centre and working out. Flatten the top of the meringue using a wet palette knife to give a smooth top. Place in the oven for 2 hours. Remove from the oven and cool fully before using.

Place the cream and vanilla bean paste in a bowl and whisk with a food mixer, or an electric whisk on high speed, to soft peaks.

Place one disc of meringue on a cake stand or a large serving plate and spread with one-third of the cream, then scatter one quarter of the sliced fruit over the top. Cover with another disc of meringue, then repeat with a layer of cream, more fruit, another meringue disc, then the last of the cream and half the remaining fruit. Finish with the last meringue disc and decorate with the last of the fruit.

Heat the last 100g of caster sugar in a pan until golden-brown and liquid all the way through. Add the flaked almonds and stir to combine, then drizzle over the top of the gâteau.

Chill for 3–4 hours before serving.

Index

e returr
tar